Maxcy Gregg's
Sporting Journals 1842-1858

Maxcy Gregg's
Sporting Journals 1842-1858

Edited & Introduced by
Suzanne Parfitt Johnson

Foreword by
James Everett Kibler, Jr.

Green Altar Books
Shotwell Publishing

Produced in the Republic of South Carolina by

SHOTWELL PUBLISHING, LLC
Post Office Box 2592
Columbia, South Carolina 29202

www.ShotwellPublishing.com

Cover Image: Currier & Ives. Quail Shooting. [New York: published by Currier & Ives, between 1856 and 1907] Photograph. Retrieved from the Library of Congress, <www.loc.gov/item/2001703779/>.
Frontispiece Image: Oil painting of Maxcy Gregg by Ann Coles, from the original by Scarborough; private collection of Suzanne Parfitt Johnson
Cover Design: Hazel's Dream / Boo Jackson

ISBN-10: 1-947660-25-X
ISBN-13: 978-1-947660-25-0

10 9 8 7 6 5 4 3 2 1

CONTENTS

FOREWORD

MAXCY GREGG, NATURALIST
JAMES EVERETT KIBLER, JR.

IN *LEE'S LIEUTENANTS* Douglas Southall Freeman wrote that Maxcy Gregg was "culturally one of the best-furnished men of the Confederacy. Few knew the Greek dramatists or the philosophers so thoroughly. Perhaps none combined so precise a knowledge of botany, of ornithology, and of astronomy. The equipment of his private observatory in Columbia would have been the envy of many a college. A scholar he was, a scientist and a gentleman." Freeman then asked the following question before Gregg's first main trial by fire at Gaines Mill – but "was he a soldier? That day would show. He would open the battle" (I, 518). At the end of that day, Freeman concluded that Gregg had given "an unequivocal answer" in the affirmative. A soldier he was indeed! (I, 535).

What concerns us here, however, is not his mettle as a soldier, but the depth, breadth, and range of his enquiry into the nature of the world around him. His "Sporting Journals," published here for the first time, gives just as unequivocal an affirmative answer to the question of how well-informed, precise, and deep were his enquiries into Nature – data and recordings that are extremely valuable to us today. I conclude that his journals, beyond the tallies of how many shots and how many bags of game he achieved, show considerable talent at describing the natural world and a gift of close observation, and careful, precise descriptions that place him in the company of celebrated naturalists like Catesby, Bartram, Michaux, and Audubon, all of whom informed his work, and with whom he frequently notes his agreement or disagreement. His records are of far more than "sport" and need to take their place as supplementary to the works of those great naturalists. His journals also give significant new details in areas the masters never touch. They are just that important.

As a grandson of Jonathan Maxcy, the first beloved president of South Carolina College, Gregg's enquiry into the nature of things was part of his intellectual and cultural inheritance. The college from its founding was a centre

i

of scientific study. John Drayton, the college's founder in 1801, was at the same time naturalist, botanist, classicist, social historian, military enthusiast, author, meticulous keeper of journals, sportsman, and lawyer. Gregg would follow Drayton closely in all these endeavours. The early faculty counted men like botanist Stephen Elliott among its number that could boast a Francis Lieber and a Thomas Cooper. Elliott published his *Sketch of the Botany of South-Carolina and Georgia* in 1821 and 1824. Drayton himself edited and translated from the Latin Thomas Walter's eighteenth century treatise *Flora Caroliniana*, and his manuscript thereof was among the first books formally accessioned by the college library in 1804. The library was particularly rich in the great works of botanists and naturalists, some of which were gifts by Drayton of personal annotated copies that included John Shecut and Michaux.

When Gregg was a student, the college's professed aim was to help form a gentleman who would be equally and comfortably at home in his drawing room and in his fields and woods. As his journals show, Gregg was such a man. His contemporary and "intimate friend"[a] at the college, Wade Hampton III, was another. Gregg shared Hampton's love of sport. Any hunter today will feel kinship with Gregg's frequent comments upon enjoying dry clothes or "a hot bath for my feet," trying to become a better marksman, enjoying the company of his dogs and horses, and after a long day, feeling the camaraderie of the camp that included "copious draughts of…peach- and apple-brandy with honey" or "plentiful corn whisky." As with Hampton, Gregg was aware he was in the great sporting tradition of the English landed gentry. We know this because a journal entry references the English sporting procedures outlined in Col. Hawker on Shooting[b] with the advice to shoot "with both eyes open & fixed on the object, in the English sporting style." Gregg, something of a meticulous perfectionist in most areas of his life, is exasperated by a missed shot and is constantly trying to improve his aim. Because, unlike his friend Hampton, Gregg was not to the manor born, it was as if he felt he had to try harder.

---

a   Hampton's description. In Wade Hampton's letter of 6 January 1836 to Peter de la Torre, he further notes that Gregg "is one of the smartest young men in the state". Hampton Family Papers, South Caroliniana Library, University of South Carolina.

b   The first American edition of Hawker, edited by William Trotter Porter in 1846, is dedicated to Wade Hampton III. Porter called him "the most accomplished sportsman of my acquaintance," and hoped that like Hampton's father he would distinguish himself "as much in Society as on the Turf and in the Field." Porter comments on Hampton's fame for his "exploits as a horseman and a shot." As editor of the sporting journal, New York *Spirit of the Times*, Porter was arguably the most influential sportsman of the day in America.

Beyond his entertaining descriptions of hunts and the habits at camp and on the trail, one is likely to be impressed by the insatiable curiosity of the man – a curiosity he shared with all the great naturalists. At one point he exclaims that for the life of him, "I cannot imagine" what this particular new "mountain bird was." He is always questioning, as when he writes of Table Rock Mountain, "I think those smaller Pines, which on my former visit I remarked for the peculiarity of their appearance, are the same species with the larger Trees, which are evidently the *Pinus Pungens*." He corrects Michaux that the mountain is in South not North Carolina, but agrees with Michaux that *Pinus pungens* is the only tree on Table Rock. At another location in the high mountains, he takes issue with Michaux over the height of balsam firs. They are not the forty to forty-five feet "assigned by Michaux," but instead trees of eighty feet are of "no uncommon stature."

Gregg also refers to other authorities (including Richard Harlan's *Fauna Americana* and John D. Godman's *American Natural History*) but also shows that he learns from and values local amateur naturalists, planters like George B. Pearson, the botanist, plant-collector of "Fonti Flora" plantation in Fairfield District, South Carolina; Nathan Sims of Union District, whose large "Deer Park" on the Tyger River boasted white deer; and the mountaineer woodsmen William Bridges and Sim Burgess. He had important local resources like Dr. Robert W. Gibbes of Columbia to whom he takes a sample of an ore from the high mountains that Gibbes identifies as "the oligistoxide of iron." The antebellum scene of which Gregg was a part was replete with knowledgeable scientist-specialists in many areas, men of considerable talent and accomplishments from Gibbes and his fossils, to John Bachman and his birds and mammals, and from J. Perkins Barrett, the supplier of specimens to Agassiz, to Henry Ravenel the mycologist.

Gregg considered himself to be primarily an ornithologist. He is always saying he is escaping outside to "go ornithologising," so his many references to Audubon come naturally. Audubon first came to South Carolina in 1831 and visited Columbia in October 1833, where he met Thomas Cooper and spent the night in the house of Dr. Robert W. Gibbes. Audubon called Gibbes "a man of taste and talent." South Carolina College during this time became one of three American colleges to subscribe to his great *Birds of North America*. Gregg would have been eighteen and a student at the college when Audubon made his brief visit in 1833. Whether or not Gregg ever met Audubon is not known, but the influence is unmistakable. Audubon was a compulsive journal keeper and kept careful records of his bird observations, kills, and the specimens he collected that remind one of Gregg's. Gregg would have had access to the great Audubon bird folios at the college library. Because Gregg refers to Audubon's figures and descriptions in November 1843 and the seven volume octavo edition did not begin appearing until 1844, he must have used the Elephant Folio.

Gregg's journals show he knew Audubon's texts very well. Of one bird which Gregg encounters, he says that Audubon saw it too, but the bird was "never obtained by Audubon." Gregg says he also failed to obtain it. Of another bird, Gregg notes that its size and colour differ from Audubon's description. At one point, he cites a particular source in Audubon as "Audubon's 7th vol. of N[orth] A[merican] Birds, Miniature Edition" – perhaps an edition Gregg himself owned.

Gregg's immersion in and fascination with nature, however, include far more than ornithology, as his constant journal references to flora will attest. His descriptions of the "Pink Beds" and "Indian Pink Root Beds" of the high mountains of North Carolina are the valuable, careful, and precise observations of a gifted naturalist. Gregg says that Mount Pisgah gets its name from this plant. He notes collecting specimens of the "cones, etc." of the male and female balsam. As his journals progress from year to year, his descriptions of the flora and landscape become fuller and more engaged (and engaging). His close descriptions of the wilds of the French Broad and Big Pigeon River regions of North Carolina are among the earliest and best accounts of a difficult terrain. These descriptions include flora, fauna, weather, and landscape features in an attempt to portray the full experience. Charleston author, William Gilmore Simms, who visited the same area of the Balsam Range some three years after Gregg, noted in his own mountain journal of fall 1847 that he was exploring where few white men had gone before and miles beyond "what the conceited world calls civilisation." One of these travelers was Gregg. Simms's descriptions of the hunt camps in the Balsams are remarkably similar to Gregg's, down to the hunters' imbibing of the same peach brandy. Simms's journal thus attests to Gregg's accuracy.

Gregg's considerable skill as a writer shows in his elaborations upon the habits and character of the people he encounters in his journeys. He is thus again more than the ornithologist and sportsman he considered himself, but instead as well a good student of Nature in all her manifest forms. This inclusiveness leads him to describe his fellow human beings. He realizes they are a part of nature too and one with the whole and unity of creation. At times Gregg in this capacity turns social historian in much the same way that John Drayton did in his *A View of South-Carolina as Respects Her Natural and Civil Concerns* (1802). A good example, for instance, is Gregg's description of the Mount Pisgah mountaineer, the "capital woodsman" William Bridges. Mr. Bridges, says

Gregg, is a "very ingenious sort of a Jack at all trades" who "has a musical turn also." Gregg continues that in Bridges' cabin, he saw and heard for the first time a mountain dulcimer with "its antediluvian-sounding notes." He learns from Bridges the nature of bear, turkey, deer, panther, and catamount. Bridges kills "on an average 10 or 12 bears in a year" and has killed seventeen panthers in the last eight years.

Gregg thus shows that he learns from and values both the "high" (men like Dr. Gibbes, Michaux, Audubon, *et al*) and the "low" (men like Bridges, Nathan Sims, and mountaineer Sim Burgess). As we have said, he was admirably fitted by his culture to be equally at home in drawing room and woods and fields. We have to recall that botanist, lawyer, author John Drayton provided the model of the complete man of culture, the complete gentleman – an achievement to which Gregg apparently aspired.

It is clear from his journals that Gregg is more than a casual student of nature and human nature, from birds to bears, from catamounts to fox squirrels. He is more than the meticulous scientist-recorder of data. He is instead a great lover of the world around him who is never happier than in his immersion in Nature. His law profession which provides the daily bread, he finds by contrast to be, as he calls it, the "confinement" of the "rascally law business," the "tedium of the Court," and "the drudgery of the law." He is never happier than when "ornithologising."

From the journals' beginnings, we note the monthly periodicity of bird missings and baggings that tell us something of the presence of such rarities in South Carolina as the Mississippi Kite and the ivory-bill woodpecker – or the relative commonness of other species. Even this rather tedious data is valuable to the naturalist today. But as the journals progress, we are struck by the engaging precise descriptions of the appearance of a comet or of the Aurora Borealis over the city of Columbia, careful accounts detailing colour, latitudes, and longitudes. It is hard to forget Gregg's descriptions of the month-long "great flights" across the sandhills and over the city of vast flock after flock of passenger pigeons on their migration from northeast to southwest – a migration that lasts from mid-February to mid-March.

It should also be noted that Gregg's range of exploration, though small in comparison to those of Michaux, Catesby, and Bartram, spans a diverse area from the South Carolina coast to the highest peaks of North Carolina. His travel accounts include the Santee River system and the woods and streams south of Columbia to the Santee Canal. They include his usual touches of local social history such as "dining on a Pilau" in the Santee rice region, or of a fishing expedition down the North Edisto River, or of close descriptions of bird life in the Congaree Swamp that over a century later is to become the Congaree Swamp National Park, or of forays along the Broad and Tyger River systems north of Columbia.

One cannot omit noting Gregg's painful description of killing an ivory-bill in the swamps below Columbia. On 12 February 1844, after "an eager pursuit thro wet cane breaks & other swamp obstacles," and two missed shots, Gregg succeeds in bringing down the bird "which gave ample proof of its fierce spirit & wonderful tenacity of life." This description recalls Audubon's story of the capture of an ivory-bill which he ties by the leg to the leg of a table, only to find the next morning a demolished table. The modern reader notes with regret the killing of birds by ornithologists like Gregg and the insatiable bird killer Audubon himself, but this was the way of the science of the time.

Balancing this seeming callousness on Gregg's part are his descriptions of his horses Buckeye and Granby and his dogs Bruno, Fan, Brant, Ranger, and Lara. For Gregg hunting involves not just the pursuit of game, but, then as now, the company and close knowledge of animals whose individual personalities Gregg comes to know. Like the best of hunters, Gregg gives credit to the various aptitudes of each of his animal companions. He notes their interrelationships, health, and their accomplishments in which he takes pride. Of "poor Brant," a canine favorite of long standing, Gregg records, he died at last with convulsions and "was buried beside Fan in the corner of the garden." Of Bruno, he says the dog was shot in the leg with pellets, with the "perpetrator of the outrage unknown." Horse nature is equally fascinating. A Pumpkin Town, South Carolina, native rides what Gregg describes as a "broken down but fiery spirited Charger, of such remarkable character & action, that we over-laughed ourselves, until it became painful." Gregg's journals are likely to humanise him for us in ways that his illustrious battle record may fail to do.

The journals provide yet another example of the refined intellectual culture of the antebellum South from a time before that world was "kicked to pieces," in the immortal words of Gregg's fellow journal keeper and Carolina contemporary, Mary Boykin Chesnut. In Gregg, one sees the qualities of the renaissance gentleman of Western tradition happily united with the bravery and mettle of the warrior. It would be difficult to find a better example of this combination in the annals of the great conflict in which Gregg gave his life.

INTRODUCTION

One aspect of the serious study of the natural sciences was the keeping of a journal, and Maxcy Gregg was diligent in writing his findings. On Saturday, April 9, 1842, he wrote the first entry into one of two Sporting Journals, spanning sixteen years, now archived at the University of South Carolina's Caroliniana Library. "Rode Buckeye in the evening below Granby, intending to visit Sunday's Pond, but seeing negroes at work near it, turned back to the Granby Marshes where I found little water & less cover. There was a single snipe there, which I killed. At Cayce's Pond I fell in with Tom Seibels, Jake Seibels, & one of Jake's brothers, who were fishing. While we remained there, two Didappers attracted our attention by fluttering along the water. I took three very long shots at one of them, & believe he dodged percussion every time." These are simple lines expressing seemingly minor events in a day more than one hundred and seventy-five years ago, but for the twenty-six year old who wrote those sentences, they represented a quest for personal knowledge and freedom from the constraints of various obligations.

At the time this first journal entry was made, Maxcy Gregg was an attorney working for his father. He lived, as he had done since his birth, in his father's house on Senate Street in Columbia, South Carolina, with his parents and his two sisters. Like other young men of his social class in the antebellum South, his life was one of duty – to his family, to his job, to the local militia, to politics, and to societal etiquette and codes of behavior. These journals, published here for the first time, add a new dimension to the life of a Civil War brigadier general, and for the reader a glimpse into the past.[1]

------

1 To his parents Cornelia Maxcy and James Gregg, the birth of a second son, Edward Fisher Gregg about 1822, was followed by that of two daughters, Julia deBerniere Gregg in 1823 and Cornelia Manning Gregg in 1826. Maxcy's unmarried sisters remained part of the Gregg family household throughout their lives, but his brother Edward did not. Like his father and his brother, Edward Fisher Gregg attended South Carolina College. Unlike his brother, in December of 1841 Edward received his diploma. Rather than follow his father and older brother into the field of law, Edward Gregg chose to study medicine. After his graduation from the University of Pennsylvania in 1845, Edward "went West to practice. Suddenly, correspondence ceased and nothing more was

Born on the 1ˢᵗ of August 1815, Maxcy Gregg's path through life was relatively predictable. His father, James R. Gregg, was an educated professional; his mother, Cornelia Manning Maxcy, was the daughter of the first president of South Carolina College. Their children would be educated, and the first-born would follow the path set by his parents. Maxcy Gregg would, like his father, be a lawyer, a States' Rights man, and would serve as an officer in the Richland Volunteer Rifle Company, one of Columbia's local militia units.

Maxcy Gregg attended South Carolina College where he excelled in a number of subjects, including Greek literature and philosophy. In his journal entry for May 9, 1842, he quoted lines from the Athenian playwright Aristophanes' *Wasps*. Gregg was, in fact, so well versed in Greek that he occasionally sprinkled his correspondence with quotations. In a letter written October 16, 1862, from Camp Barnes in Berkeley County, Virginia, to his South Carolina friend William Gilmore Simms, Gregg "engage[d] in a discussion of Grecian history…in which he [drew] freely from the original Greek of the dramatists, making an amusing commentary of his own." That discussion was continued by Gregg in another letter he wrote to Simms from Winchester on the 11ᵗʰ of November. Gregg quoted "from memory, sundry passages in the original," from a Greek tragedy.[2]

Gregg also excelled at college in botany, and it was then that he began a lifelong study of nature, ranging from songbirds to astronomy, as reflected in his *Sporting Journals*. He would have preferred a career in the field of science, but

---

ever heard of him." The family never knew his fate and were left to surmise that his life had ended abruptly from an unknown cause. McCarty, Louise Miller, compiler. *Footprints: The Story of the Greggs of South Carolina*. Winter Park, Florida: Orange Press, 1951, 100.

2 Guilds, John Caldwell, general editor. *The Writings of William Gilmore Simms* (Centennial Edition, Volume III). Columbia: University of South Carolina Press, 1972, 219n. Maxcy Gregg did not receive his diploma from South Carolina College. After he and his classmates took their final examinations at the conclusion of their senior year in 1835, the faculty met and determined that William Blanding and Maxcy Gregg should receive first and second honors; however, despite much deliberation, the faculty could not reach a consensus on which young man ought to take which honor. The final determination of standing fell to a draw 'by lot,' with Maxcy Gregg winning the proverbial coin toss. This procedure fell far short of the righteous young Gregg's sense of propriety and justice. Maxcy spoke privately with Professor Henry J. Nott, Chairman of the Faculty. As a matter of principle and personal honor, Maxcy explained, he was compelled to refuse the acceptance of an honor based not on scholastic achievement but rather the draw of a straw. Unsatisfied with Nott's response, Gregg then verbally accosted him during Chapel, in front of the assembled students and faculty, removing all possibility of a quiet resolution of the case. Professor Nott warned the uncompromising young Gregg that his refusal to deliver the required speech at commencement exercises would result in the loss of his diploma. Gregg stood fast, and despite his father's and grandfather's legacies at the college, he was made an example of and his diploma was withheld.

as the eldest son he was obliged to follow the course designed by his father, and so the obedient son "never told him of his taste, but studied law and followed in his footsteps to the end." Gregg did not veer from his lot in life despite the fact that he described his profession as "rascally law business" and a tedious "drudgery." A neighbor observed of him that he was "one of the tidiest of men, and was always dressed in, generally, a full suit of black, with the uncomfortable standing collar of immaculate white… As a lawyer his character was unsullied, and his reputation was never smirched by undertaking a case in the least disreputable."[3]

He found a place for himself in politics as an intense Southerner and a States' Rights supporter. Although he rarely mentioned political activities in his journals, Gregg represented Richland District at numerous conventions throughout the state and the South. While James Gregg served in the South Carolina General Assembly (1822-1845) and as mayor of Columbia for one term, Maxcy Gregg did not enter the local political arena (although his name was mentioned for governor in 1860 and 1862). Holding no personal aspirations for political office, Gregg was "indifferent to the prizes of ordinary political ambition." Politics, Gregg wrote in his journal, were "machinations" which consumed much of his free time as he and his fellow South Carolina secessionists pushed and pulled the Palmetto State towards separation from the Union.[4]

Serving as an officer in a state militia unit was also a duty which took up much of his time. Gregg was interested in military science and "studied all that books could teach concerning the art and practices of war." When the United States entered into hostilities with Mexico he sought, and received, a commission with the United States Army. After placing his ring on his mother's finger, he left his father's home, not to return for more than a year. Although Major Gregg

---

3 Louise Miller McCarty, *Footprints*, 98. Robertson, Mrs. A.G. "Gen. Maxcy Gregg." *Confederate Veteran Magazine*, Volume VIII (1900), 429.

4 Palmer, Benjamin Morgan. *Address Delivered at the Funeral of General Maxcy Gregg*. Columbia, South Carolina: Southern Guardian Steam-power Press, 5. When his name was proposed for governor of South Carolina in December of 1860, William Gilmore Simms wrote to William Porcher Miles, "The Executive Chair is now a seat of equal dignity & responsibility & not, as heretofore, a mere Constabulary. It is difficult to say where the proper man is to be found, who can properly fill it. Some of those spoken of are mere bladdery blatherskites, others again are able enough, but odiously selfish; Maxcy Gregg has been spoken of, but he, though admitted to be bold, brave & able, is yet personally unpopular, I hear." Oliphant, Mary C. Simms, and T.C. Duncan Eaves, editors. *The Letters of William Gilmore Simms*, Volume IV (1858-1866). Columbia: University of South Carolina Press, 2012, 281.

saw no action, a special section of his journal is devoted to his experiences in Mexico, and the lessons he learned through recruiting and training a regiment served him well in 1861.[5]

It was only when these and other "affairs of one sort or another" allowed that he was free to take up his Blunderbuss, mount one of his horses, and often accompanied only by a few dogs, participate in the activity which gave him the greatest personal satisfaction – exploring the natural sciences, particularly ornithology.

Gregg's ease with nature might have been influenced by his grandfather. In one of his sermons delivered to the students of South Carolina College where he served as president from 1804 until his death in 1820, Jonathan Maxcy held that "Nature is an external display of god. Powers and causes are hidden and invisible, and the proper objects of intellect. In studying into the works of nature, we should avoid speculative hypotheses, and be guided wholly by facts." The study of nature was viewed as "a spiritually uplifting pastime" and "a means to better understand God's order." Gregg was not an overtly religious man, and the reader will find no references to either God or spirituality in his journals, but he found, like his grandfather, solace in nature. Maxcy attended church at, alternately, Trinity Episcopal and First Presbyterian, with his family. His *Book of Common Prayer*, archived at the South Caroliniana Library, contains his name, the date April 8, 1854, and pencil markings of responses written by Julia to accommodate her brother's increasing deafness.[6]

Gregg was conscientious about maintaining subject boundaries in his logs. He rarely mentioned his immediate family or offered much in the way of an opinion on politics. He was easily able to separate and compartmentalize those other aspects of his life from his hunting and specimen collecting expeditions. Not only did he keep track on a daily basis of the numbers of shots fired and birds brought down each time he went out by himself, as well as by all other members of a hunting party, he tallied his own numbers every several months. Between October of 1842 and March of 1843, for instance, he went out "ornithologizing"

---

5 Macaulay, Neill Webster. "*Maxcy Gregg, Lawyer, Soldier and Savant.*" Unpublished manuscript, 5-6; Maxcy Gregg Folder, Vertical File, South Carolina Confederate Relic Room and Military Museum (SCCRRMM), Columbia, South Carolina.

6 Maxcy, Jonathan. "An Anniversary Discourse, Delivered to the Students of the South Carolina College, on Sunday, December 1ˢᵗ, 1816." *Collegiate Addresses; Being Counsels to Students on Their Literary Pursuits and Future Life by the Rev. Jonathan Maxcy, D.D.* (Romeo Elton, editor). London: Longman, Brown, and Co., n.d., 136. Taylor, David, editor. *South Carolina Naturalists: An Anthology, 1700-1860.* Columbia: University of South Carolina Press, 1998, 6.

a total of sixteen times, once in January, three times in February, twice in March, and five times each in November and December. During those months he fired 128 times, and listed numbers of specimens obtained for each month individually. He also kept track of the number of individual birds shot during each of those months, noting in conclusion that he had identified ten species and thirty "individuals." He was also careful to give credit for bringing down a bird where the credit was due. Bruno, one of his hunting dogs, and a hawk each received acknowledgement for bringing in partridges.

Although judged in modern terms one might conclude that Maxcy Gregg was merely a hunter whose preferred target was birds, in his time the ornithologist learned the science through the collection and study of specimens, and Gregg considered himself an ornithologist. It was a time, also, when "there were acknowledged scientists doing good work, [and] there was a belief that virtually anyone could become a naturalist, regardless of age, education, or economic class. Commonly naturalists were clergymen, doctors, or politicians who pursued the study of natural history with vigor but most often as a personal interest." In order to identify both flora and fauna by their common and Latin names, Maxcy Gregg turned to the works of various published naturalists from either his own extensive library or that of South Carolina College. John James Audubon was taken from the shelf when he needed to identify the plumage of a bird. When confronted with a Balsam Fir tree, the *Abies balsamifera*, Gregg referred to the French father-and-son team of botanists, André and François André Michaux, who had collected and identified North and South Carolina specimens in the late 18th century and early 19th century. And when attempting to identify a "mouse, a female, [which] was larger than the common Mouse, more stoutly built, with a tail shorter in proportion & blunt at the end; it's color lighter & more reddish, its eyes prominent, large & resembling somewhat those of the flying squirrel; its feet & toes, with sharp claws, seemed also adapted to a life of climbing," he looked to *Fauna Americana, Being a Description of the Mammiferous Animals Inhabiting North America* by Richard Harlan and *American Natural History* by John Davidson Godman.[7]

In order to collect a wide sampling of specimens the ornithologist required varied and diverse landscapes. Gregg had the advantage of relatively close access to coastal areas, pine forests, swamplands, and mountainous regions. Among his favorite places to hunt was the old town of Granby. The settlement was at one time a trading post dating back to 1733 when it became one of a small number of townships established by the governor of South Carolina. Granby was one

---

7 David Taylor, *South Carolina Naturalists*, 6.

of the sites frequently visited by Maxcy Gregg, perhaps, in part, because of its association with the Revolutionary War, in which two of his ancestors fought. Gregg also noted, on January 20, 1858, environmental changes he observed as the abandoned town reverted to nature. "There is now little left to mark the site of the old Town of Granby. All the Houses are gone. The old oaks & Cedars about Mrs. Hane's House & most of the India trees have been cut down. And the little grave-yards of the Hane & Seibels families are close pressed by the Cotton-field, the soil where the houses & gardens once were being fresh and rich. Aleck Taylor, who is now the owner of the Old Town, has thrown within his fence the little Marshes which used once to be my favorite Snipe grounds, but which for many years, from being thrown open to cattle, had become bare of cover. The cover is now thick, and a high growth of broom-straw adjoins the marshes."[8]

In addition to his interest in ornithology, Maxcy Gregg was an ardent amateur astronomer. With his personal collection of "astronomical instruments and globes" he observed and documented in his Sporting Journals several comets, a meteor, and an aurora borealis. From the observatory Gregg built into the roof of the family's Richland Street home, it was not only the stars that were visible. His little cousin, Susan Maxcy, "his pet and constant companion" in the mid-1850s, related an incident. "One evening I remember following him to the observatory and his giving me a spyglass to make my own observations, and I suppose by way of keeping me quiet. Coming down the steps, he found me spying into the neighbor's tea table. My, he was indignant! And I, disappointed that I didn't get a better look."[9]

---

8 John Gregg settled in the American colony in the mid-1700s, accompanied by his wife, "one Dutch servant, and five negroes." During the American Revolution their son James defended the land accrued by his family, serving as an officer in the First South Carolina Regiment. After the expiration of his term of enlistment, Captain Gregg aligned himself with Francis Marion's guerilla band. Retribution by British soldiers and Loyalists was forthcoming, and Maxcy Gregg's grandfather found himself "forced, for a considerable time, to conceal himself in Poke Swamp, where he slept in a hollow log, fed by his family, occasionally visiting his residence under cover of darkness." Undeterred, he continued to participate in raids even as his home was burned, leaving his wife and children homeless. Gregg, Alexander. *History of the Old Cheraws*. New York: Richardson and Company, 1867 (reproduction, n.d.), 86, 383.

9 Last Will and Testament of Maxcy Gregg, 1862; Series S108093, Reel 0023, Frame 00707, South Carolina Department of Archives and History (SCDAH), Columbia, South Carolina. Louise Miller McCarty, *Footprints*, 98.

One surprising element of his journals is Gregg's observations on his personal health. Like most South Carolinians, he suffered his share of fevers. He wrote of being ill in January of 1844 "with a kind of nervous type of tertian" fever, which was most likely malaria. Even after two weeks, he had not "recovered [his] health & strength completely." The Low Country of the Palmetto State had a well-deserved reputation for being "notoriously unhealthy." Malaria was prevalent in the swampy Low Country, that area being afforded the title of "the most malarious area on the Atlantic coast." Like yellow fever, malaria was a mosquito-borne disease, recognized as being seasonal, with the "sickly season" precisely defined by one Charleston doctor as June 21 to October 21. Others expanded the "time for retreat" from the 10th of May to the 10th of November. Maxcy Gregg merely kept an eye on the weather and avoided travel to the Low Country until the first "hard frost" had been reported.[10]

Medical professionals attributed contaminated air to be the cause of malaria and various fevers, making a connection to stagnant water, though not to mosquitoes. As early as 1844 James Gregg, in his capacity as Senator representing Richland District, was notified that it would be a "dangerous experiment to the health of the town" of Columbia, and "injurious to [the] health" of her citizens to re-open the Columbia Canal (another area favored by Maxcy Gregg for his excursions), which had been abandoned for navigation after the railroad became the main means of transporting goods between Columbia and Charleston. Mr. Gregg was warned by a local doctor that "dampness and heat in all warm climates are universally considered as furnishing malaria, and wherever Canals exist – however much effort is made to keep water in them, there will be much stagnant water constantly exposing surfaces, for evaporation, and deadly miasma."[11]

Treatments for fevers varied and included "bloodletting, taking sometimes 72 ounces from a patient," "snake root and musk," potassium citrate, calomel, quinine, morphine, and laudanum. Gregg was once prescribed calomel to treat a case of grippe which affected him "in the shape of a sort of chill & fever." He noted that he was "not sure but the remedy was as bad as the disease, for I have been left in a wretched state of languor." Gregg was fortunate that lethargy was his only reaction to the mercury he ingested. In April of 1843 when "suffering under the most violent cold [he] ever remember[ed] to have been attacked with," Maxcy was even more anxious to escape from the house on Senate Street, for after being confined, he confessed in his journal, "my gun now gives me a very

---

10 Waring, Joseph Ioor. *A History of Medicine in South Carolina 1825-1900*. Columbia, South Carolina: The R.L. Bryan Company, 1967, 37.

11 Report to the General Assembly, Series S165029, Volume ND00, Page 00120, SCDAH.

agreeable relief." A serious cold, "the first symptom of which being a strange sensation in the chest," had the forty-three year old housebound for nearly three weeks, preventing him from "using [his] gun."[12]

In 1860 Gregg resorted to the surgeon's knife for an unknown problem. After a month spent recovering, he regarded the operation as successful although he noticed an increase in his deafness, which had, by that time, become so severe that he was considering leaving the courtroom and trying, he wrote a cousin in Louisiana, "a new life before I am too old." Before he became hard of hearing Gregg was able to identify the vocalizations of a variety of birds but uncertain of others. The Bartram Snipe, he knew, produced a "rolling whistle when disturbed." Hearing a song from a bird in a pine tree and not recognizing it, Gregg shot the bird, a Red-eyed Vireo, "merely in order to make an identification." Another that attracted his attention was a bird that uttered "various strange notes" which he initially "attributed without hesitation to Frogs." It was found to be a *Rallus elegans*, a Fresh Water Marsh Hen.[13]

Gregg's most serious health crisis occurred in November of 1845 when his hunting excursions were "to be interrupted for a long time, by an accident which came near being fatal." On Thursday the 27th, as he was returning from a Master of the Lower Battalion militia muster, he felt as if he were suffering from a "bad cold." The following day he awoke in the middle of the night and as he got up from his bed he "fainted & fell into the fire, burning [his] head, neck & right hand very dangerously. [He] came to with the pain & started up, probably just in time to save [his] life." Maxcy was not suffering from a "bad cold," as he initially thought. He had measles and a high fever. Although he recovered from his bout with measles and the serious burns he suffered, Gregg made no excursions during the winter of 1845-1846. He endured about two months of "close confinement & great suffering" during which his mother was his constant nurse. He withstood "much pain & constraint, in restoring partially, by mechanical means, such as springs & bandages, the flexibility of the

---

12 Joseph Ioor Waring, *A History of Medicine in South Carolina*, 20n, 31.

13 Marshall-Furman Papers (Mss. 2740, 4042), Louisiana State University Libraries (LSU), Baton Rouge, Louisiana; transcript by Robert K. Krick, June 2014. Gregg's deafness has been cited as a contributing factor to his confusion during the battle of Fredericksburg where he received his mortal wound. James Gregg also experienced deafness, and although he traveled to New York in 1844 for treatment, the doctor determined that he was too old to undergo the recommended surgery.

fingers, & presenting distortion of the neck." It was not until the end of January of 1846 that he was able "to walk out, with [his] hand in a sling & [his] neck wrapped up."

Maxcy Gregg would have been the first to admit that, while proficient, he was not an excellent marksman. He took it all in stride, however, and often, whether intentionally or not, added a humorous touch in describing his failures. When his attention was attracted by two Didappers "fluttering along the water," he took "three very long shots at one of them" but believed the bird "dodged percussion every time." On another occasion when he spied a Solitary Sandpiper, he became "over-anxious to get it, & firing nervously, only broke a leg the first shot, and missed the bird as it flew off." After taking seventeen shots and bringing down six birds, Gregg admitted he had "made bad shooting." His shooting was also "bad" when he took twenty shots and brought down five swallows.

Hunting involved not just the pursuit of game, but the employment and companionship of animals, much cherished by the hunters themselves. Gregg most often went out riding one of several horses, including Buckeye, Granby, and Camden. He was generous in his comments on the accomplishments of his dogs. Bruno exhibited "great style" in driving a flock of Kildees, and when raising a covey of partridges he treed them "in the most dashing style." Fan was also a capable retriever. On one occasion while on an all-day hunt with his uncle, the two men headed toward the Congaree River where they "hitched [their] horses, threw off [their] great coats, & took it afoot down the River." On finding a small flock of Green-wing Teal, Maxcy fired and "crippled" one of them. Fan swam to retrieve the duck from the opposite side of the pond where it fell. Unfortunately, Fan's success was diminished when she and another retriever both got hold of a rabbit, and "pulling for it, tore it so much" that it had to be abandoned. By August of 1845 Ranger was added to the group. While shy on his first two outings, the puppy "at last seemed to acquire courage amongst the pack of Dogs, Children & Shooters in which he found himself, & began to fetch birds a little, being his first attempt in that way." Under the tutelage of a professional, Ranger soon "took to fetching out of the water readily, having Bruno's example to encourage him in swimming." The puppy was a fast learner and "with Bruno's example before him, acquitted himself very creditably in fetching out of the water." Just as Ranger was making progress, Maxcy was laid up following his bout with measles, and by the time he was able to return to hunting Ranger showed "the great loss he suffered in his education" and had to be "trained anew to the simple matter of fetching birds."

Robert Pringle Mayrant was one of Gregg's most frequent companions on his hunting forays, and the two made several expeditions with other friends as the "Santee Squadron" down the Congreee and Santee rivers to Charleston. It was on one of these excursions in October of 1843 that Maxcy first observed and came to covet Mayrant's "large Blunderbuss" which Mayrant had purchased from Columbia merchant William Glaze at his store, *At the Sign of the Drum*. Another of Maxcy's most frequent hunting companions was his mother's brother, Hart Maxcy. The two men, accompanied by their dogs, often participated in all day's hunts. Following the death of James Gregg in 1852 the Gregg family lived with Hart Maxcy, his wife, and children, at their farm in the country just north of Columbia. During the two years the Greggs lived at Rockwood Maxcy had the opportunity to share his love of nature with Hart's children. The habits of a rabbit were examined for nearly a week by Jonathan, Ashley, Martha, and Susan under the tutelage of Uncle Maxcy, who also allowed the boys to fire at targets. It is apparent in his interaction with the children that "courage, honesty, and strength, were tempered with the softer graces of gentleness and love."[14]

In 1854 Maxcy's sisters, Julia and Cornelia, received an inheritance from their bachelor uncle Elias Gregg. With this unexpected gift they purchased the Richland Street house, and the family moved back to the city proper. It was "by no means a pretentious home, outstanding only on account of the occupants and fine library." The Gregg home was "noted for its hospitality, delightful entertainments and dinner parties attended by 'a feast of reason and a flow of soul.'" Julia and Cornelia were "accomplished ladies known in their day as outstanding in influence and good works, both private and public."[15]

In addition to the six Greggs, the household included a varying number of slaves between 1833 and 1865. In 1833 James Gregg mortgaged his farm, using as collateral his eleven slaves, Peter and his wife, Leah, "one other negro woman, Hester, and her two children, Harriet and Dennis, one other negro woman, Liza, and her child George, one negro girl named Rhode," and "one negro boy named Pleasant, but whose name may be changed." The property was again mortgaged in 1842 with "a negro man named Isaac, about seventy-one years of age," held

---

14 Benjamin Morgan Palmer, *Address Delivered at the Funeral of General Maxcy Gregg*, 4.

15 Louise Miller McCarty, *Footprints*, 97, 98. The sisters' various public services included knitting socks for soldiers during the Civil War.

as collateral. Of those slaves, four remained in bondage to the Greggs until the war brought an end to slavery, and each is mentioned by name in the Sporting Journals.[16]

The opportunity to escape from his obligations and his family for more than an afternoon or a day was a rare treat for Maxcy Gregg. He was accompanied by Peter on a twenty-eight day hunting excursion to the mountains of North Carolina in 1843. Early in the journey Granby became lame, and Peter fell off to accommodate the injured horse. While Gregg continued on to the mountains, Peter made his way at his own pace to Greenville where he spent time visiting his mother, while nursing the horse back to health. Peter was also the caretaker and veterinarian to Gregg's dogs. When Brant "took the distemper" in 1844 he was treated with opium, as prescribed by Peter Hawker in his *Instructions to Young Sportsmen, In All That Relates to Guns and Shooting*. When this treatment failed, Peter "rubbed [him] down the spine regularly with an ointment of red-pepper." After tearing a gash in his skin Bruno was held by Gregg while Peter sewed the wound and "fixed on with bandages a plaster of tar & grease." Through Peter's ministrations, the dog recovered. Peter exhibited an "unfortunate love of the bottle," for which Gregg seems to have made no judgement.

Gregg wondered if Leah, Peter's wife, might have been intentionally starving one of his dogs in retaliation for his decreasing the stray-cat population, but ultimately decided that she would not do such a cruel thing. Pleasant came to the family when he was young. Among his duties was pouring tea for the family each afternoon. Five years younger than Gregg, he was with the brigadier general throughout his Civil War service and maintained a vigil at Gregg's deathbed.[17]

His final entries in his Sporting Journal coincide with Maxcy Gregg's increased involvement in the secession movement and his role in the Civil War. Through the decades, from college debates and the turbulent 1840s and 1850s, he "maintained his silent watch...knowing that truth [would] experience a resurrection, and [he] calmly waited for the historic moment when the revolutionary sword should again cut the cords of political bondage, and set his country free." Gregg not only viewed a political showdown as inevitable, he was

---

16 Miscellaneous Records (Columbia Series), ST 0417 (LDS #22669), Volume H, 397-398; ST 0419 (LDS #22671), Volume M, 173-174, SCDAH.

17 Leah and Peter, who had been with the Greggs from as early as 1833, were most likely among those who made the sea voyage to Liberia with forty-three year old Julia Gregg and the American Colonization Society in the fall of 1866. After the war Pleasant, who adopted the surname Goode, became involved in politics, being elected president of the Colored Democratic Party. Following his death in 1870 he was buried at Trinity Episcopal Church graveyard.

perfectly willing to do what he could to hasten its onset. After complaining to his cousin, Henry Marshall, on August 13, 1860, that "the Southern people seem infatuated in their attachment to the Union," Gregg penned and sent to friends a draft of an ordinance of secession. When the final Ordinance was approved on the 20th of December, Maxcy Gregg was an enthusiastic signatory.[18]

Gregg was accurate in his prediction that "the North will not willingly release its prey, but that as soon as the double dealing & vacillation of [President] Buchanan has reached its term, a serious effort will be made to subjugate the Southern States by the use [of] a naval force, combined with the occupation of such important ports & fortresses on the coast as may be practicable. I think it likely that I may have a place in the army during the war." Within two weeks of South Carolina leaving the Union, Governor Francis W. Pickens appointed him colonel of the first regiment of South Carolina troops mobilized to defend Charleston Harbor from the anticipated reinforcement of Union-held Fort Sumter. Stationed on nearby Morris Island Gregg's regiment, which consisted of ten companies of South Carolina riflemen – some of the companies made up of longstanding militia organizations, others newly-formed for the war – witnessed the shelling of Fort Sumter which began on the 12th of April, though they took no part in the artillery duel. Their orders were to monitor the coast for an anticipated landing by Federal troops.[19]

Just one week after the surrender of Major Anderson and his troops at Fort Sumter, Colonel Gregg led about half of the First South Carolina Volunteers to Virginia where they remained until their six-month term of service expired. Their first test under fire occurred on the 17th of June at Vienna where they ambushed and routed four companies of the 1st Ohio Regiment under the command of Brigadier General Robert Cumming Schenck.

Back in Richmond not long after that engagement, Gregg's regiment was mustered out of service. He remained in the Confederate capital where, within a month, he had recruited eleven companies which were mustered in to Confederate service as the First South Carolina Infantry (Provisional). This regiment remained in Virginia after Gregg was promoted to the rank of brigadier general in December. Assigned to South Carolina, the Twelfth, Thirteen and

---

18 Benjamin Morgan Palmer, *Address Delivered at the Funeral of General Maxcy Gregg*, 6.

19 Marshall-Furman Papers, LSU; transcript by Robert K. Krick. Brigadier General Maxcy Gregg's role in the Civil War has been documented and written about in various publications, most notably and extensively in Robert K. Krick's "Maxcy Gregg: Political Extremist and Confederate General" from *The Smoothbore Volley That Doomed the Confederacy* (The Louisiana State University Press, 2002).

Fourteenth South Carolina Infantry regiments became Gregg's brigade. There, for the first time, he served under the command of Robert E. Lee. In April of 1862 Gregg and his troops were transferred to Virginia where the brigade was brought up to full strength by the addition of the First South Carolina (Orr's) Rifles and the First South Carolina Infantry.

To Gregg's dismay, he had missed both the first battle of Manassas in July of 1861, and November's Battle of Port Royal near Beaufort in his home state. However, his leadership skills were unquestionably combat-proven in June of 1862 while leading his brigade as an element of Major General Ambrose Powell Hill's famed Light Division. The cost, however, was high. During the battle of Gaines' Mill on June 27th, one hundred and forty of the brigade's 854 casualties were killed.[20]

Action in the second battle of Manassas was also fierce for Gregg's brigade, and its performance contributed heavily to the achievement of the Confederate victory there. While maintaining the vital left flank of Lieutenant General "Stonewall" Jackson's corps on the 29th of August, Gregg and his troops repulsed six assaults by Federal units attempting to break their line. Reminded through a message from MG Hill that his position was a critical one, Gregg responded that though his men were running out of ammunition, his South Carolinians would hold the position, if need be, "with the bayonet."[21]

---

20 All fourteen members of the color guard of the 1st SC Infantry were either killed or wounded in the fierce fighting at Gaines' Mill. Those killed included Privates Alfred Gaillard Pinckney, P. Gasden Holmes, Thomas Hagerty, John O'Rourke, Thomas Gascons, William Tobin, and another whose name remains unknown; Color Sergeant James H. Taylor; and Color Corporal Edmund T. Shubrick Hayne. The wounded were corporals Thomas J. Howard, George M. Cotchett, and William L. Durst; and 1st Sergeant Rufus N. Richbourg. The fourteenth member of the color guard was Color Sergeant William W. Gregg, a cousin of the general, but because he had been taken ill, was not on the field but instead in a Richmond hospital. On the morning of the 27th of June, which happened to be William Gregg's eighteenth birthday, he was still ill, but hearing the sounds of battle, walked out of the hospital. "Trembling from weakness, his cheeks flushed with a fever that would have kept most soldiers safe in bed, he passed along the lines inquiring for Gregg's brigade. He struggled on, hoping to find his regiment, regain his flag, [and] go into action with his own color guard..." Unable to find the First South Carolina Volunteers, the young man stumbled in among the Eighth Alabama Regiment of Wilcox's Brigade (Longstreet's Division). Here he "took a musket, went into the ranks and fought amongst strangers. After the battle they bore testimony that he fought with great gallantry, until he yielded up his life for the cause so dear to him." *Anderson Intelligencer* (Anderson, South Carolina), April 18, 1900.

21 McCrady, Edward Jr. "Gregg's Brigade of South Carolinians in the Second Battle of Manassas." *Southern Historical Society Papers*, Volume XIII (1885), 34. Just days prior to the battle of Cedar Mountain Maxcy Gregg learned of the death of his mother on the 2nd of August. In order to validate a codicil to his 1861 will, he made a hurried run to Culpeper Court House on the 9th.

By now his brigade was considered among the best in the army. Their next engagement, a nightmarish fight in darkness and under a torrential rain, took place on the 1st of September at Chantilly. Hard marching followed as the rival armies vied for position. A footsore trek to Frederick, Maryland, was followed by a tramp to Harpers' Ferry where the Light Division received the official surrender of Union troops there after a short artillery barrage. A rapid seventeen-mile march to Sharpsburg on September the 17th brought Gregg's troops directly into action on the field of battle. Only the timely arrival and hard fighting by the Light Division saved General Lee's army from disaster at the hands of General George B. McClellan's numerically superior army.

In October, anticipating a winter respite from fighting, Lee's army settled into bivouac in northern Virginia. The Light Division, and Brigadier General Maxcy Gregg's Palmetto Brigade, found themselves camped near Berryville where rumors began to circulate among Gregg's troops. It was whispered by several members of the Fourteenth Regiment that the entire brigade might return to South Carolina to assist in the defense of Charleston, which was under threat of a naval attack. Gregg, anxious to return to his native state with his troops, wrote to General P.G.T. Beauregard, Commander of the Department of South Carolina, Georgia and Florida, to share with him that "the Troops of my command have been in high spirits lately. From a report brought from South Carolina, of Col. [James] Chestnut's [sic], declaring his belief that an application which you had made for Gen A.P. Hill's division to be sent to the Coast of South Carolina would be successful... Since the 1st of October, I have been looking every day for news of an attack in Charleston against which place the enemy have the strongest notions for sending a great force. It is natural therefore that like all my Officers & men I should strongly desire to take part in the defence of our own State...or if the whole Division of Gen. A.P. Hill cannot be spared from Virginia; I still cling to the hope that you may endeavor to obtain my Brigade." Gregg was confident enough in the likelihood of being sent south that he wrote a friend that he and his brigade might be sent to Charleston "in time to engage in its defence, in the event of assault." Before Gregg's request for a transfer could be answered, however, the Light Division was again on the move.[22]

Gregg's men, so often placed at the most critical point of the battle line, were held in reserve during the battle of Fredericksburg on the 13th of December 1862. The Union troops of Brigadier General George Meade broke through the Confederate line in the woods, and as the Federals advanced, a deadly

22 Unified Papers and Slips Belonging in Confederate Compiled Service Records, Maxcy Gregg, NARA. John Caldwell Guilds, *The Writings of William Gilmore Simms*, 219n.

minié ball found its mark, mortally wounding the forty-seven year old. With his last telegram to South Carolina governor Francis W. Pickens, Gregg made clear that his loyalty was to his home state. "I am severely wounded, but the troops under my command have acted as they always have done, and I hope we have gained a glorious victory. If I am to die now, I give my life cheerfully for the independence of South Carolina, and I trust you will live to see our cause triumph completely."[23]

Maxcy Gregg died at 5:00 a.m. on Monday, the 15th of December 1862. Six hours after his death, his body had been prepared, dressed in his regimental uniform, and placed in a coffin. After lying in state in Richmond, his embalmed body was taken home for burial. A eulogy was delivered by the Reverend Benjamin Morgan Palmer at First Presbyterian Church, and his body was then interred on the 20th of December beside his parents at Elmwood Cemetery in Columbia. It was said of him by a peer that he was imbued with a "resolute, chivalrous spirit. To say that he does not fear an enemy, would be low commendation. He fears nothing under Heaven, but a base reputation." William Gilmore Simms wrote of him, "His patriotism was ardent and his politics consistent. He was of the straightest school of State-rights politicians. He was an accomplished scholar, of high rank in his profession, a high-toned gentleman. *Sans peur et sans reproche!* His name, henceforth, is monumental in his native State."[24]

It is not surprising that Maxcy Gregg maintained a journal for at least sixteen years. He was a "self-contained and reticent" man who, "in the seclusion of his study, surrounded by the great immortals who survive in books, not only found companions congenial to his taste, but drank in the wisdom of the past." His Sporting Journals offer a unique glimpse into the leisure activities of a young man of antebellum South Carolina. They offer, too, the rare opportunity to see Columbia and other areas of the state through the lens of time. It is hoped that with the publication of Maxcy Gregg's Sporting Journals, his name will now be counted among the noted naturalists of South Carolina.[25]

---

23 "Historical Notes." *South Carolina Historical and Genealogical Magazine*, Volume 7, Number 4 (October 1906), 181.

24 *The Camden Journal* (Camden, South Carolina), March 16, 1842. John Caldwell Guilds, *The Writings of William Gilmore Simms*, 220n. *Without fear and without reproach!*

25 Benjamin Morgan Palmer, *Address Delivered at the Funeral of General Maxcy Gregg*, 4, 5. Immediately following the death of their brother, sisters Julia and Cornelia became reliant on extended family for emotional, though not financial, support. The entire Gregg family had been especially close to their Maxcy-Leverett cousins, who relocated from Beaufort to Columbia in the spring of 1862. Not long after the funeral of Brigadier General Maxcy Gregg, Reverend and Mrs.

Gregg's penmanship is clear, concise, and without embellishments. He employs characteristics typical of the antebellum era, such as using a dash in place of a period to end a sentence and capitalizing nouns seemingly at random. Several verbs used in the past tense ('staid' for 'stayed', and 'past' for passed, for example), seem to the modern reader to be misspelled, but in the mid-19th century were entirely acceptable. Because his writing is easily read, few changes have been necessary in order to clarify grammar or composition for the ease of the reader.[26]

Leverett, feeling "so sorry for the forlorn state of Julia and Cornelia," invited the sisters to make their home with them on a permanent basis, and within months the Richland Street house was sold. During Major General William T. Sherman's occupation of Columbia in February of 1865, the Leverett home was pillaged. The uniform Gregg had been wearing when mortally wounded was found among Cornelia's possessions. His gold epaulettes, "splendid but old fashioned things," were stolen, as were "his crimson sash [and] the pants he was killed in." His uniform coat was not taken, but three buttons were forcefully removed and taken. In 1866 Julia Gregg moved to Liberia where she worked as a teacher for ten years. She and Cornelia later moved to Europe where they found it less expensive to live. Before moving back to the United States permanently, they lived for a while at the Waldensian commune at the foot of Mont Blanc. The two sisters died in Fredericksburg, Virginia, within two years of each other, while living at the home of their cousin, Susan Maxcy Latimer, the little girl who had been caught looking at neighbors through Uncle Maxcy's telescope. Before her death on the 7th of January 1896, Cornelia burned what was left in her possession of her brother's correspondence. The Gregg sisters were buried at Hollywood Cemetery in Richmond. Taylor, Frances Wallace, Catherine Taylor Matthews and J. Tracy Power, editors. *The Leverett Letters: Correspondence of a South Carolina Family, 1851-1868*. Columbia, South Carolina: The University of South Carolina Press, 2000, 182, 388-389, 391.

26 The South Caroliniana Library has digitized the journals, which are available to viewers on their web site. See http://delphi.tcl.sc.edu/library/digital/collections/max.html

Sporting Journal

Resumed, Sunday, 12 Nov: 1848

from Memoranda on loose sheets &c.

Fri. Nov. 14. 1845 Maigrant was about to make a
short cruise down the River, and I agreed to
accompany him as far as Threewits' Ferry, not
having more time to spare. Accordingly, we
embarked in the Nimrod at Granby, a
little after mid-day, taking with us Charles
Henry, William Macomb, Stephen, & Guard.
Maigrant spoke of having lately seen seventy
Turkeys on the Sandbar above the mouth of
Gill's Creek. Charles Henry & I took a
tramp thro the adjoining woods in search
of them, but found no signs of Turkeys.
Afterwards, I took another tramp with
Maigrant thro the swamp & Cotton wood thicket
at the head of the Big Lake, with no better
success. I fired this day but one shot,
at a Dove, which I brought down, but did
not get & do not count. We encamped

APRIL - SEPTEMBER 1842:
THE TOWN OF GRANBY AND THE COLUMBIA CANAL

Sat. April 9, 1842. Rode Buckeye in the evening below Granby[27], intending to visit Sunday's Pond, but seeing negroes at work near it, turned back to the Granby Marshes where I found little water & less cover. There was a single snipe there, which I killed. At Cayce's Pond I fell in with Tom Seibels, Jake Seibels, & one of Jake's brothers, who were fishing. While we remained there, two Didappers attracted our attention by fluttering along the water. I took three very long shots at one of them, & believe he dodged percussion every time.

6 shots

     1 snipe
     1 Redwing Blackbird (male)

Fri. [April] 15 [1842]. Rode in the evening with J.J. Seibels[28] to the Granby Marshes, taking Buckeye myself, & lending him Granby. Finding no Snipes, we proceeded to Sunday's Pond, where I shot a Green Heron, which lodged in a

---

27 One of Maxcy Gregg's favorite places to hunt was the old town of Granby, a small town settled by several German-speaking families of Swiss descent. By 1748 the community included a corn mill, a small garrison, and a house and store owned by Wade Hampton (1754-1835). During the Revolutionary War Saxe-Gotha (the original name of the settlement) was the site of Fort Granby, an outpost which was held for a time by the British until it was taken in May of 1781 by 'Light Horse' Harry Lee, the father of Robert E. Lee. Located on the west bank of the Congaree River about a mile and a half south of Columbia, by the early 1840s the area was "low and swampy." *South Carolina: The WPA Guide to the Palmetto State*. Columbia, South Carolina: University of South Carolina Press, 1988, 214.

28 John Jacob Seibels was a classmate of Maxcy Gregg at South Carolina College where both were members of the Clariosophic Society. In later years the Seibels had a home on Richland Street, not far from the second home of the Gregg family. In 1854 John J. Seibels was appointed Ambassador to Belgium.

bush not easily approached thro the bog, & which Lara, the only dog with me, was not sufficiently trained to find & fetch. So I had to leave the bird there. On the way back, heard for the first time this spring, the Chuckwillswidow.

2 shots   1 Green Heron   By J.J.S.   1 Dove

Thurs. [May] 5 [1842]. Riding Buckeye in the evening, over the old fields along the Steam-mill Branch, I discovered a solitary bird which I took for a Bartram Snipe. Gallopped home for my gun, & returning, searched for the bird for some time unsuccessfully. When I was beginning to fear that I could not find the Bartram, shot one of a pair of Solitary Sandpipers, which I strangely enough took for Spotted Sandpipers. Found it at last, feeding along the old field, one or two hundred yards from the spot where I had first seen it. I was however, over-anxious to get it; & firing nervously, only broke a leg the first shot, and missed the bird as it flew off. After that it was very shy, & difficult to approach. I got within a long range at last, by creeping along a gulley, but the instant I showed myself over a tuft of weeds, it flew off, I missed it, & could not find it again. From its appearance, I think it was a Bartram Snipe, tho I was led to doubt about it from not hearing the rolling whistle of the species when disturbed. Possibly the Bird may have been the Charadrius Pluvialis, or Marmoratus: tho I think not.

4 shots   1 Solitary Sandpiper

Mon. [May] 9 [1842]. For some time past, the water running out of Everett's Pond, being obstructed by the mound thrown up along side of the excavation of the Railroad,[29] and only partially percolating thro the sand, has been forced to spread itself out into a little Pond, in a low part of the field. Riding by this

---

29 In 1842 a second railroad line, from Branchville to Columbia, was completed, adding sixty-six miles of track in the state and an increase in property values and business in the capital city. Columbians turned out on the 28th of June 1842 for a barbeque and ceremonies marking the arrival of the first train to arrive in Columbia from Charleston. The railroad between Charlotte and Columbia followed, being completed around 1845. Construction slowed until the 1850s, but by 1860 the state was home to more than a thousand miles of train track.

place Sunday evening, I saw five diminutive Sandpipers, feeding in company with a Lesser Yellowlegs, & several Solitary Sandpipers, which last however, by a strange mistake, I took for the Totanus Macularius, as I had done when I killed one a few days before; perceiving at the same time something unusual, but not thinking of seeing <u>Solitary</u> Sandpipers sociably assembled. So mounted Buckeye before sunrise this morning, & galloping out followed by Fan found the same party of Little Sandpipers at the same place, together with several Solitaries, & Yellowlegs. With three shots, which I fired before I picked up any Birds, seeing their reluctance to quit the Pond, I killed two Yellowlegs, & two Solitary Sandpipers, but only a single one of the diminutive species. The Little fellows proved a very difficult mark, for with half a dozen more shots, I got but one. A clamorous Kildee kept pestering me for a long time by dogging my steps with its φωνὴν Χαράδρας ὄλεθρον τετοΚυίας[30] until incensed beyond endurance, I fired at it three times & killed it. Finally, took three shots to kill a Spotted Sandpiper, & when I got it in my possession was greatly puzzled to tell what it was. After an hour or two spent in this sport, rode back, & arrived about as early as I usually get out of bed.

15 shots

    2 Lesser Yellowlegs
    2 Solitary Sandpipers
    1 Spotted Sandpiper
    2 Little Sandpipers (Sringa [Calidris] Pusilla)
    1 Kildee

Mon. May 30 [1842]. Rode in the evening down to the old warehouse below the old Ferry Landing, & spent some time in firing at marks with buckshot. The size I used was T.T.G. of which my gun chambers four. I found that by putting the

---

30 The Greek passage is from Aristophanes' *Wasps* (line 1034), and translates as 'the voice of a death-bringing torrent'. It was not uncommon for Gregg to intersperse letters to friends with a Greek or Latin passage. He was "well versed" in several languages, including French, German, Italian, Spanish, Latin, and Greek. He was also "intimate with the classics, especially Greek literature." The identification and translation of the Greek text is courtesy of Marcus Hines. Shand, Robert W. "Incidents in the life of a Private Soldier in the war waged by the United States against the Confederate States, 1861-1865," 6. Robert W. Shand Papers, South Caroliniana Library, University of South Carolina (SCL, USC). *Cyclopedia of Eminent and Representative Men of the Carolinas of the Nineteenth Century* (Volume I). Madison, Wisconsin: Brant & Fuller, 1892 (Reprint 1972), 91.

shot down in regular tiers, with paste board wads between, they were thrown with far greater closeness and regularity than when I dropped them down pell-mell. Eleys Cartridges of Mould shot are I think a failure – unless those which I have got are bad ones. The reason I made the trial this evening, was that I expected to go over to John Englishe's with Gen. Hopkins the next day, on a hunting & fishing Expedition – in which however we were disappointed. After finishing my trials at the mark, & on the way back, I missed several Martins & a Nighthawk.

5 shots

Sat. [June] 4 [1842]. Having seen a family of four or five Little Screech Owls after dusk the evening before, on the road to Mrs. Fleming's field, just beyond Rocky Branch[31], I determined to visit the same spot this evening & watch for them. So mounted Buck-eye – rode to Everett's Pond – & on the way back, waited for the owls until the gathering dusk forced me to give up the hope of meeting with them again.

Fri. [June] 24 [1842]. Rode Buck-eye in the evening to Everett's & the Wetweather Ponds.[32] The rail-road is now so far completed, that for a few days past the [train] cars have run up to Columbia. A great fire swept the tract of land below it, about two weeks ago, from the corner of Henry's field to Hampton's Middle Ponds[33] & across to the Bluff road.[34] The weather before that time had been quite dry – since then, it has been wet. On my way back, towards dusk, a Chuckwillswidow flew up from the road this side of the Hill on which Hayne's negro house once stood, & lit on the lower limb of a large Pine. I brought it down with a one-handed shot from the saddle, to the great discomposure of Buckeye.

1 shot   1 Chuckwillswidow (female)

31 Rocky Branch, a tributary of the Congaree River, runs eastward on the southern side of Columbia.

32 The Wetweather Ponds were not specific sites but rather ponds created during especially rainy spells, and therefore referred to as 'wetweather'.

33 Hampton's Middle Ponds were located southeast of Columbia, lying in the low land east of the Congaree River.

34 Bluff Road is an extension of Huger Street which traverses southeast of Columbia.

Fri. July 29 [1842]. On Sunday, the 3d of this month, as I was riding out in the morning, & passing the Grove between the College & Rocky Branch, I observed a Crow besieged by a Mockingbird on a Pine tree. The moment I scared the crow off, the Mockingbird darted at him & treed him again; & being reinforced by a Companion of his own tribe, continued to worry the poor Crow in the same way, as long as I could keep them in sight. Proceeding to Everett's Pond, & amusing myself in watching some Cranes there, I saw a bird suddenly start up before Bruno in the South-eastern edge of the Pond, & flutter along the surface of the water for about 30 yards, uttering a cry of distress, & counterfeiting lameness; it then dived & I saw no more of it. At the first glance, & sound of its note, I imagined it for a moment to be a Telltale; but after it disappeared, I concluded it must be a Didapper, & made Bruno hunt for its nest for some time, tho without success. In the search, he started a young rabbit, which, perhaps without any good reason, I was inclined to take for a Marsh Hare. The next Sunday, Bruno caught a young rabbit near the Pond, after a fair & hard race thro the bushes. About 8 or 10 days since, as I was riding in the evening thro Randolph's lane, I saw an immense flock of Martins, which had settled in the fields of corn, on the stalks, & remained a little while, apparently for the purpose of resting in their flight from the river swamp back to the Town; the flock being mostly composed, as I think, of young Birds. A day or two after, in a moonlight evening, sitting in our front Piazza, I heard the twittering of a great multitude of swallows, which I suspected, tho I could not be certain of it, were in the air, & on a southward flight. However that may be, since that time I have seen no more of the great flock of townbred Martins, which were in the habit of roosting on the trees back of the Court House. Took up my gun this evening, after a long interval, & rode Granby down to the Brickyard. Coming back to Wade's field,35 I had the pleasure of discovering an employment for Bruno suited to his genius. A flock of a dozen Kildees, or more, were about the field; I set Bruno to driving them, which he did in great style, giving me several shots on the wing, some of which I killed at a pretty long distance. Saw but few Night-hawks, which, with the Martins, appeared to be travelling southwardly. Made bad shooting.

17 shots   3 Kildees

     2 Nighthawks

     1 Martin

---

35 'Wade's field' most likely refers to a piece of property belonging to Wade Hampton III, who was himself an avid hunter and an acquaintance of Maxcy Gregg. In 1836, while a student at South Carolina College, Wade Hampton wrote that Gregg was "an intimate friend of mine, & [he] is one of the smartest young men in the state." Hampton Family Papers, SCL, USC.

Mon. Aug 15 [1842]. The first few days of this month were remarkably cold, the wind remaining steadily at N.E. with drizzly rain for three or four days. Winter clothing & fires became comfortable. Accounts were published in the papers of numerous Icebergs having been met with at sea in pretty low Latitudes.[36] Did they cause the unseasonable cold here? For more than a week there has been rain every day, so that I have been prevented from going out shooting as I wished to. On the morning of the 8 Aug. I saw a Golden Crowned Thrush walking about in the yard under my window, apparently catching insects. It is the first time I remember ever to have seen the Bird any where but in retired woods. This evening, rode Buck-eye down to the Canal[37], & hitching him at Wade's field, remained there shooting until a gathering Storm rendered it necessary to gallop home. Saw few Martins – but a good many Barnswallows. Late in the evening, a flight of Nighthawks appeared for a few minutes. All these birds were travelling steadily Southwards. My shooting was bad – but I wounded some birds witch [sic] I did not get. Lara was with me, but would not fetch.

20 shots

4 Barn Swallows
1 Bank Swallow

---

36 According to *The Edgefield Advertiser* of June 15, 1842, "We understand that a live Yankee is building a steam tow boat for the purpose of going among the icebergs now so plenty in the Atlantic, and towing them to the West Indies, New Orleans, and even to Calcutta, should the experiment in other places succeed. He 'calculates' that one good fat iceberg, of the Greenland breed, will bring a thousand dollars in the West India market."

37 Constructed between 1820 and 1824 "as a means to navigate around the rapids of the Broad River where it joins the Saluda River to form the Congaree River," the three-mile-long Columbia Canal vastly improved the navigability of the rivers, and, as a result, the economy of Columbia. The project, which was completed at a cost of $206,000, involved constructing a dam across the Broad River on the northern edge of town, a brick and granite guard-lock, and a series of four locks. The locks, the largest in the state, were sixteen feet wide, 100 feet long, and lifted the chambers of each about nine feet. During the height of its use, the canal "transported over 30,000 bales of cotton a year past treacherous shoals and rocks." By 1842 rail transportation had made the Columbia Canal all but obsolete. The Columbia Canal National Register of Historic Places (NRHP) Nomination Form, South Carolina Historic Preservation Office (SCSHPO), South Carolina Department of Archives and History (SCDAH). Moore, John Hammond. *Columbia and Richland County: A South Carolina Community, 1740-1990.* Columbia, South Carolina: University of South Carolina Press, 1993, 91.

Mon. Aug. 29 [1842]. Riding out the evening before, I had seen at the larger Wetweather Pond a small party of Wood Ibises. I was struck at the first glance by the singularity of their appearance, with their solemn pace, stooping over, & carrying their huge bills slanting before them. They seemed very wild, & flew off without giving me any opportunity of observing them at leisure. Before sunrise this morning, galloped Granby off for the Pond, & found the Ibises again. There were four of them. I had left all my dogs at home, not to be in my way. Hitched at a distance, approached the Pond with great caution on the northern side, & by creeping in the high grass with which the Pond is covered, got within 40 or 50 yards of the Birds. They seemed to have been walking backwards & forwards in an open space of water – but on my approach, began to stop & watch. Crouching as I was in the grass, bareheaded, I could just see their heads by rising a little, and they could not exactly make me out. I waited my opportunity when two got in range, and then, having a charge of 16 Buck shot in tiers in one barrel, fired away with it, and knocked one Ibis over. The other barrel, loaded with a cartridges of No. 4 I reserved – but the Survivors of the party, flying off with a terrified croak, tho they made a circle, did not come near me. When I rode Granby in after my dead bird, he took fright at it, & forced me to dismount in water half-leg deep to pick it up. Both wings of the Ibis were broken, & one shot had pierced its breast – yet its dying struggles in the water were long. Passing Everett's Pond on the way back, missed a Kingfisher flying. Home about 8 o'clock. Dr. Gibbes,[38] whom I met up town, & to whom I offered the Ibis, told me he had never seen one, and asked me to give it to Trewet to be preserved, which in the afternoon I did.

2 shots   1 Wood Ibis (Tantalus Loculator)

---

38 Doctor Robert Wilson Gibbes (1809-1866) was a Columbia physician "of national reputation" who served as Assistant Professor of Chemistry at South Carolina College, and as Intendent, or Mayor, of Columbia from 1839 to 1849. He had numerous hobbies, including ornithology, and he had a collection of birds "all prepared and mounted by himself." (Maxcy Gregg did not practice the art of taxidermy.) In 1857 Robert Gibbes sued the mayor and the police chief of Columbia for barring him, as the editor of the newspaper *The South Carolinian*, from a public meeting of the City Council. The freedom of speech trial was held in the Court of Common Pleas with Maxcy Gregg acting as one of two attorneys representing E.J. Arthur and John Burdell of Columbia. The case was won by Mr. Gibbes. Both Dr. Gibbes and Maxcy Gregg were Directors of the Columbia Athenaeum in 1859. Robert Gibbes served as Surgeon General of South Carolina during the Civil War. He owned an impressive art collection which, along with his home, was burned by General Sherman's troops during their visit to Columbia in February of 1865. Woodward, C. Vann, and Elisabeth Muhlenfeld, editors. *The Private Mary Chesnut: The Unpublished Civil War Diaries*. New York: Oxford University Press, 1984, 49n. LaBorde, Maximilian. *History of the South Carolina College*. Columbia, South Carolina: Peter B. Glass, 1859 (Carlisle, Massachusetts: Applewood Books reprint, n.d.), 195.

Tues. [September] 8 [1842]. Having passed the Wetweather Ponds two evenings last week without seeing anything of the Ibises, I supposed they had abandoned the spot as dangerous; but riding by on Sunday evening, I scared up two, which sailed round overhead for some time, apparently reluctant to leave the Pond. Had the third been killed by somebody else since my last meeting with the party or had he been mortally wounded by my shot? Early this morning, gallopped out to the pond on Granby, but found no Ibises. Proceeded to Hampton's Middle Ponds, where I saw a good many Summer Ducks, but having left all my dogs at home for fear of frightening the Ibises, made no great exertion to get a shot where I could not have got the Ducks out if I had killed them. Missed a White Crane, on the wing, & on the way back, by Wm. Flemming's field, a Sparrowhawk.

2 shots

SUMMARY FROM APRIL TO SEPT. 1842

Month	Apr.	May	Jun.	July	Aug.	Sep.	Total
Times out	2	3	2	1	2	1	11
Shots fired	8	24	1	17	22	2	74
Chuckwillswidow			1				1
Nighthawk				2			2
Martin				1			1
Barnswallow					4		4
Bank Swallow					1		1
Redwing Blackbird	1						1
Wood Ibis					1		1
Green Heron	1						1
Kildee		1		3			4
Snipe	1						1
Lesser Yellowlegs		2					2
Solitary Sandpiper		3					3
Spotted Sandpiper		1					1
Little Sandpiper		2					2

14 Species

Individuals, 25

Mills, Robert, and Marmaduke Coates. Richland District, South Carolina. [1820] Map.
https://www.loc.gov/item/2007627903/.

NOVEMBER 1842 - MARCH 1843:
A WEDDING IN GEORGIA AND THE CONGAREES

Fri. Nov. 4, 1842. At my Aunt Burroughs'[39] in Telfair where I had arrived with Hart on the 2[d] after a journey of 233 miles, performed in 6 days. Went out Possum hunting after night with Jonathan, & Hart's boy Dave, taking a gun, & two mongrel dogs. Proceeded as far as the Quarter, with our Lightwood torches – heard some Owls, but found no Possums, & came back by 10 o'clock.

Sat. [November] 5. Having made an appointment with William Manning to meet on the other side of the [Altamaha] river & hunt, set off in the morning with Jonathan & Edward,[40] the latter of whom had escaped from his mother by stealth; & mounted behind me in the woods. About a mile the other side of the River, beyond Music's, heard W.M. blowing up his Dogs in the Swamp and found his Cousin, John Ashley[41] in the road. An owl having been disturbed, lit in a Pine tree. I was armed with an old shackling double barrel, tied up with twine, & out of order in the locks. With this I fired a load of buckshot at the Owl, immediately after which a Hawk (the Red-shouldered, I believe) came up, lit on

---

39 Desire Burroughs Maxcy Ashley (1796-1886) was Maxcy Gregg's maternal aunt. For Maxcy Gregg a family wedding in Georgia was an opportunity to hunt with cousins. Hart Samuel Maxcy (1807-1875), Gregg's maternal uncle, married Miss Mary Martha Manning, the daughter of Martha Ashley and Lawrence Manning, on the 6th of November 1842. The Gregg and Maxcy families gathered for the festivities at the Telfair County home of the groom's sister, Desire Burroughs Maxcy, and her husband Cornelius Raines Ashley.

40 Edward Ashley, Maxcy Gregg's first cousin, was the son of Cornelius and Desire Burroughs Maxcy Ashley. He was about seven years old in 1842.

41 John Ashley, Maxcy Gregg's first cousin, was also the son of Cornelius and Desire Burroughs Maxcy Ashley. John was about thirteen years old in 1842.

a dead tree, made a great screaming, and went off again. Having loaded with smaller shot, I endeavored to find the owl again, but failed; & Wm. Manning having collected his Dogs, we went to driving. After one or two unsuccessful drives, a Deer was started & ran up along a branch leading into the Sandhills. My stand was on the hill commanding one side of this Branch – the Deer, a small Doe or Fawn, passed under the hill, within 40 or 50 yards of me. I fired one barrel while the Deer was in some bushes – then had a fair chance with the other barrel, but on pulling trigger found that the shackling old piece had not come to a cock. By the time I could cock, the Deer had got into bushes again, & I fired at a disadvantage, tho I probably wounded it. During the drives, W.M. had killed a Turkey – and on our way home, we jumped up a Deer from some grass & bushes before us, which we followed for some time without success.

3 shots

By me.   Nothing   By W.M.   1 Turkey (Hen)

Sat. Nov 5. Having dined at Mrs. Manning's, in the afternoon returned across the river with Jonathan & Edward. Near Music's treed a black fox squirrel on a high pine. After firing 9 shots at it, (4 with buck-shot) I was obliged by the failure of ammunition & the approach of night to retire discomfited.

9 shots

Tues. [November] 8 [1842]. Hart's wedding was on the 6th. The next day a rain. Fair to-day. Out driving in the morning with W. Manning, John Ashley, and Jonathan – a negro driver along. Our course was westward, up the River Swamp, in which we made a very long drive after a Deer which refused to run out to the stands, & got off at last up the Swamp. W.M. had a shot (running) with his rifle, but missed. Then drove for a long time again, a sort of hummock or swamp extending out towards the Hills. The Dogs were trailing all the while, but the Deer was not started. A flock of Turkeys were found, one of which W.M. killed. Made two or three more short drives, equally unsuccessful, & came back to a late dinner. This was my last hunt in Georgia – for the next afternoon we came across the River to Ashley's, & the following morning set off on our Journey home, which we accomplished in six days, by a route slightly differing in some parts from our former one, but about the same length, 233 miles. The Country between the ferry by which we crossed the Oconee [River], 6 miles above Dublin,[42] & Ashley's is a vast expanse of open Pine woods covered with thick grass, abounding with the Saw Palmetto, Salamander Hills & Gopher holes & intersected by sluggish swamps, with dark colored muddy streams. On the South side of the Ocmulgee,[43] the Country rises into Sandhills, not extending however, I believe, very far from the River. The Streams running northwards into the Ocmulgee are said to be very short – beyond their sources, the Country slopes down into a flat again, towards the Saltilla. The afternoon of our first days journey homewards, we saw a Deer in the woods – the next morning we saw two parties, one of 3 or more, the second of 5. A very large hunting party had been lately out as we understood, coming from the Counties above Down into Telfair, and killed 109 Deer. William Manning told me that a White Deer, of small size, is known to range the woods some 5 or 6 miles from his mother's house, and that another small deer, white on one side, has been seen there also, supposed to be of the stock of the old White Deer. He told me too, that the Sandhill Crane is sometimes seen in the Pine woods, but is exceedingly shy – what food it seeks there, he could not say. Before going over to Wm. Manning's, the day of the wedding, I went out in the old field before the house with Ashley & the Boys, & having dug at a Salamander Hill down to the Burrow, set a steel-trap for the Salamander, but it did not catch him. In the Swamp of the Oconee River where we crossed it above Dublin – in that of the Ocmulgee at different places – & in that of Turkey (or as called on the Map, Palmetto) Creek, I found that species of Pine, resembling the white Pine, which I first noticed in our journey to Telfair in May 1840 in the Swamp of the Ocmulgee near Hartford.[44] Nobody could give me any other name for it than Short leaf Pine. At Evans, two miles this side of Hamburg,[45] I was told that some Gophers are found on this side of the Savannah [River], but no Salamanders. On our route in Georgia, we found the Salamander Hills extending further up the Country than the Gopher holes.

By me.   Nothing.   By W.M.   1 Turkey (young Gobler)

---

42 Dublin was a small community in Laurens County, Georgia.

43 Gregg is most likely referring to the Little Ocmulgee River, which is in Telfair County, north of the Ocmulgee.

44 Hartford was a small community on the east bank of the Ocmulgee River in Pulaski County, Georgia.

45 Founded in 1821, Hamburg, South Carolina was a small commercial center and transportation hub on the east bank of the Savannah River, across from Augusta, Georgia.

Sat. Nov. 19 [1842]. Having about dinner time to-day seen some birds fly by my Grandmother's,[46] which I suppose must have been Golden Plovers, took up my gun in the evening & walked out to find them. After searching for them without success over the old fields on the Southern limit of the Town,[47] as I was passing towards Randolph's fields, 4 of the birds flew hurriedly from the direction of the Canal toward the old Croft house. The Party I had seen before, was much larger & hearing several guns popping in different directions, I concluded the poor Plovers had been much worried. Continued my search till night about the old fields, but found no more of the birds. In a Pine thicket at the upper edge of the Town, after Sunset, suddenly startled some kind of Hawk, or more likely Owl, & missed it with both barrels, shooting very badly. Afterwards startled it again among the Pines, & fired thro such a thicket as gave me no chance to kill it. Weather now excessively cold – until the frost 10 days since, the fall had been remarkably mild.

3 shots.

Thurs. Dec. 22. The dissipation of the session had given me no time for shooting lately. Cornelia Brantley,[48] being on a visit at our house with her sister Margaretta, had impressed me as an escort & kept me in constant service. What time I

---

46 Maxcy Gregg's maternal grandmother, Susannah Hopkins Maxcy, was the daughter of Ezek Hopkins, a Revolutionary War naval officer (whose brother, Stephen Hopkins, was a signer of the Declaration of Independence), and the widow of Jonathan Maxcy. She lived with the James Gregg family immediately after the death of her husband on the 4th of June 1820. By 1840 she had made her home with her youngest son, Hart Maxcy, where she resided until her death in 1850 at approximately 82 years of age.

47 The southern boundary of Columbia in 1842 was Lower Boundary (Heyward) Street.

48 Maxcy Gregg was perhaps a bit smitten with Cornelia Brantley. Not long after this visit, he named his new hunting dog 'Brantley'. Despite the charms of the 'beautiful little Coquette' and his success at escort duty, Gregg remained a confirmed bachelor.

had to spare, was consumed in Militia duty,[49] political machinations,[50] & idling. Having seen the beautiful little Coquette off by the Rail-road cars the morning before, rode down in the evening with William DeSaussure to Gen. Hopkins' on a sporting expedition. This morning, started early for a Duck-hunt – being joined on the road by a young Grey, entered the Swamp about a mile below Allen's Mill & divided our forces, Hopkins & I going to the right, DeSaussure & Grey to the left. A slight freshet occurring lately, had probably carried most of the Ducks down the river – for we did not find very many. The day cloudy, Hopkins & I rambled about for some time thro the intricacies of the swamp, without any other success than the slaughter of a Barred Owl by me. Coming across Jesse Lykes[51] at a house he was putting up, we were joined by him for the rest of the day. Meeting at last with DeS. & Grey we crossed the Creek (Raiford's) at the Alligator-hole ford, & divided again. Hopkins & I hunted towards the Jumping Gut, from which on my approach I started a number of English Ducks. I fired both barrels, & may have done execution with both – but from my situation in the thicket & Cane-break, I did not know the effect of my shot, & should have gone off empty handed, had not Albert informed me that a Duck had fallen out in the field, where Fan after some search found it, curiously concealed in the grass at the edge of a little thicket. Collecting our party again, with the exception

---

49 Serving in the South Carolina militia was a legal 'duty' of all physically sound white males between the ages of eighteen and forty-five. Individual participation was required at six musters annually in company, regiment and battalion drill and training exercises. Maxcy Gregg would have been enrolled, at the time of his eighteenth birthday, in one of the several Richland District militia companies. He chose the Richland Volunteers, a pseudo-police force tasked with confronting and putting down "insurrectionists, outlaws, and the slave and Indian population." In 1841 Captain Maxcy Gregg was elected colonel of the Twenty-third, to which the Richland Volunteers were attached. Stauffer, Michael. "Volunteer or Uniformed Companies in the Antebellum Militia: A Checklist of Identified Companies, 1790-1859." *South Carolina Historical Magazine* (88), April 1987, 110.

50 In addition to his militia duty, Maxcy Gregg spent a great deal of his time outside of the court room in 'political machinations,' a civic duty which followed in the footsteps of his father. James Gregg served alternately in the Senate and Legislature for twenty-four years. In 1842 South Carolina politicos sought to repeal the Tariff of 1842, the 'Black Tariff,' which reversed the terms of the Tariff of 1833 (the 'Tariff of Abominations') and the Clay Compromise, and which led to the short-lived Bluffton Movement led by Robert Barnwell Rhett. Not for the last time South Carolina extremists, including Maxcy and James Gregg, pushed the Palmetto State towards nullification and secession from the Union.

51 Jesse G. Lykes, a successful planter, was born about 1815 and living in Richland District with his wife, Caroline, and their daughter in 1850.

of Grey, at the Cup Island Pond, we embarked in a heavy Bateau[52] lately placed there by the General, & went over to the Island. We got no game, however, and the only incident by which to recollect the occasion, was my slipping by a false step over the edge of the boat, & getting one leg & one arm in the water – luckily where it was shallow. On the way out of the swamp, in passing thro an old field of broomstraw, we saw a Blue Hawk prowling about, & after a little while alighting on the ground. I gallopped up, dismounted, & approaching, brought the Hawk down as it rose. Had a late & wild ride back.

9 shots

1 English Duck (fem)	By the rest of the Party Nothing
1 Barred Owl	
1 Blue Hawk	

Fri. [December] 23 [1842]. Weather clear & excessively cold. Ice in abundance all day. There have been a good many Deer in the Swamp this year, so we set off in the morning provided with buck shot for a drive, & at Allen's Mill joined company with Fed Lykes,[53] Matthew Howell[54] & Dr. Mayo.[55] Lykes had three hounds of no value, with which he drove the grounds where Deer were expected to be found, while the rest of us were strung along in stands near the Jumping Gut, in an extensive field. My stand was at the "Elm Tree." The dogs were on trail for a long time, but were too slow to bring the Deer out, & we had at last to give up the drive. Old Mr. Jas. Hopkins, who is as keen a sportsman as any boy, joined us at the stands, with his man Peter. Turning our operations against the Ducks, we proceeded, after eating a snack, to the Cup Island Pond, where however the Ducks were too few & too wild for us all. I killed on a tree in the western part of the Pond, a Barred Owl, so large that I was not sure but it was a Horned Owl, till Fan brought it to me. On the way back, in passing thro an extensive wood, in which are situated the "Wood Ponds" two or three Cat Squirrels showed themselves, one of which, firing

---

52 A bateau is a shallow, flat-bottomed, carved out boat.

53 Frederick Lykes, a planter born about 1806, was living in Richland District with his family (on property adjacent to that of Jesse Lykes) in 1850.

54 Matthew R. Howell, a planter born about 1796, was living in Richland District in 1850.

55 William T. Mayo, born around 1817, was a physician residing on property adjacent to the Lykes with his wife and young daughter in 1850.

from Granby's back, I brought down. Before getting out of the Swamp, we parted Company with Lykes' party. Old Mr. Hopkins continued to lead the rest of us in search of Ducks until all hope was at an end. Some time before Sundown, a vast body of Crows commenced passing in a Southerly direction. The flight continued within our observation until some time after Sunset, the train reaching without interruption as far as the eye could reach either way. I should think 20 or 30,000 a moderate estimate of the number seen. We got back late, after a very cold ride.

6 shots

| 1 Barred Owl | By the rest, | Nothing |
| 1 Cat Squirrel | | |

Sat. Dec. 24 [1842]. Weather colder still. Took our ease by the fire until about 11 o'clock, when we rode out into the fields southwest of Cabin Branch after Partridges. We found but a single Covey, & that in the woods. The day was a very blank one with me, for I got to missing & could not stop. We spent about three hours in Lark & Dove hunting, but found all these Country Birds as wild as if they had been be-devilled for a week by all the School boys of a Town. The Partridges have probably either not yet left the woods, or been driven by the severity of the weather to take shelter in the least exposed situations.

18 shots

By me Nothing	By W.D.	1 Lark	By Gen. H.	3 or 4 Doves
		7 Doves		
		1 Kildee		

Sun. Dec 25. A sleet & freezing rain last night. Cleared off in the Course of the day. Set out for home with DeSaussure in the afternoon, & rode the distance pretty rapidly. At Lykes' Pond we stopped to shoot at some Mergansers, one of which DeS. winged; but all our efforts to get it afterwards, altho assisted by Fred Lykes with a water dog, & altho we fired 3 or 4 shots at it, failed. As we got down towards Cane Branch about dark, we suddenly observed our shadows projected by a vivid light, & looking round, saw in the South eastern quarter of the Heavens, near the Horizon, the largest & most brilliant meteor[56] I have ever seen. Its course appeared to be southwest – it soon burst – its light was much like moonlight, but of a more glittering nature.

3 shots

Sat. [December] 31 [1842]. Off about sun-rise for an all day's hunt with Hart. He rode Brownie, I Granby. Day brilliant & freezing. Proceeded by Sunday's Pond to the Congaree Neck,[57] where we hitched our horses, threw off our great coats, & took it afoot down the River. Finding no Ducks in the River, we went up the Creek, & a little way above its mouth discovered what I took for a flock of 4 or 5 Summer Ducks. I think that they flew off for on making a circle & approaching the point where we expected to come on them, nothing was to be seen but a pair of Green-wing Teal, both of which I crippled with my first barrel; one of them I shot again as he made off down stream – the other got out of our sight for a while, but at length we espied it lying dead under the opposite bank, where Fan swam over & got it. Followed the Creek up to the Main Road, scaring up one small party of Ducks only – & then seeing a large boat coming down, gave up the farther advance along the Creek, & returned to our horses. In the mean time, we had killed some Doves & Robins in our progress, coming across numbers of both. After getting our horses, we went into the Plum-thickets, where we hunted Doves for a while, & then went down to the Creek to eat some bread & cheese. Afterwards went over into the belt of timber on the River again, to look for Robins among the Wild Orange, India, & Hackberry Trees. They were not as thick however as we had found them in the morning, when we were reserving our ammunition for Ducks. Returned in good time, & got home a little after Sunset. We found but a single small party of Partridges to-day, near the Bend of the Creek, & I got but one shot. We started several Rabbits in different parts of the neck, where their breed is probably beginning to recover

---

56 In addition to his interest in ornithology, Maxcy Gregg was an ardent amateur astronomer. With his personal collection of "astronomical instruments and globes" he observed and documented in his Sporting Journals several comets and a meteor. When the family moved to Richland Street in 1854, Gregg cut a space in the roof in order to construct a small observatory. He learned to be mindful when loaning his telescope to children after one of his little cousins was caught spying on neighbors from the observatory. Last Will and Testament of Maxcy Gregg, 1862; Series S108093, Reel 0023, Frame 00707, SCDAH.

57 The Congaree Neck is that part of the river where the Broad and Saluda rivers join and form the Congaree River.

from the loss suffered in the Great May freshet of 1840. One we raced on horse-back for some time, but it gave us the dodge at last. I wounded very severely a Red tail & a Marsh Hawk, both of which, after falling, managed to fly off. I wounded also another Marsh Hawk that flew pretty high over my head; & may have killed some Doves & Robins that carried off my shot.

26 shots
    By me   By Hart
        2 Greenwing Teal   4 Doves
        1 Partrtidge   7 Robins
        5 Doves
        3 Robins

Wed. Jan. 25 [1843]. After a good deal of cold weather, it has been for some days rather warm & hazy. Rode in the afternoon to Taylor's Ponds, at the Northernmost of which I shot a Greenwing Teal on the wing, and dispatched it with another shot in the water. Proceeded on foot, & at the fourth pond shot another Greenwing, as it rose singly – but it fell in a thick place where I could not make Fan find it. Returning for Granby, rode into the Pond, & made Fan find the Duck. From the long lapse of time since I had hunted about these grounds, my familiarity with them turned out to have diminished more than I should have expected – & walking thro the weeds & grass proving warm & tiresome, I rode round the remaining Ponds with exactly the result that was to be anticipated – frightening several ducks & getting no fair shot. They were principally Teal, tho there were a few large Ducks. Took a stand for flocks coming to roost, but without success. Home rather late.

6 shots
        2 Greenwing Teal (Drake & Duck)

Mon. [February] 13 [1843]. Warm, hazy weather. Rode in the afternoon to Taylor's Ponds, where I met Hawes & a young Hooper, who had walked down. Hawes told me of a Marsh Hen – a bird of singular habits – which he had lately heard, & had a glimpse of, about the ponds – running in the grass & excessively hard to be put up. Before long, after firing at some Partridges, we heard some of these birds uttering various strange notes, some of which I should if not better informed have attributed without hesitation to Frogs. After many vain attempts to put some of them up with Fan & Hooper's Pointer, Bob, we at last flushed one over a small sheet of water, & Hooper shot it. I found it to be the Fresh Water Marsh Hen – Rallus Elegans. If it is a resident here, it is strange that I never noticed it before. Perhaps I may have mistaken its notes, if ever heard, for those of frogs. While I was wading about after some of the Marsh-Hens, the Dogs got after a Rabbit, which I shot swimming in a ditch – but Fan & Bob both getting hold, & pulling for it, tore it so much that I did not bring it home. Towards Sun-set we separated & took stands for Ducks coming to roost. After I had been some time at my post among the Pond, lying toward the East, Fan put up an English Duck within 30 or 40 yards of me, which I killed – but the moment I felt its weight, I concluded that it had been pining with an old wound, its flight having also seemed feeble. On examination afterwards in the Kitchen, it was pronounced sick & thrown away. We did not see many Ducks this evening – Hawes killed one – Hooper had several shots, but brought none down. DeBruhl,[58] who not long since bought the Plantation from Black, is now digging a large ditch in the edge of the swamp near the Bluff, with the view of draining the Ponds – in which it is hoped he may be disappointed.

6 shots

By Me.	By Hawes	By Hooper
1 English Duck (fem)	1 Eng. Duck	1 freshwater Marsh Hen
1 Rabbit		

By Hawes & Hooper - a few Partridges

Tues. Feb. 14 [1843]. Weather quite warm. Rode in the afternoon with Hart, down to Granby, where the marshes, destitute of cover, give no promise of Snipes this season & to Sunday's Pond, where we found a Covey of Partridges.

7 shots

2 Partridges	By H	2 Rusty Blackbirds
1 Redwing Blackbird		

---

58 Jesse DeBruhl was a prominent political and social figure in Columbia. This reference likely denotes the DeBruhl-Marshall House at 1401 Laurel Street.

Sat. Feb. 18 [1843]. Walked in the afternoon with Hart to the Canal, & as far as the Lower Basin. Found no Partridges, but started five Rabbits. The first was set by Fan in the Marsh south of Randolph's fields, & got away under the fire of one of Hart's barrels & both of mine. It seemed to be badly wounded. I had not been able to aim freely, from its running out towards & beyond Hart. The second was missed by both of us in the Broom straw field this side of the Basin. The third, starting from the Marsh to the East of the same field, I think I wounded. The fourth was set by Fan towards the north edge of the field, & when it ran out, was followed by her so closely, that neither of us ventured to shoot. The fifth Fan set in the head of the little Marsh which lies west of the Double Dee Springs – but the cover of matted grass was so thick, that it was a long time before it would move out – at last, it imprudently took to the open field, and I shot it. Saw no Robins this evening, tho some are to be found now about the Eastern edge of the Town – to which quarters they are probably confined by their fondness for the berries of the Orange Trees about Wm. Bay's & Dr. Percival's.

9 Shots

   1 Rabbit   By Hart   1 Brown Titlark
   1 Dove

Wed. [March] 1 [1843]. Out on foot in the afternoon, with Hart. In the little Marsh which heads in the Western part of Randolph's south field, found a few Snipes & a Woodcock – the last, Hart shot sitting – each killed one Snipe on the wing. Going down the Marsh, my attention was caught by something that looked like a bird's nest, on a bush. Breaking off the limb it was fastened to, for the purpose of examining it, I was surprised to find no opening in the mass, but did not observe that a mouse was clinging to a twig close to the nest, till Hart saw it as I brought the limb to him. The Mouse, seeming paralysed by fear, allowed us to secure it. On pulling the nest to pieces, it appeared to be solid, composed of coarse grass on the outside, & finer within. The remains of a young Mouse were imbedded in the middle. The old mouse, a female, was larger than the common Mouse, more stoutly built, with a tail shorter in proportion & blunt at the end; it's color lighter & more reddish, its eyes prominent, large & resembling somewhat those of the flying squirrel; its feet & toes, with sharp claws, seemed also adapted to a life of climbing. I carried this strange mouse home with me, & put it in a canister on my Mantelpiece – but in the night, it got out, & drowned itself in my hand-dish, from which Pleasant[59] removed it without my knowledge, & threw it away, so that I lost the opportunity of examining it as closely as I wished to. I could not identify it by the aid of Harlan & Godman[60] – it seems to come nearest to the Arvicola Xanthognathus. Proceeding by the Canal, & turning to the Marshes that unite in Waring's Field, we found a number of Snipes, that kept us engaged till after sun-down. The Marshes are mostly very bare of cover now, from the fields having been turned out for a good while, to be grazed over by the cattle of the town – but in the place I used to call Intermarsh, the cover remains thicker, protected by the mire – & there, Fan made two or three steady sets at Snipes, a thing I do not remember ever to have seen her do before. I got four Snipes about these shooting grounds of my school-boy days, before, yielding to Hart's impatience & the gathering darkness, I left them. The Robins have within the last week or two, been fusilladed by the boys about the trees of Wm. Bay & Dr. Percival, but seem scarce elsewhere – at least, on this side of the Town.

18 shots
    5 Snipes

By H.
    1 Woodcock
    1 Robin
    1 Snipe

Sat. Mar. 25, 1843. Walked in the evening with Hart, by Waring's field, the Canal & across to Dr. Fisher's[61] Pond. Found but a very few Snipes, one of which I shot at the marsh south of Randolph's fields. Hart had a shot at a pair of Summer Ducks in the Pond. We met with few Robins – they keep mostly to the Eastern side of the Town. Weather pleasant to-day, tho not warm. For most of this

59 Pleasant was enslaved to James Gregg from as early as 1833. In 1843 Pleasant was twenty-three years old.

60 Gregg refers to two books from his library, *Fauna Americana, being a description of the mammiferous animals inhabiting North America* by Richard Harlan, and *American Natural History* by John Davidson Godman.

61 Dr. Edward Fisher (1792-1869) led a "long and blameless" life in Columbia. He was admired by James Gregg to the degree that his son was named for the doctor. *Charleston Courier* (Charleston, South Carolina), September 2, 1869.

month, it has been unseasonably & excessively cold, with much bad weather – snowing four times, first on the 7th when it lay two or three inches deep – again about ten days afterwards, when a little fell mixed with rain – again on the 19th when it came down pretty briskly for about two hours, but in consequence of having been preceded by a rain, melted, altho the day was cold enough – and lastly on the 21st at which time the quantity was small. As the month of February was very mild, & gave a start to vegetation, it seems likely that much fruit will be killed. About ten days ago, after a week or more of bad weather, a Comet[62] suddenly appeared in the west one fair evening, with a prodigiously long tail. There have been but few clear evenings since to observe it. When I first saw it, which was not till the 17th the tail seemed 40 or 50 degrees long, extending from within 40 or 50 degrees of the Sun's place, to a point beyond the feet of Orion, & tapering at both ends the narrowest towards the head – no nucleus discernible. However, the haze towards the horizon might have hidden a part of the train.

5 shots

   1 Snipe

By H. 2 Robins

---

62 This comet was also observed by Virginian Edmund Ruffin who was at the time touring South Carolina at the behest of the State to conduct an agricultural and geological study. Ruffin commented in his diary, regarding the comet and the family with which he was boarding, "They are evidently alarmed at the appearance, & consulted me as to what it was a sign for." Mathew, William M., editor. *Agriculture, Geology, and Society in Antebellum South Carolina: The Private Diary of Edmund Ruffin*, 1843. Athens: The University of Georgia Press, 1990, 148.

Summary from Oct. 1842 to March 1843

Month	Nov.	Dec.	Jan.	Feb.	Mar.	Total
Times out	5	5	1	3	2	16
Shots fired	15	62	6	22	23	128
Blue Hawk	1					1
Barred Owl	2					2
Robin	3					3
Dove	5			1		6
Partridge	1			2		3
Snipe					6	6
English Duck	1			1		2
Greenwing Teal	2	2				4
Rabbit				2		2
Cat Squirrel	1					1

10 Species   Individuals 30

SUMMARY FROM OCT. 1842 TO MARCH 1843

Month	Nov.	Dec.	Jan.	Feb.	Mar.	Total
Times out	5	5	1	3	2	16
Shots fired	15	62	6	22	23	128
Blue Hawk		1				1
Barred Owl		2				2
Robin		3				3
Dove		5		1		6
Partridge		1		2		3
Snipe					6	6
English Duck		1		1		2
Greenwing Teal		2	2			4
Rabbit				2		2
Cat Squirrel		1				1

10 Species
Individuals, 30

Barred Owl from *Birds of America* (1827) by John James Audubon

April - September 1843:
A Journey to the Mountains of North Carolina

Tues. April 11, 1843. Spring very backward. Some little snow, or frozen rain, fell as late as the 6th of this month. Since that time it has turned warm. On the 1st day of the month, I saw the first Martin of this year. Confined in Court,[63] & suffering under the most violent cold I ever remember to have been attacked with, my time passed heavily enough, and my gun now gives me a very agreeable relief. Rode in the evening to the Granby Marshes. Shot a Dove by Cayce's;[64] & started some Snipes, together as I believe, with some Pectoral Sandpipers (but without distinguishing the latter) at the little plash on the same side of the road with his house. At the more easterly of the Granby Marshes, I killed a Pectoral Sandpiper, a sitting shot; and altho I had observed something peculiar in the appearance of the birds, it was not until after I killed it that I ascertained that it was not a Snipe. There was a flock of these Sandpipers, perhaps 20 or 30 in number that I continued to hunt about the Granby Marshes for some time; they would sometimes fly off; then I would find them again unexpectedly; they seemed rather tame, & generally rose with a soft whistling note. I missed several shots, both on the wing, which did not surprise me, & on the ground, which did; but happening once to get a fair chance at the flock as they were wheeling round very low, after being alarmed by a sitting shot, I brought down six. This was at the little Marsh, to the Eastward. I shot a snipe at the same Marsh; and a Kingfisher, towards the upper end of Cayce's Pond, which falling on the other

---

63 Maxcy Gregg was often required to travel out of town, most often on horse-back, and while many aspects of his career appealed to him, he very often felt 'confined' by the tedium of it. In addition to private clients Gregg was a member of the Court of Appeals which met at least twice a year in Richland District and was responsible for examining those who were seeking admission to the South Carolina bar. In 1857 Gregg "directed the examination on pleading and practice, which was rigid and exacting." *The Anderson Intelligencer* (Anderson Court House, South Carolina), April 20, 1876.

64 The Cayce House in the old town of Granby was constructed around 1765.

side, Fan swam across & brought to me. Having met with these Sandpipers now, I feel confident that the bird given to me by George Hawes,[65] 31 March 1841, & which then took for one of this species, tho doubtingly, was so in fact.

13 shots

1 Dove	1 Kingfisher
1 Snipe	7 Pectoral Sandpipers (Pectoralis Sringa)

Thurs. Apr. 13 [1843]. Rode over the river in the evening, in search of the Pectoral Sandpipers. Shot one, on the wing, at the little Marsh by Cayce's. There was but a small party there, in company with a few Snipes. Not finding any of the Sandpipers at the Granby Marshes, proceeded to the Sunday's Pond. Here I found that the pretty little fringe of wood which used to surround the pond, has just been destroyed – only a few desolate trees left standing – the Pond too is half drained, tho that was begun some time ago. Returning to Granby, I came upon the flock of Sandpipers unexpectedly, at the upper, or Larger Marsh; and firing from my horse as they rose, killed two. I thought I had killed a third; but if so, it disappeared. After finishing my search for it, I again found the flock, unexpectedly, on the other side of the Marsh; & taking a sitting shot, killed three. The rest merely flew across the Marsh; & pursuing them, I killed four more at a shot. Only two now remained, which flew a little way off & lit near the cross fence to the west of the Marsh. Following and putting them up, I shot one; the solitary survivor made his escape. These birds seemed more tame this evening than before. Their habit of crowding together in feeding, as well as when alarmed, is calculated to prove very fatal to them. The Granby Marshes are now very bare of cover – the grass is springing up, but is still low & thin. Got home rather late – fired on the way, a somewhat random shot at a Rabbit, from Granby's back.

10 shots   11 Pectoral Sandpipers

---

65 George E. Hawes was a medical doctor who, although born in South Carolina in 1817, had moved to Florida by 1850.

Fri. Ap. 21. The Crows have lately been doing mischief at the farm,[66] where the corn has just come up. Mounted Buckeye, early in the morning, & accompanied by Hart on Granby rode out to try & circumvent them. They proved too wary however – I got one shot on the wing, but it was rather too far. In the woods between the Eastern field & the well, we saw a great number of Bee Martins passing about among the tops of the trees. Somehow or other they looked very small – perhaps from keeping principally about the tops of high pines – they were silent; & their appearance made us doubt what they were. So I shot one for my own satisfaction. I found it about the usual size.

2 shots   1 Bee Martin

Fri. Ap. 21 [1843]. Evening. Rode out with Hart after the Crows again in the evening, but met with no better success. I fired once, but think there was nothing but powder in the barrel I used – at least the report was faint, & no execution done.

1 shot

Mon. [July] 17 [1843]. Resumed my gun after a very long interval of time, during which I had the misfortune to lose poor Fan, who died on the 17 June of some kind of paralytic disease. Set off a little before Sun-rise this morning on a journey to the Mountains, mounted on Buckeye, and accompanied by Peter,[67] on Granby. For the sake of shade, instead of taking the main road to Winnsboro,[68] which I wished to visit, followed a Sandhill road, passing by Stack's on Cane

---

66 In addition to the house on Senate Street, James Gregg owned one hundred acres of land along the Rocky Branch southeast of South Carolina College where Maxcy Gregg Park is now located. At various times crops grown on the thirty acres of improved land, valued at $2,000 in 1850, included corn (400 bushels in 1850) and oats (100 bushels). A few dairy cows and mules were maintained on the property, as well as a stable for Maxcy's horses.

67 Peter was one of James Gregg's slaves, formerly the property of Josiah Kilgore of Greenville. In 1843 Peter was about 46 years old. He often acted as veterinarian to Maxcy's dogs and horses.

68 Winnsboro, considered "one of the most pleasant and flourishing villages in the state," was the county seat of Fairfield District. Located about twenty-five miles north of Columbia, both Maxcy Gregg and his father periodically did legal work there. Mills, Robert. *Statistics of South Carolina*. Charleston, South Carolina: Hurlbut and Lloyd Publishers, 1826 (Reprint, The Reprint Company, Spartanburg, South Carolina, 1972), 539.

Creek, & crossing Cedar Creek at John Waring's. A few miles this side of Cedar Creek, killed a Black Fox-Squirrel, which after taking two cartridges & a loose charge of birdshot to dispatch it, lodged on a twig which caught under its arm, & remained in the tree. Arrived at Winnsboro about 3 o'clock & stopped at Gamble's.[69] Granby fell lame early in the day – had a shoe taken off, supposing that it pinched him – but as he still continued lame, the shoe was put on again, & Peter proceeded to doctor his shoulder. Took tea with Boyce,[70] & went with him & his wife[71] in the evening, to hear Cary, the Washingtonian lecturer.[72]

3 shots   1 Black fox squirrel.

---

69 Mr. F.J. Gamble, a native of North Carolina, managed a hotel at the corner of Congress and Washington streets in Winnsboro in 1850.

70 After attending South Carolina College, William Waters Boyce (1818-1890), a Charleston native, studied law and established a practice in Winnsboro. Boyce was elected to the United States House of Representatives in 1853. He was opposed to secession, which he referred to as a "stupendous madness." He resigned his seat in Congress when South Carolina seceded from the Union and, despite his opposition to secession, was elected to the Confederate Congress. In 1864 Boyce advocated petitioning the Federal government for peace terms, a stance which made him a pariah in his home state. His prediction that the South would lose the war came all too true to those living in Winnsboro when Sherman and his troops spent several days there during the Carolina Campaign. After the war Boyce opened an office in Washington, DC. Maxcy Gregg's friendship with William Waters Boyce dated back to their college years. Gregg served as sixteen-year-old Boyce's second in a duel in downtown Charleston (at the intersection of Meeting and Broad streets) in December of 1835. After Boyce's opponent, William Whaley, shot and put him "hors de combat," Boyce fired, putting a "ball…through the beaver hat of a gentleman who was sitting on his horse with one leg across the saddle." Doffing his hat and bowing to Whaley's second, Gregg and his opponent drew their pistols and fired. Pinckney took a ball to the thigh, while Gregg was hit in his vest pocket where the bullet was stopped by several metal objects, resulting in severe bruising but nothing permanent. Pursley, Larry E. "William Waters Boyce: Conscience of the Confederacy." *The Sandlapper Magazine*, December 1981, 30. *Memphis Daily Appeal* (Memphis, Tennessee), January 5, 1963. Alexander Cheves Haskell Papers, SCL, USC.

71 William Waters Boyce married Miss Mary Pearson of Fairfield District around 1840.

72 Mr. Carey was a member of the Washingtonian Temperance Society, an organization also known as the Washingtonian Total Abstinence Society. The association was founded in April of 1840 in Baltimore, Maryland. Mr. J.F. Carey, himself a recovering alcoholic, lectured throughout South Carolina in the spring and early summer of 1843 on the "the evils of intemperance, which never fail to arouse and reclaim the drunkard." Mr. Carey's lecture tour of the State was only slightly tinged by the rumor, utterly false, according to *The Edgefield Advertiser*, of his having "Abolition principles." This speaking engagement most likely took place at Winnsboro's Thespian Hall, located on Washington Street near the Town Market and Clock Tower. *The Edgefield Advertiser* (Edgefield, South Carolina), May 10, 1843; January 4, 1843.

Wed. July 19 [1843]. Having been detained in Winnsboro a day by Granby's lameness & having failed in the object of my visit, which was to see if Boyce would be willing to take charge of the South Carolinian,[73] from which it is necessary for Pemberton[74] to retire, on account of his health – rode on this morning 18 miles, to Steele's, about a mile above Dr. Pearson's, on the Monticello road.[75] On the way fired with one hand from my saddle at a couple of Partridges, & missed them clear. Early in the afternoon, a rain came up, which cooled the excessive heat of the air.

1 shot

In the evening, rode on, 10 miles, to Nathan Sims,[76] two miles beyond Shelton's ferry, arriving just in time to escape a shower. Enjoyed the visit very well. Old Sims is quite a character, & told me a vast deal about his Deer & his Bees. He had kept deer about 38 years, & has perhaps 30 now, besides fawns, in a Park of 500 acres, surrounded by a high rail fence. Many get out – & return again – there being no deer in the Country for many miles round. There has been a white doe in the Park for many years, the offspring of a mother of the ordinary color. This white Doe has had several white fawns – one of which, a young Doe, now turning red, I saw together with 4 or 5 other Does & Fawns about Sims' house. The inclination of the Bucks' horns forward, is owing, Sims says, to the Bucks' bending them in the velvet, by rubbing them on the inside of their thighs. The number of points no criterion of age. He has never known Deer to kill snakes, as some hunters report.

---

73 *The South Carolinian* was a weekly newspaper published in Columbia between 1838 and 1852.

74 Mr. A.H. Pemberton, editor of the *Augusta Chronicle* before his association with the *South Carolinian*, died on the 20th of July 1847 after a "protracted illness, in which he suffered much." *The Edgefield Advertiser*, July 21, 1847.

75 After traveling west from Winnsboro for about fifteen miles, Gregg turned his mount north on the Monticello Road, which ran from Columbia through the small community of Monticello in Fairfield District, and north to Union, South Carolina.

76 Nathaniel ("Nathan") Sims (1778-1844), born in Hanover County, Virginia, became a well-to-do planter on Tyger River, Union District, a short distance northeast of Gordon's Bridge (Roger's Bridge in the journal). His plantation was about four miles north of the village of Maybinton where Gregg visited in August. Nathan Sims' son, Benjamin F. Sims (1811-1859), inherited the deer park less than a year after Gregg's visit. (Courtesy Dr. James E. Kibler)

Fri. July 21. Granby's lameness was now so much increased, that I was obliged to make a very short day's journey with him. Various opinions, from judges good, bad, & indifferent, indicated various diseases in the foot, pastern, or shoulder. Most voices were on the side of Swinney. But Gage, by tapping the shoe all round, & observing when the horse flinched, discovered the seat of the disorder to be on the inner side of the foot, near the heel, & pronounced it either to be gravel or a prick in the foot. After riding about 5 miles, to the Cross Keys,[77] dismounted Peter, & proceeded 5 miles further to the Cross Anchor,[78] to dinner. In the evening went on to Mrs. Hobby's about 6 miles. I had left a letter with Gage for David Johnson, requesting him if he got home in time, to join me in Greenville.

Sat. 22. In the morning, leaving Peter behind, with instructions to proceed slowly to Foster's, in Greenville District, where he expected to find his mother, & there await my return from the mountains, rode on by Woodruff's, Westmoreland's, & Anderson's Bridge, on the Enoree [River], to Josiah Kilgore's,[79] Peter's former master, about 17 miles. In the evening, 14 miles to Greenville, & stopped at Long's Tavern, where I found Elias Hall.

Tues. July 25. I had staid two days at Greenville, and on the second day had gone to Paris Mountain with Dick Harrison, in his buggy without our guns. The distance from the village to the foot of the mountain, at its north western angle, was about 7 miles. We ascended on foot, & explored the summit of the Southern ridge, which we followed for more than three miles. A haze in the air

---

77 The Cross Keys House in Union County was built in 1814 at the intersection of Old Buncombe and Old Ninety-Six roads for the influential Bobo family. After fleeing Richmond, Confederate States' president Jefferson Davis and his cabinet dined at the Cross Keys House.

78 Cross Anchor was built by the captain of the British ship Salley, "on which Barrum Bobo had been the purser." The Cross Anchor House was destroyed by fire in 1932. Neuffer, Claude, and Irene Neuffer. *Correct Mispronunciations of Some South Carolina Names.* Columbia: University of South Carolina Press, 1987, 16.

79 Josiah Kilgore, Junior, was born about 1790. In 1850 he was living in Greenville, South Carolina, and occupied in farming (with real estate, including sixty-three slaves ranging in age from six months to sixty years old, valued at $20,000) with his wife and their twenty-year-old son.

prevented our view of the Mountains of the Blue Ridge from being very distinct – the Table Rock[80] being the only Mountain that I could make out perfectly well – tho I thought I could distinguish Caesar's Head[81] too. The view was fine – but disappointed me, because I expected it to be finer. The height of Paris Mountain above its base, I should conjecture to be 7 or 800 feet. While on the summit, a rain coming up from the Blue Ridge, drove us for shelter into one of the cabins which are perched up there, the owner of which greatly provoked Dick (to whom the clambering had given a keen appetite) by his inhospitality in not inviting us to take a very scanty family dinner with him. This morning, at a late hour, set out with Dick for the Mountains. Elias Hall, to our disappointment, could not go with us. Met Peter as we left the village, who reported that Granby had the gravel, & was getting better. Rode 10 miles, & dinner at the house of a Mr. Lynch, grandson of the old Lynch from whom "Lynch's Law" took its name.[82]

---

80 Table Rock, as described by Robert Mills in 1820, was "a mass of granite, rising from the vale, through which a rapid river winds its turbulent way; there is a steep ascent from the torrent, covered with trees, to the base of the rocky wall; then ledges of stone, rising almost perpendicular, and at length, hanging over at top, so that they seem to totter to their fall. Indeed, a large triangular mass stands separated from the rest by deep fissures, and resting upon a very slender base." Bert Hendricks Reese recounted the entertaining myth of how Table Rock and The Stool, an adjacent prominence, got their names. "In the days of extreme witchcraft, the witches had planned a convention and needed a place to meet. They chose the flat top of our mountain. The morning session had ended and it was time for lunch, but they had no table on which to spread their lunch. They bewitched the wind and commanded it to blow the rock clean. The wind blew – and it blew and blew until there was nothing left on the rock. So, they spread their lunch on it. But, there were no chairs and they knew their mighty Wizard, the Old Man of the Mountain, must be provided a place to sit. So the witches made ready the little hill into a stool for their ruler. He sat on this stool and ate from the table of rock. So, this welded the name Table Rock to the mountain and The Stool to the nearby hill, and the wind is still keeping the rock clean." Robert Mills, *Statistics of South Carolina*, 579. Reece, Bert Hendricks. *History of Pumpkintown-Oolenoy*. Greenville, South Carolina: A Press Printing Company, Incorporated, 1970, 15.

81 Caesar's Head is another mountain at the foothills of the Blue Ridge Mountains.

82 As a lawyer, Maxcy Gregg would have been familiar with the original meaning of 'Lynch Law,' "the assumption of extrajudicial authority," which is attributed to Virginian Charles Lynch (1736-1796), a Quaker who, though he did not take up arms until late in the war, served his country during the American Revolution. In 1780 Mr. Lynch was appointed a "civil and military authority" in his neighboring district, two hundred miles from the official court at Williamsburg, by Governor Thomas Jefferson, and in that capacity was "clothed with authority for emergency acts to break up [a] conspiracy of desperadoes who burned and plundered the homes of the Continentals without mercy." When Charles Lynch uncovered a plot that had been hatched in his community "for the purpose of overthrowing the Continental Government," he used the powers invested in him by the governor to have the conspirators arrested, tried and judged, not in a courtroom but at his home, by a jury of three other men appointed for that purpose by Governor Jefferson. Those convicted were "sentenced to receive 39 lashes on his bare back, and if he did not

In the afternoon, rode 14 miles further to Hodge's. It ought to be called Hog's.

Wed. July 26. A hard rain before daylight in the morning. Rode 18 miles to dinner at Jas. Britton's, 5 miles beyond Flat Rock,[83] & 2 beyond the new & ill-looking little village of Henderson Court House.

In the evening, left the Asheville road, & proceeded in a Westerly or N. Westerly direction, 8 miles, to Wm Britton's, on Mills river. The valley of the French Broad [River] where we crossed it, presented a most beautiful landscape – the beau ideal of a farm. We had a slight sprinkle of rain on us this evening. Wm. Britton, who is a great hunter, was unluckily suffering under chill & fever (contracted in a journey to Augusta) or we should have obtained his Company, & had the advantage of his skill & experience as a woodsman. He directed us however to the residence of Wm. Bridges, near the Balsam Mountain, who, he informed us, was a great hunter, & teller of hunting stories.

Thurs. 27. In the morning, rode about 17 miles to Bridge's. Our course was at first south & S.West for about 12 miles, passing several miles up the valley of Boylston's Creek – then 2 miles up Davidson's River in a N. Westerly direction, & about 3 miles up Avery's Creek, in a northerly direction – when we ascended the Pine-Spur Ridge to Bridge's house, which stands at a considerable elevation.

After dinner, Bridges, who has an oat harvest on hand, & therefore made some difficulty about leaving home, agreed to go with us to the Balsam Mountain the next day – & I ascended the Pine Spur Ridge with Dick Harrison, from the summit of which we obtained a view of the Balsam Mountain, with the Looking-glass Rock in the fore-ground. By the time we got down, Dick was too tired to continue our Walk down the gorges of the Mountain after Pheasants as we had proposed, & I strolled a short way by myself, but stopped on the side of the Mountain, brought up my journal, & returned early.

---

then shout 'Liberty forever' to be hanged by the thumbs until he gave utterance to that patriotic sentiment." Wikipedia contributors. "Lynching." Wikipedia, The Free Encyclopedia (Last viewed February 25, 2015). Rowbotham, Sally Smith. "Col. Charles Lynch and the Lynch Law." *Daughters of the American Revolution Magazine*, Volume 96, Number 1 (January 1962), 15, 16. Charles Lynch was the brother of John Lynch, for whom the Virginia town of Lynchburg is named.

83 Flat Rock, North Carolina, a popular summer resort of many South Carolina families of wealth, was located near Asheville.

Fri. July 28. Set off in the morning for the Balsam Mountain, with Bridges & his wife's uncle, Ed. Steward. Our general course was nearly west – the distance to Bridge's Camp on the Balsam about 10 miles. The Mountain is according to Bridges exceedingly difficult of access by any other route. Our path led first up & along the Pine-Spur ridge for three miles or more, when we descended & crossed the Eastern fork of Looking-glass Creek – a small knob was then to be surmounted before reaching the western fork, after which we ascended & followed the Trail ridge for 2 or 3 miles, passed Bridge's near Camp, which is 6 miles or more from his home, & surmounting a pretty steep ascent of about three quarters of a mile, got on the Pisgah ridge, which connects the lofty Peak of Pisgah, which was in view some dozen miles or so to the N. East, with the still loftier Summit of the Balsam. After following for about 3 miles the Pisgah Ridge, which rising higher & higher, gave us magnificent prospects, we descended a little way, crossed the Big Pigeon river, & found ourselves at Bridge's Camp in the edge of the Balsam Mountain, & about 4 miles, as he told us, from its highest part. At the Camp, we separated for a short hunt, the day being well worn. Dick & I went northwesterly, into the skirts of the Balsam – Bridges & the old man took a different course. A light shower or two of rain fell while we were out. I shot a Mountain Boomer – Dick got two shots at a Doe, & missed her both with his rifle barrel & his buckshot. When we met at the Camp, Bridges reported that he had seen up Pisgah Ridge two Bears & a Deer. At night, having toasted some fat pork, roasted the Boomer, & made coffee, we supped & laid ourselves down under the Camp where after hearing abundance of hunting stories from Bridges, we fell very pleasantly asleep.

1 shot   1 Mountain Boomer

Sat. July 29. Rose pretty early, & set out hunting – Bridges & the old man went into the Balsam, Dick & I up Pisgah Ridge. Our ascent was rendered rather difficult in places by thickets of Laurel & other undergrowth – but we advanced slowly, eating huckle-berries, & enjoying prospects. About two miles from the camp, I put up a pack of Pheasants, & as soon as I could draw a load of buck-shot & put in small shot, pursued them down the laurel-covered side of the Ridge, but without success. Dick did not go beyond this point. I ascended about three quarters of a mile further, & took a stand according as I supposed, to Bridges' instructions. It was however, rather too far up. While there, it rained a good deal, after the capricious fashion of the Mountain. I shot a Mountain Boomer however – & was somewhat surprised at the number of small birds of different kinds occurring at that elevation – an elevation considerably greater I should think, than that of the White-top Mountain, altho the growth of trees, owing perhaps to superior richness of soil, does not exhibit near so stunted & rugged an aspect. At length, Bridges called me from the Ridge below, & I proceeded to join him, killing by the way, a Pheasant, on the ground, in the Laurel thicket on the side of the ridge. Dick & the old man had gone on to the Camp, neither they nor Bridges having killed anything. We descended to the Big Pigeon, & went on after them to the Camp, which is within 20 yards of the river.

2 shots   1 Pheasant (about 2/3 grown)
               1 Mountain Boomer

In the evening, after taking our snack, I shot another Boomer, close to the Camp, & we separated for another hunt – Bridges & I going into the edge of the Balsam, across the Pigeon at the head of the falls, & on Pisgah Ridge, while Dick proceeded in another direction into the Balsam, & the old man set about gathering balsam with his "spunge" as they call the iron instrument used for that purpose – in which occupation Dick came near shooting at him for a Deer. Bridges & I set one of his great bear-traps, in a bear-path, leading thro an infernal Laurel thicket – and about the end of our hunt, he started, with his solitary Cur, Trim, an old Buck, at which I might have had a beautiful shot if I had happened to be in the right place. After we had supped, & turned in for the night, a hard rain came down, & made us rather uncomfortable, as our bark roof, owing probably to the accumulation of Balsam straw on it, leaked freely, & our fire was nearly put out, & could with great difficulty be kept up. My cloak, which I had brought up the Mountain, strapped on my back, was now of great service to me, as well as to Dick, who had troubled himself with no incumbrance of the kind.

1 shot   1 Mountain Boomer

Sun. July 30. Set off homewards in the morning, which was raining. We loitered awhile for the purpose of collecting specimens, (cones &c) of the male & female Balsam – but to Bridges' surprise were very unsuccessful, not being able to find any fresh cones of the Male Tree. Bridges & I remained behind together, looking for a Balsam Bird, as well as specimens of the Balsam – but could not find one. This Bird, according to Bridges, is about the size of the Robin, with a very stout bill, & a short tail – plump made, & with its breast speckled – living much about the Balsam Trees, & laying 4 blue eggs, about the size of the Cat-bird's. Its note a short whistle, resembling one of the low cries of the Panther. I cannot imagine what it is. However, while in unsuccessful search for one, I killed a Rose-breasted Grosbeak, one or more of which I had heard, if not seen, the day before. When we got up with Dick & the old man, we found that they had got into a brood of Turkeys, & Dick had shot one of the young ones. I killed another, at a long distance, on the wing, with small shot, & missed one, still farther off, with buck-shot. Bridges took a stand with Dick, & called up the brood, till Dick killed three more of them. He thought he killed the old hen too, but she could not be found. Dick also missed several shots. I got no more shots at the Turkeys – but missed a Swallow-tailed Hawk, flying high over head. Leaving the Turkeys at last, we came pretty rapidly down the mountain. By the time we got to Looking-glass Creek, what between fatigue, wet, sore feet, & hunger, I found myself nearly broken down, & the remainder of the walk, during which some sharp showers of rain fell, was a most severe labor. What I never remember to have experienced before – even the perspiration caused by the exercise seemed cold. Trim started a Deer in the Laurel on Looking-glass Creek, but we could not get a sight of it. After we got back to Bridges, copious draughts of his peach-& apple-brandy, with honey[84] – dry clothes, & a warm bath for my feet, restored me to comfortable sensations.

4 shots   1 Turkey-Poult (about a 2 pounder - larger than any of Dicks.)

              1 Rose-breasted Grosbeak (Coccoborus Ludovicianus)

                         young male - or possibly female.

By R.H.   4 Turkey Poults

Mon. July 31. Dick having commenced tiring of the Mountains, much sooner than I wished to leave them, we had intended proceeding to Caesar's Head to-day, but rainy weather kept us at our host's.

---

84 Although there are no indications that he was a heavy drinker, Maxcy Gregg was not averse to alcohol. He, perhaps, learned to make his own peach brandy with honey from William Bridges while on this trip to the mountains. In November of 1862, when it was particularly difficult to obtain alcohol in the Confederate States, Gregg wrote his South Carolina friend, William Gilmore Simms, from bivouac in Virginia: "Let me exhort you and the friends in your circle, to cultivate native resources. Was not the honey of Hymettus famous for long ages that knew not sugar? And can any drink be better than the distilled juices of the peach, old and mellow?" *The Writings of William Gilmore Simms, Centennial Edition* (Volume III). Columbia, South Carolina: University of South Carolina Press, 1972, 219n.

The Balsam Mountain takes its name from the Pines with which it is covered. Two species seem to be confounded by the Mountaineers here. The Abies Balsamifera – from which they obtain the medicinal resin – is called by them the female Balsam. Another tree – which I think is the white – or possibly the Black Spruce – is called the male. This tree grows intermixed with the other, & seems the most abundant & rather the largest. No resin is obtained from it. The two, according to Bridges, are always found in company, and no other Pine is found on the mountain. This may account for the trees being taken, notwithstanding the difference in their appearance, for the same species. The heights attained by the Balsam Fir here, is much greater than the 40 or 45 feet assigned by Michaux[85] to it. 80 feet is I think, no uncommon stature.

The Balsam Mountain, giving rise on its Eastern & Southern side to the French Broad, & several of its tributaries, & on the North & West, to the Big Pigeon, & other head waters of the Tennessee, is according to Bridges of vast extent, & never had been thoroughly explored. He told stories of several hunters who had attempted to cross it, from one side to the other, but after cutting their way thro the tangled undergrowth which seems to distinguish this Mountain, for days at a time, had been compelled by the failure of their provisions, to turn back. It is only very lately that these wild regions have commenced to be visited by Sportsmen from a distance. Bridges has guided some parties to the Balsam – and into a place called the Pink Beds,[86] which he described as an extent of flat, tho elevated Country, lying as I think, some 8 or 10 miles distant from Bridges' house, in the direction of Mount Pisgah, taking its name from the abundance of Indian Pink root[87] found there, & forming a great resort at times for game. Of this place – the Pinkbeds – we had heard in Greenville – & thought of visiting it, but Bridges dissuaded us from doing so at this time, as he said we should not be likely to find much game there. On the Balsam Mountain we found the tracks & beds of Deer in great abundance. Bears too seemed to be in the greatest plenty, from the tracks, the scratches on the bark, & the broken branches of Services

---

85 André and François André Michaux were the French father-and-son team of botanists who collected and identified North and South Carolina specimens in the late 18th century and early 19th century. They published their findings in *Historie des arbres forestiers de l'Amérique septentrionale* (*The North American Sylva*).

86 The Pink Beds were native Phlox carolina which bloom in July. Visitors to the Blue Ridge Parkway south of Mt. Pisgah Visitors' Center can view the Pink Beds. (Identification courtesy of Dr. J. Dan Pittillo, former member of the faculty of Western Carolina University, March 12, 2015.)

87 Indian Pink Root is identified as Spigelia by Dr. James E. Kibler.

upon which the Bears had been getting berries. Twice I thought I found Panther tracks – and Bridges reported having found one also. These animals appear to flourish in the inaccessible vastnesses of this Wilderness. Bridges says that he has killed 17 during an eight years residence in his present situation – and describes them as much fiercer, & more ready to attack men even when unhurt, than I had supposed them to be. From his account, he has been more than once in danger from their attacks. Besides Panthers & Wild Cats, he says that there is an animal occasionally met with on the Mountain, of an intermediate size, which he calls a Catamount, & describes as more slender built & with a longer tail than the Wild Cat. He kills on an average 10 or 12 bears in a year – and having had all his dogs but one killed by some bad neighbors, depends more on his traps now than formerly. Sufferer as he has been tho by the rascality of his neighbors in this respect, he seems perfectly ready himself to kill any hounds that might be brought into his presence by interlopers, to frighten away the game.

The numerous birds met with so high up here, surprised me – and none more than the Swallow tailed Hawks, parties of which were often sailing about in view. They are seen every Summer, according to Bridges, & their flights are supposed to portend bad weather – tho as for that matter I suspect that there is never any great confidence to be reposed in the weather here, and that any thing else might do for a sign as well as the Hawks. Snowbirds, old and young were abundant. I noticed besides Robins, the Yellowhammer & the Downy Woodpecker – the Carolina Titmouse (unless it were the Parus Athicapillus). The Indigo Finch – Waxbird – & amongst other Warblers, the Blackthroated Blue. Bridges spoke of a Gray Eagle, sometimes seen about the Mountain, a very powerful Bird larger than the Bald Eagle, & not having its feet feathered down to the toes. Can this be the Falco Washingtonii? However, he stated the measurement of one, across the wings, as only 6 feet 10 inches. He says he has seen about 8, & killed 3 or 4, one of them having been caught in a steel trap. According to Bridges, no snakes are found in the lofty region to which we ascended. He showed me, from Pisgah Ridge, a bare spot towards the head of a lofty gorge, which he said was occasioned by a great stream of water, which had fallen there during a storm, not very long ago, & swept soil & trees in a vast wreck down the Gorge. But the strangest part of his story is, that the trace of the destructive torrent is lost all on a sudden, & that there is no discovering what became of the water.

This Bridges, besides being a Capital woodsman, is a very ingenious sort of a Jack at all trades. He has constructed a Mill, turned by the water of a little mountain rill, which not being sufficient to supply a continuous power, he has by a simple, but most ingenious contrivance, made the machinery regulate itself

– when the water in the reservoir falls to a certain point, it stops working the mill, fills up, & commences again, without the necessity of being attended by a Miller.

He has a musical turn also - & in his cabin, I saw for the first time a dulcimer, & heard its antediluvian-sounding notes.

He handed me some specimens of ore, which he supposed to be lead, to be examined on my return home. He said that the [Cherokee] Indians in the western part of N.C. the remnant of whom were about to be removed to the west in a few days, had been in the habit of getting lead from somewhere about the Balsam Mountains, and that he thought he had discovered the place, this ore being found there in vast masses. If it should prove to be lead, he wished to obtain a grant of the land. After my return however, Dr. Gibbes at my request examined the ore, & pronounced it to be the oligistoxide of iron.

Tues. [August] 1. Made a late start & proceeded by Gash's Bridge on the French Broad, about 10 miles this side of Bridges, & by the Blythe's Gap road, to Caesars head – a distance represented to us by Bridges as about 20 miles, but which we found about 26 or 27. On the way we saw 2 or 3 Ravens & some turkey Buzzards collected at a spot where we could discover no remains of their feast. I missed two shots at one of the Ravens on the wing. We had intended to stop at Caesar's Head, but finding that Howard, the keeper of the tavern, was out on a Camphunt, proceeded 4 miles further, to Douthitt's, who also turned out to be away from home. This compelled us to come 5 miles further on, to Pumpkin Town,[88] where we did not arrive till after dark.

2 shots

Wed. 2. In the morning, after despatching a letter to Elias Hall, requesting him to come up on Thursday or Friday, rode about 3 miles with Joe Berry Sutherland,[89] & his brother James, for whom we called at his house, to drive the Chestnut Ridge. The Dogs (6 pretty good looking hounds) got amongst two broods of

---

88 Pumpkintown was a small community located about five miles from Table Rock. Corn was the main crop grown in the area, although pumpkins were also cultivated for cattle feed.

89 The Sutherland family settled Pumpkintown in the late 1700s. The family built a hotel to accommodate tourists visiting Table Rock.

Turkeys, & kept giving tongue after them for a long time, we supposing that they were running a fox, even after we discovered the Turkeys. Dick missed a Poult – I ran old hen on the wing, a long shot; but quickly afterwards discovering either the same, or the other old Hen almost concealed in the top of a Pine tree, brought her down with a load of buckshot. She was a pretty large Hen, in very good order. We could not succeed in calling up the Poults, as the other old Hen remained unhurt, & giving up the drive, we returned to dinner at Pumpkin Town.

2 shots   1 Turkey (old Hen)

Wed. Aug 2. In the evening I strolled out a little way, by the Oolenoy [River], & brought up my journal in the woods. Saw no game.

Thurs. 3. Rode with Dick in the morning 5 or 6 miles to Sim Burgess' in the cove, coaxing along with some difficulty 4 of Joe Berry & Jem Sutherland's hounds. Here we left our horses, & got Sim Burgess, his brother John & a young fellow named Aites to go driving with us. Having crossed the Slicking, the rest of [us] wound up round the further side of the Buzzard-rock Mountain, while Sim Burgess drove it up on the Slicking side. Aites stationed Dick on Flat rock Creek below me; me, just under the Peak of the Buzzard rock, & himself went a little way down the mountain, on my right. I soon heard the report of Aites' gun, & immediately a large Buck came running by me at full speed, within the distance of some 50 yards or so. I fired both barrels; at the second shot, the deer seemed to stagger a little. Aites and John Burgess soon came on in pursuit, having let loose an old short-legged hound of Corbin's, which we had taken up on the road, famous for tracking & running down game. I went to a stand above the Flat Rock Creek, not far from my former stand; & soon heard some of the Dogs open below me, & saw a handsome Buck come up the mountain side, & stop behind some bushes about 30 yards below me, to look round. I fired at him, & what with the smoke & the bushes could not for my life see what became of him. While looking about, astonished & perplexed, I heard Sim Burgess calling me, & running about 100 yards up the hollow, found him holding the Buck down, with some of the dogs about him; & hastening to his assistance, cut the Deer's throat with my hunting knife. We at first supposed this Deer, in which we found 7 shot – my charge was 12 – to be the same as the one shot at before; but discovered our error when Aites & John Burgess coming back, reported that they had tracked the first deer a mile or more by his blood. So gutting &

hanging up the Buck I had killed, we all set out in pursuit of the other. The day, which had commenced pretty clear, with a cool wind, had by this time become rainy. The two curs of Sim Burgess followed the track faithfully, & we went on in rapid pursuit, often finding blood on the bushes, & coming to some places where the Deer seemed to have fallen down. Dick not keeping up with the speed at which we advanced, lost his way, & remained behind. The rest of us kept up the chase as far as Allen's & Kennemore's Mill, on the East fork of French Broad, over the most diabolical route the old Buck could have selected. This was about 5 miles from the place where I had shot at him. There the increasing rain threw the Curs out & forced us to desist. The hounds had unluckily got before us, & appeared to have overtaken the Buck & to have been whipped off by him. Corbin's old hound alone kept on. We never caught sight of him. The Mountaineers seemed to think we had got after the old Rocky Mountain Buck, a celebrated animal said to have baffled all pursuit, tho shot at by most of the Hunters in the Country. Sim Burgess said he did not think Aites had hit him at all, tho he had shot within about 20 yards – but that the hunt was given by me. Near the Mill, our remaining hounds made a fresh start, & we left them in the woods. We returned by a pretty good path, infinitely more pleasant to my tired limbs than our former track, which was of a most fatiguing nature – & in which, by way of variety of game, we had come across a Rattle Snake, which Sim B. shot with his rifle. On the way back, great piles of drift wood, & a rent in the side of a mountain, similar to that which I had seen at a distance from Pisgah Ridge, were pointed out to me in a hollow which has its slope towards the waters of the East Fork of French Broad. The storm which caused this was said to have happened a year or two since. Arriving at the place where we had left the Buck, & not finding Dick, we went on, Sims & J.B. carrying the Buck down the mountain alternately, a distance of about a mile & a half; and the rest of the way to Sim B's – towards two miles – on a pole between them. I was too nearly broken down to attempt doing my share of the carrying, & Aites did very little, under pretext of a sore shoulder. At Burgess', where we arrived toward night-fall, wet and cold enough, we found that Dick, after wandering about for some hours, wofully lost, had at last got back, taken his horse, & returned to Pumpkin Town. I warmed & eat [sic] some dinner, while the Mountaineers were skinning the Deer. Then paying them a dollar, as the price of the quarter I owed them for doing my share of the carrying, & loading Buck-eye with a hind & fore quarter in a meal-bag, rode on after night to Pumpkin Town, where a hot bath for my feet, plentiful draughts of corn-whiskey (called "Pumpkin Town Particular") & dry clothes, did me great service. The fore quarter of venison I left at Jem Sutherland's as I came by.

3 shots   1 Deer (Buck)

Sat. Aug. 5. Yesterday being wet & cloudy, we staid mostly in-doors. Elias Hall & Sam Earle came up in the evening. This morning it cleared off. Earle went down to his brother, Edward's. The rest of us, with Joe Berry, set out for the Table Rock. On the way, our dogs got off after a Deer, or something else, & only two of them came back to us. I rode with Elias by the foot of the Giant's Stool, for Corbin, a grim looking old hunter, with whom I had made a sort of engagement the day before, to go bear-hunting to the Sun Perch. We found that he had gone up the cove, expecting us to meet him there. Dick voted very strongly against going to the Sun Perch, having little fancy for any further Mountain rambling, since his bewildered adventures on our last tramp. We concluded, however, to ascend the Table Mountain, & try to communicate with the bear-hunting Party. Joe Berry, with Mat Keith[90] & two other Mountaineers, accompanied us a part of the way up, & took our horses back. We went on, & blew our horn as a signal, both from the ridge which connects the Giant's Stool with the Table, & from the summit, but could neither see nor hear any thing of Corbin's party. I had much difficulty in getting Dick & Elias up the Stairs, as they both became dreadfully nervous. I had to carry up their guns, & all the baggage. Drive too, one of our two Dogs, refused to ascend the stairs, & I had to carry him up the first flight. I believe he found some way of scrambling up the side of the rock afterwards. When at last on the summit, after taking a survey from the Cedar Tree, now dead, I proceeded to place Elias at a stand near the head of the Whip & Spur Gap, & Dick near the Spring, while I drove the top of the Rock. But I did not succeed in finding even the track of a Deer. I started a wolf, fox, or some smaller varmint, which darted away thro the bushes so fast that I could draw no aim on it. The Dogs pursued it but for a short time. Afterwards we proceeded along the ridge beyond old Maverick's tenantless Cabin, & returning to a little Camp built near the Cedar Tree by a man who is working on the steps for Sutherland, spent the night there. There was some rain in the evening. Our fire was much too hot & smoky for our little cabin. Elias was particularly annoyed, as the temperature of his system had been raised by the deep draughts from our bottle of "Pumpkin Town Particular."

Sun. Aug. 6. In the morning, after a rather watery Sun-rise, a fog swept over the summit of the Rock. Descending by the Steps, & going round to the Pool at the Base, we fired some rounds at marks. Towards noon, we returned to Pumpkin

---

90 Cornelius Keith was an early settler of the Oolenoy River area, arriving there in 1756 from Loch Lomond, Scotland. Four Keith brothers (William C., Thomas J., John R., and E.M. Keith) served in Company A of the First South Carolina (Orr's) Rifles, one of the five regiments commanded by Brigadier General Maxcy Gregg in the Civil War.

Town. Elias was so broken down, (notwithstanding he had had the benefit of the whole bottle of whiskey, with the exception of a small draw which I gave Drive to steady his nerves in coming down the Stairs) that he had to stop at Keith's & get a Colt which he rode bare-backed the rest of the way, much to the amusement of Dick & myself. Dick however, was pretty well tired down too. I noticed at this visit, that the Pine which grows most abundantly on the Table rock – indeed I believe the only one – is the Pinus Pungens, which Michaux says grows on the Table Mountain in <u>North Carolina</u>, making a mistake probably of the State. I think those smaller Pines, which on my former visit I remarked for the peculiarity of their appearance, are of the same species with the larger Trees, which are evidently the Pinus Pungens.

Dining at Pumpkin Town, we set off for Greenville, by the upper road. Elias was mounted on Whistle Jacket, a broken down but fiery spirited Charger, of such remarkable character & action, that we over-laughed ourselves, until it became painful. We called at Edward Earles', and were joined by him & Sam Earle in the ride from there to Greenville, in the course of which we were overtaken by a light shower of rain.

Tues. Aug. 8. After waiting for Dick one day, which I spent in visiting Judge Gantt, about 6 miles south of the Village. I was disappointed this morning by learning from Dick that he could not set off with me for Columbia, on account of the sickness of his servant. So determined instead of taking the direct route to call at David Johnson's again. Peter had arrived the day before with Granby, whose lameness was much diminished, some gravel having worked out of his foot. This morning, the Blacksmith, Cobble, pronounced that he was suffering from a contracted heel, & prized it open, while he shod him with a broader shoe. Set off about 9 o'clock, & rode 14 miles, to Kilgore's.

In the afternoon, rode about 10 miles, by Westmoreland's to Dr. Woodruff's, getting caught in a hard shower by the way. At Dr. Woodruff's, I saw two birds flitting about which from the glimpses I had, I took for Baltimore Orioles.

Wed. Aug. 9. Rode in the morning to David Johnson's, & found that he had just gone off a day or two before. Dined at his house.

In the evening, rode over to Gage's, & spent the night with him. A light shower of rain towards Sun-set. Shot a nighthawk by his cabin.

1 shot   1 Nighthawk.

Thurs. Aug. 10. Granby having become too lame to keep up with me any longer, set off by myself about 10 o'clock, intending to get back into the Columbia Road at the Cross Keys. But arriving at Murphy's Bridge, 3 ½ miles from Gage's, I found the Tiger [Tyger River] risen four feet over the Bridge. So got a new shoe put on at a Blacksmith's, in place of one which Buckeye had cast, & returned to Gage's to dinner.

In the afternoon set off towards Unionville, intending to proceed to Judge Johnson's in search of David, but was compelled by a storm of rain, which I barely escaped, to stop at Unionville. Peter, who set out some time after me, was caught & soaked – besides having some difficulty from the rise of the waters at the Bridge over Fairforest, & at a little Branch near Union C.H.

Fri. [August] 11. Leaving Peter behind, to come on by slow journeys, rode about 25 miles to dinner at Maybinton[91] – crossing Tiger at Roger's Bridge.

In the evening, rode on 11 miles to Lake's, crossing the Ennoree at Henderson's Bridge.

Sat. [August] 12 [1843]. A very cloudy morning, which turned into a sunshiny, sultry day. Started very early, & rode about 20 miles to dinner at one of the Lorick's, the nearer to Columbia. At Cannon's Creek, about 29 miles from Columbia, I saw several young Ardeae Caeruleae, in the white dress – the furthest inland that I remember to have met with them. When within 18 or 20 miles of Columbia, I came across some hunters, who were at stands along the road for Deer. Passing them, & stopping when I heard the hounds, I came very near getting a shot at a Doe, which crossed the road, from the Drive towards the River, within 150 or 200 yards of me.

In the afternoon rode home, 13 miles. Buckeye, having lost his fore-shoes to-day, & having his hoofs much broken became lame. By the end of the day too, a swelling of a very serious appearance had formed just behind his withers

91 Maybinton, a thriving town with a hotel, churches, academies, shops, and manufactories, was several miles west of the Broad River in Newberry District. It was settled by the Irish Maybin (Mebon) family before the American Revolution. (Courtesy Dr. James E. Kibler)

– something of the kind having been threatened when I first reached Greenville. I apprehended a fistula – but it turned out to be a bad sort of saddle-bruise or blood-blister, which was cured by poulticing & lancing.

Thurs. Sept. 7 [1843]. Slowly recovering my strength, after the attack of "Grippe" which seizing me about a fortnight after my return from the Mountains, & laying me up for a week, had completely prostrated me. Walked, rather late in the evening, with Hart, over to my Grandmothers, to shoot Nighthawks, taking with us Bruno & the puppy (since provisionally named Brant, as an abbreviation for Brantley) & calling out Pronto Strobel there. Weather exceedingly hot for September – saw but few Nighthawks – I missed two. I shot a Yellowhammer flying, which fell close to the hut at the back corner of Fenton's lot.

3 shots   1 Yellowhammer

Thurs. Sep. 28. The weather has been excessively hot all this month, till within a day or two that it has turned cooler. Mounted Granby in the evening (he has got over all lameness, & I keep him barefoot to toughen his hoofs) and rode to Hampton's Middle Ponds, where I remained at a stand till nearly dark, & saw only two Summer Ducks pass up. I missed a Nighthawk, & fired two shots at a bird which I suppose was a Night Heron – being probably of the same species with those large croaking birds which used to excite my curiosity at the same place 3 or 4 years ago. It fell on the other side of the sluice,* below the old burnt Mill – & there being no bridge now, I was obliged to trust to Bruno's exertions. He had a long fight with the wounded bird, which croaked in the most formidable manner – but he came back without it, & I could not tell whether he had killed it, or, what was more probable, been worsted in the battle.

3 shots

* I had not at this time found out the path for getting round below the sluice. I think some more water ran thro that way then than now (Oct. 1844) & the undergrowth in the edge of the swamp was rather thicker.

Summary from April to Sept. 1843

Month	Ap.	Jul.	Aug.	Sep.	Total
Times out	4	19	17	2	42
Shots fired	26	12	8	6	52
Nighthawk			1		1
Bee-Martin	1				1
Rose-breasted Grosbeak		1			1
Kingfisher	1				1
Yellowhammer	1				1
Dove	1				1
Wild Turkey		1	1		2
Pheasant		1			1
Snipe	1				1
Pectoral Sandpiper	18				18
Fox Squirrel		1			1
Mountain Boomer		3			3
Deer			1		1

13 Species
Individuals, 33

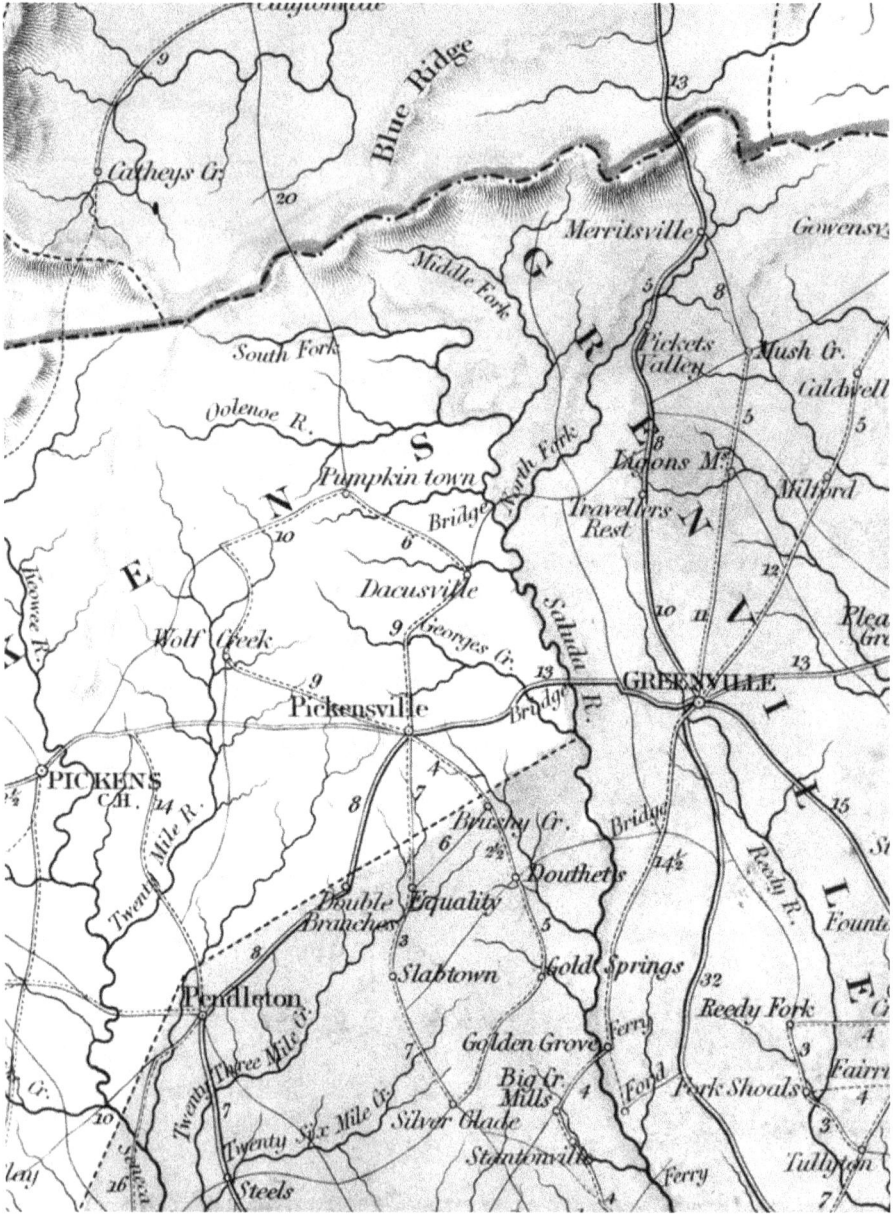

Burr, David H. Map of North and South Carolina exhibiting the post offices post roads, canals, rail roads &c. By David H. Burr; Late topographer to the Post Office. Geographer to the House of Representatives of the U.S. [London, 1839] Map. https://www.loc.gov/item/98688532/.

October 1843 - March 1844: The South Carolina Low Country

Mon. Oct 2. 1843. Rode out in the evening with the intention of visiting Taylor's Ponds – but finding the entrance changed by DeBruhl, & it being late, gave that plan up & went over to the burnt Mill. Fired no shot.

Mon. [October] 9. Rode in the afternoon with Mayrant[92] down to Granby, with the hope of seeing Summer Ducks fly up & down the river in the evening, in which we were disappointed. Sailed about in his new Boat for awhile, but the wind being very baffling on the water, tho steady enough above the Banks, we were obliged to land some distance below the ferry & walk up. Lara, after swimming the river several times, warmed his blood by a long fight with Mayrant's big Cur, Guard, until both were quite willing to stop. Weather coolish now, but no frost yet. I missed a Sparrowhawk on a high tree at the Lower Steam-boat landing.

1 shot

Tues. Oct. 10. In the evening, rode by Everett's Pond, & there fired two shots at a Didapper, beyond all reasonable distance, & more by way of experiment than anything else. Went on to Hampton's Middle Ponds, & riding up to the Creek, just below the broken Culvert at the Rail-road, flushed unexpectedly a flock of

---

92 Robert Pringle Mayrant was one of Maxcy's most frequent companions on his hunting forays. Both men were particularly fond of duck hunting. Mayrant, as Gregg refers to him, was born on Sullivan's Island in 1808. In adulthood he stood five feet, ten inches in height, had light colored eyes, brown hair, and a florid complexion, no doubt due to his obesity. Robert Mayrant and his family lived on the northeast corner of Senate and Bull streets, not far from the Gregg home. He was a planter of moderate success, in part attributable to his wealthy father-in-law.

some 6 or 7 Summer Ducks. I brought one down, which fell on the other side, & making off wing-broken, required another shot to stop it. Bruno got it out of the marsh with some difficulty, having to climb a slimy log in swimming water, which lay in his way. Remained at a stand below the Old Mill till Dusk, but got nothing. Missed one shot at a Kingfisher. I have been suffering for 4 or 5 days under a most violent cold.

5 shots   1 Summer Duck (young male, or fem.)

Sat. 14. Coldest day yet this fall. Thermometer 44 at Sun-rise, 52 a little after sun-set. Some frost reported, tho I saw none. Mounted Granby in the morning, & set off for an all day's hunt. Found Taylor's Ponds almost entirely dried up. Shot a Winter Falcon there on the wing. Past the Big Lagoon, which was very low, with no Ducks in it, & the Eastern Bank of which has been cleared & planted to the water's edge since I was at it last. Towards Gill's Creek, Bruno got into a Covey of Partridges, which he treed in the most dashing style, & one of which he caught in some thick grass. Hitching Granby in the Swamp, I hunted down to the mouth of the Creek on foot, encountering some formidable Cane-brakes on the way. Killed four Summer Ducks, the first and the second in the water, wounding at the same time with the second a third which escaped by diving, & which I afterwards killed further down the Creek. The fourth I brought down by a long shot, as it rose. Bruno brought them all out handsomely. Where the Creek enters the river, I fired a very long shot at a flock of about 7, & wounded one or more, but they all flew off. After following the river up to a point opposite the mouth of Congaree Creek, I endeavored to take a shorter cut across to my horse, but becoming entangled in Briar-patches, was forced to make great circuits, & pretty well tired down. When at last I came to Granby, mounted him joyfully, & set off homewards. In passing thro DeBruhl's Plantaton, this side of the Ponds, I saw a Marsh Hawk rise before me with something heavy in its talons, & pursuing it to where it had lit, forced it to a second flight. It lit again, on the ground; & before I could get near it, a Redtailed or Redshouldered Hawk – a Redtail I think – made at it & robbed it of its prey. The Marsh Hawk, reluctant to abandon it, kept flying round & swooping at the Redtail, until I gallopped up & frightened both away. My attention was engrossed in marking the spot where the prey was left; & there I found a Partridge, alive, tho wounded, & able to attempt its escape by running. In the road, this side of DeBruhl's gate, I shot a Partridge which sat for some time before me, & when shot, flew into the field where I found it dead, & where Bruno put up some more Partridges, two of which I missed. Home without further incident.

13 shots

4 Summer Ducks	Caught by Bruno - 1 Partridge
1 Partridge	Taken from Hawk, 1 Partridge
1 Redshouldered Hawk (young)	

Wed. Oct. 18. Rode in the evening by Everetts to Hampton's Middle Ponds, where no Ducks past up. Weather coolish & very dry. Frost enough last Saturday night to kill most of the Cotton. I shot a Dove, but Lara tore it so much in fetching it from where it fell across the Creek, that I threw it away.

2 shots   1 Dove

Fri. 27. Mayrant & I had been planning a voyage in his boat down the river, as far as the Rail-road Bridge; & fixed upon this day for setting off; but in consequence of a N.E. storm, I considered the scheme as suspended. Mayrant however called for me in the morning, & rousing me from bed, informed me that the weather was clearing off with a N.W. wind. So packing up my baggage hastily, I drove down to Granby after him, & about 10 o'clock, we set sail in the Nimrod. Our crew consisted of two negroes, sent up by Bob Myers, whom we were to join at his landing, for oarsmen, tho one of them had never seen an oar before. We had on board also Mayrant's two dogs, Guard and Cora. Our armament was pretty formidable, consisting of Mayrant's great Blunderbuss, which was christened by Wash Myers the Thunderbuss – of another heavy single barrelled gun, lately bought by him at Glazes'[93] – & of my gun – all ready for action – besides a large double barrel of Mayrant's stowed in its case by way of reserve. Provisions, wine & baggage, added to the rest, made a full load for the Boat. The river having been raised by the rains, we went down with a rapid current, making some use of a sail, but more of the oars, as the wind proved baffling, which it seems to be most commonly between the banks of this river. Arrived in good time in the evening at Myers' landing, about 12 miles from Columbia by land, & more

---

93 Robert Mayrant purchased his 'great Blunderbuss' from Columbia merchant William Glaze (1800-1870) at his store, 'At the Sign of the Drum,' a mercantile which sold "watches, jewelry, silver, and plated ware, guns, pistols, cutlery, metals, and fancy goods." Hennig, Helen Kohn. *William Harrison Scarborough, Portraitist and Miniaturist: "A Parade of the Living Past"*. Columbia, South Carolina: The R.L. Bryan Company, 1927, 96.

than twice as much by water. Just below the mouth of Congaree Creek, I killed a Coot, sitting on a log. A mile or two below, I shot a Summer Duck, in the water, at the distance of about 70 yards. Mayrant had killed at Fisher's Pond before I joined him, what he called a Stone Curlew, & sent it home. I should have supposed he meant a Semipalmated Snipe, but he described it as having yellow legs. We landed at the mouth of Savanna Hunt Creek, & I walked up to Wolf's Pond, but saw no Ducks there. We discovered at the mouth of the Creek the tracks of a Deer, that seemed to have been in the habit of going down to the river there to drink. At Bob Myers' landing, we found him getting his Deck Boat, the John-Moore, ready for the voyage; & after taking a short row down the river with him, proceeded on horse-back – I on mule-back – to his house, about 5 miles off, where we found Seymour awaiting our arrival, & spent the night.

6 shots	By me	By RPM
	1 Summer Duck	1 Stone Curlew
	1 Coot (Fulica Americana)	

Sat. Oct 28. Morning cold & rather clear. Riding down to the landing, & leaving Myers there engaged in loading his boat, & Seymour with him, we proceeded in the Nimrod, now lightened of much baggage, & without the dogs, who had got lost on our road to Bob Myers' the evening before, about 3 miles down the river, to Chappell's plantation, where we landed. On the way, we came across a Ruddy Duck in the River, which did not offer to fly, but astonished me by its sleight in diving, twice dodging my shot within the distance of 30 or 40 yards. Finally I killed it by a shot from Thunderbuss, as it raised itself up to flap its wings. Landing at Chappell's, we went by his house, & hunted, I up & Mayrant down, Raiford's Creek. I killed a Cat Squirrel, frightened the only party of Summer Ducks that I saw, & getting considerably out of my way, came in sight of some Deer hunters. A Turkey, frightened by some of them, lit in a field not far from me, but disappeared under cover of the broomstraw & briar-patches. Falling in with some of Myers' servants & horses, I rode back to Chapell's House, & returning with Mayrant to his Boat, dropped a little further down the river, to the Bee Tree Landing, where we awaited the arrival of the John Moore, which was to complete its cargo at that place. While Myers remained attending to this, Mayrant & I walked over to Raiford's Creek, & hunted, he up & I down it, some little way. I missed two or three shots at Summer Ducks, being annoyed by the noisy behavior of Myers' Dog, Snap, who accompanied me as a retriever, but did nothing but bark after squirrels. I got back to the Bee Tree Landing before Mayrant, & witnessed the first experiment of letting the John Moore swing off with her full load. The Boat made a deep roll, being top-heavy – pitched the Caboose off into ten feet water – & sent the crew scampering like rats to the upper side. The Caboose was fished up, ten bales of Cotton thrown off, & we slept in the Cabin.

Mayrant & Seymour however, paid a visit to Chappell, who entertained them with woeful prognostications of the fate of the Boat, when it should reach the Devil's Pockethole, & sundry other perilous rejoins.

8 shots

    By me 1 Ruddy Duck (Fuligula Rubida)

         1 Cat Squirrel

By R.P.M. 1 Summer Duck,

         1 Cat Squirrel

        & one Redtail Hawk -none of which he got, or at least brought back

Sun. Oct. 29. Myers had the night before declared his intention of abandoning the voyage, on account of head-ache & fever, but being better in the morning, changed his mind. Seymour however, regarding the propensity of the Boat to roll over as disagreeable, the accommodations on board as bad, & the company worse – for we had bedeviled him rather too much for the first night – & alleging business – deserted. Mayrant & I took a little the start in the Nimrod, & about the time that the John Moore overtook us, discovered a large Sea Gull swimming in the river. It was pronounced by Mayrant to be of the largest kind & appeared to be sick, proving of exceedingly light weight. Myers fired two shots at it from his Boat, but did not seem to hurt it. It did not – perhaps could not fly – & rowing up in the Nimrod, I dispatched it by a close shot. While approaching it, I observed it drink water. I believe it was a small specimen of the Great Black-backed Gull, in immature plumage. Our day's voyage was about 45 miles by water, stopping below Stark's Saw Mill. We sometimes remained on board the John Moore – sometimes cruised in the Nimrod – & passed in safety the Devil's Pocket, his Elbow, his Foot track & other places of note. All the Sand bars were under water. The principal accident occurred in passing some trees with drift wood amongst them, which pulled loose the Nimrod, in which

I had been ashore to get some wood, before she had been again fastened at the Stern of the Moore. This rendered it necessary to make fast to the Bank, while Ned, the Steward, went back, swam out to where the Nimrod lay entangled, & brought her back. At one point to-day, Mayrant & Myers landed at right of a Turkey in a tree, & got amongst a large flock in a Cane brake, where they could make nothing out of them. We passed the rail-road Bridge rather late in the afternoon, Mayrant & I having given up all idea of stopping short of Charleston. We were in hopes, each succeeding night, of a hard frost, from the appearance of the weather – in which we found ourselves as often disappointed.

4 shots

> By me.   1 Great Blackbacked Gull (Larus Marinas)
>
> (in immature plumage)

By R.P.M.   1 Summer Duck   By Myers   1 Summer Duck
            2 Cat Squirrels

Mon. Oct. 30. Early in the morning, Mayrant & I, with Myers, taking the start of the Large Boat in the Nimrod, dropped down the River Duck-hunting. At the junction of the Congaree & Wateree, we ran up into a Lagoon, where I killed a Summer Duck. Leaving this place, we by mistake entered the old river on the left, instead of taking Manigault's Cut off on the right – in consequence of which, as we lost 3 or 4 miles in distance, the Moore past us without our knowing whether she had done so or not – & we did not catch up with her till quite late, when Myers & I had our hands blistered by 5 hours rowing. The most tempting shot that offered itself to-day – at a flock of English Ducks – was lost by mismanagement of which Myers was the cause. We were drifting down on the Ducks – Mayrant in the bow, under cover of a screen of green limbs – & I directing the boat at the Stern. At Mayrant's request, I was just turning the head of the boat, to give him a shot to his left – when Myers, by his blundering, led me to suppose that Mayrant desired the contrary direction given to the boat, which lost the chance, as the Ducks flew, were fired at under a disadvantage, & none got. Our day's voyage was about 70 miles, as we ran some distance into the Long Reach by moonlight, & stopped some miles below Vance's Ferry. We were amused this evening by the sly maneouvers of our Captain – old London – to leave Jesse Harris' boats out of sight behind him – cutting close all the points & shaving the Bites. Afterwards, to enliven the moonlight work, we had ballads, of which the Chorus was sung by the Crew, while Ned, in the part of the improvisatore, recited a narrative of the voyage – the passage of the Pocket hole – the warnings of Old Chappell – the desertion of Judge Seymour, & other incidents, mixed with the more fanciful parts of the song.

4 shots

By me 1 Summer Duck

By the rest nothing

Tues. Oct. 31. We made but a short day's run, for on arriving at the Santee Canal[94] – which might be 30 miles by water, Myers' boat was found too wide to pass thro the locks, & the latter half of the day was consumed in hewing off the gunwales, & getting about 2 miles into the Canal. Mayrant & I kept ahead with the Nimrod. Just above the 1st Lock, I shot a Coot in the water of the Canal. Afterwards, I killed a Didapper in a Pond on the western Bank of the Canal, where he did not seem to have a fair chance to dive. He was brought out by Jackson, Myers spoilt pet – & the Cabin Boy on this voyage. Further on in the same Pond, which seems to be of considerable size, I shot a Ring-neck Duck, or Black-head, a very long way out, where I could not get it at the time. Mayrant killed a Rabbit, at about 80 yards as he said, with the Thunderbuss – & wounded a Black-head in the Canal, which I pursued & killed as it rose & flew off. Being joined by Myers, & dragging the Nimrod over the Bank into the pond, we got my Ring-neck, the head of which was eaten off by a Cooter – & Myers shot a Coot. Young Sloan & Jake Tipton were in the Canal along with Myers' Boat, having in charge a pair of Match boats of Matthew Crawford. As they camped

---

94 Construction of the 35-foot wide Santee Canal, "one of the earliest important canals in the United States," was begun in 1793 and when completed in 1800 was twenty-two miles in length. It was planned as a faster transportation route from the midlands of South Carolina to the port of Charleston. With the increase in cotton as a crop in the early- to mid-1800s, the canal experienced greater use as a transportation corridor. Seventy thousand bales of cotton were transported by 720 boats from the inland of the state to Charleston in 1830. When Maxcy Gregg and the 'Santee Squadron' made this run in 1843 there were few roads connecting Columbia and Charleston, and to further hinder land traffic the area consisted of "sandy uplands, of wide swamps, of marshes and broad tidal streams," making travel, and especially transportation of cotton and other goods, easier by water. Irving, John B. (Reprint edited by Louisa Cheves Stoney). *A Day on Cooper River*. Columbia, South Carolina: The R.L. Bryan Company, 1969, viii.

out on the Bank, Mayrant & I preferred to make a bed & a slight shelter of Pines, & sleep on the smoky side of their fire, as a precaution against malaria.[95] Myer slept in the cabin.

7 shots

By me	By R.P.M.
2 Ring-neck Ducks	1 Rabbit
1 Didapper	
1 Coot	By R.C.M.
	1 Coot

Wed. [November] 1 [1843]. The John Moore was detained a long time to-day, in consequence of the necessity of hewing off her sides again, to enable her to pass thro the locks. Mayrant & I went ahead in the Nimrod, which we lifted round two locks & smuggled thro three. We saw many Ringnecks in a great Cypress Pond, called I believe Kirk's. Mayrant with his great gun, killed one which must have been more than 100 yards off. I killed one with my Gun about 90 yards off. But not getting any help to put the Nimrod over into the Pond, we had to leave them. By the same shot which killed one Blackhead, I wounded three others, which flew off. I do not count the one I lost, as there is the possibility of its being of some other species. We saw also & fired at a pair of Ruddy Ducks, which kept at a pretty safe distance out in the Pond, & dived at the flash. A Ring-neck lit in the Canal, which I approached under cover of the Bank. As I fired, he dived, & rising commenced flying off when I cut him down with my other barrel.

---

95 The low country of the Palmetto State had a well-deserved reputation for being unhealthy. Malaria was so prevalent in Charleston that it was afforded the title of "the most malarious area on the Atlantic coast." Like yellow fever, malaria was a mosquito-borne disease, recognized as being seasonal, with the 'sickly' season being precisely defined by one doctor in Charleston as June 21 to October 21. Others expanded the "time for retreat" from the region as from the 10th of May to the 10th of November. Maxcy Gregg merely kept an eye on the weather and avoided travel to the low country until the first frost had been reported. Those who contracted malaria suffered incapacitating fevers, violent shivering, delirium, and, in "extreme examples, destruction of red blood cells, causing death as the liver and spleen swelled, turning black." Malaria could also be recurrent, with fever coming on with no warning. Common treatments included "whiskey or boiled dogwood bark," even though there was a consensus among the medical community that quinine was the most effective treatment. Joseph Ioor Waring, *A History of Medicine in South Carolina*, 37. Adams, Michael C.C. *Living Hell: The Dark Side of the Civil War*. Baltimore, Maryland: Johns Hopkins University Press, 2014, 49, 50.

He dropped in the water, dived, & came up dying. Mayrant afterwards going ahead while I walked back to see what detained the John Moore, fired at a flock of 7 Blackheads, killed 3, & crippled 2, but got none. I walked on & rejoined Mayrant; & proceeding in company with Sloan's Boats, we stopped in a deep, swampy looking forest, about half way down the Canal, where we pitched a tent of the two sails of the Nimrod, to spend the night. Myers preferred sleeping in his Cabin. Some rain falling in the night wet my legs & woke me up – but I made up the fire anew, & on the whole we were pretty comfortable.

9 shots

      By me   1 Ringneck Duck.   nothing else got-

Thurs. Nov. 2. A cloudy morning, clearing off rather warm for this malaria region. Being placed in charge of the Nimrod, I sailed & worked her down the Canal, while Mayrant & Myers following in the Large Boat, fired many shots at fish from the bow, without getting any. At Black Oak, where as at several other Locks, we had to haul the Nimrod round on rollers, Mayrant shot in the Canal a duck which I take for the Golden-Eye – in immature plumage, perhaps a female. He knew no name for the Duck, but said he had often seen the same kind about the rice fields. He also killed, at the Lower Lock, a Bluewing Teal. In a very extensive marsh, which we passed in the morning, one the right bank of the Canal, & where Myers stopt with me a little while to hunt, I saw alighting, out of reach, a vast flock of some kind of Ducks. I saw also, a great flock of birds resembling some kind of Plovers, on which a Peregrine Falcon was making attacks. There, too, & further down along the Canal, I saw many birds like Swallows flying about – possibly white bellied Swallows, but I am inclined to think they were Black Terns. Passing thro the Lower Lock about dusk, which was as soon as the tide allowed, we ran down Biggin Creek & Cooper River by moonlight, until stopt by a dense fog, which compelled us to cast anchor in the channel before the tide was near out.

No shot fired by me.

By R.P.M.   1 Golden-Eye Duck
           1 Bluewing Teal.

Fri. Nov. 3. Our anchorage must have been, I think, somewhere near Mulberry Bluff. The Ebb tide setting in soon after Sun-rise, we commenced another run, the Nimrod, with all three sportsmen on board, taking the start. I was landed on the right bank of the river, & shot a great Horned Owl, sitting beside a ditch in a rice field. Then, taking charge of the Boat while Mayrant & Myers went ashore, I shot a Blue-wing Teal, out of a flock at a long distance. It fell on the edge of the marsh, up-stream from me, tho in an Eddy – & I was obliged to work up with the paddle against the wind till I got it. Changing again with Mayrant & Myers, I set out to follow the embankments down the river – but getting up Dockon Creek, & finding no crossing place for a great distance, I was forced some miles out of my way, & took a pretty extensive survey of several rice plantations – Roper's, Ball's, Moultries', Motts', & others.[96] I saw very few Ducks about the fields. Perhaps the high rice stubble, still remaining green, may have screened from view what were there. I rejoined the Nimrod at last, at a point several miles below the mouth of Dockon Creek – or Wappahoola, if it be so called – the two come together before entering into Cooper River. Still, my long walk had not entirely dried my legs, which had got wet from the dew on the rice stubble at my first landing. Myers I found had killed a Tell-tale, & as he said, a Marsh Hawk - & Mayrant a ruddy Duck. Overtook the John Moore by dint of rowing - & kept on till the commencement of flood tide compelled us to cast anchor opposite Carson's great plantation. Here Mayrant & I, with Jake Tipton & Sloane for oarsmen, embarked in the Nimrod, & first pursued a Didapper, at which I fired a Cartridge, aiming low. The Didapper went under as usual, but instantly rose with a leg broken, & flew off till it was brought down my by second barrel. Afterwards, we landed at Carson's Mill, & I with Jake Tipton went about a mile off to a back rice field, where no Ducks were to be found – it was not flooded. On the way, I killed a Tell-Tale. During this time, Mayrant having left Sloane to take care of the Nimrod, & strolling about to look at the place, the Driver, who had not seen Mayrant, & who seemed to regard boatmen with great suspicion, collected a dozen of his trustiest fellows to watch Sloane & the boat. On Mayrant's return, Sloane was relieved of his fears of captivity & guard discharged. I got back with Jake Tipton after sun-down – blew the horn

---

96 As the crews neared Charleston they passed a number of rice plantations and homes of some of the wealthiest South Carolinians. 'Point Comfort' was the home of R.W. Roper. Other plantations and their owners were 'Strawberry' (John C. Ball), 'The Bluff' (Dr. William Lennox Moultrie), and the site of 'The Farm,' which had belonged to Mrs. Rebecca Motte, a heroine of the Revolutionary War who sacrificed her home in order to force the surrender of the British soldiers who were using it as a fort. "Carson's great plantation" was 'Dean Hall,' the home of William Augustus Carson which now is open to the public as Cypress Gardens, a 170-acre nature preserve.

for the Nimrod – & got on board the John Moore. With the Ebb Tide & a fine moonlight, we ran on to the mouth of Back river – 15 or 20 miles I suppose – where anchor was cast.

7 shots

By me   1 Great Horned owl (Strix Virginiana [the Great Horned Owl])

           1 Blue-wing Teal

           1 Didapper   By R.P.M   1 Ruddy Duck

           1 Tell-Tale

                                    By R.C.M.   1 Tell-Tale

Sat. Nov. 4. With the morning's Ebb tide, Mayrant, Myers & I set off in the Nimrod for Charleston, taking in Ned as an oarsman, & leaving Capt. London to follow with his Boat as fast as he could. The distance by water – being probably 25 miles – was accomplished by the Nimrod in about 6 hours – arriving between 1 & 2 o'clock, soon after the commencement of flood tide. The day very warm, - the only very warm one since our leaving Columbia. I rowed all the way, till we got to Town Creek, where I took a seat in the bow for shooting. Ned relieved Myers at the oar. Mayrant steered. Our sail was of little use, for want of a breeze. In the morning, I saw one Bald Eagle on a distant tree near the mouth of Back River, & another flying, making three in the course of the voyage. I also shot at a pretty large bird flying past, before we left the John Moore, which Mayrant pronounced a Sheldrake, adding that it was a kind of Duck. A Bird larger Still flew by, which was called a Loon. We also saw 5 or 6 Golden-Eye Ducks flying by, conspicuous from the white speculum. We also saw on the way, several Porpoises, Sharks, Cranes & Gulls. I omitted to mention in its place, that on the first day we were on the Santee Canal, we saw flying overhead a Bird which I should have taken for an Anhinga, but which some of the party present at the time, knew as a Cormorant. So much for new game seen on the voyage. I killed three Gulls in the course of the morning, the last of which I brought down like the rest from the wing, but was obliged to despatch by a second shot in the water to save a troublesome chase. They were all, I believe, young Ring-billed Gulls – but so different in plumage from Audubon's[97] figures & descriptions, that I am not without some little doubt. On arriving in Charleston, we separated –

---

97 John James Audubon (1785-1851) was well-recognized as the premier American ornithologist. Audubon was also a skilled artist and author of *The Birds of America*, an illustrated book to which Maxcy Gregg referred in identifying birds.

Myers, who had been with us about as long as we could well have agreed with him, going to the Planter's Hotel,[98] Mayrant & I to Stewart's.[99] In the afternoon, I went with Mayrant to the wharves, taking our guns to shoot Gulls – but finding that Myers had sent the Nimrod off to meet the John Moore, we were obliged to give our shooting up, & spent the rest of the afternoon in looking for Guns & Cartridges in the Shops. A very bad supply for such a city.

8 shots

> By me   3 Ring billed Gulls (Lari Zonorhynchi)

> By the rest nothing.

Sun. Nov. 5. We staid but one night in Charleston, having no decent clothes with us, & not thinking it quite safe to remain longer, as there had been no frost as far down as the City, & there was a good deal of malignant fever on the Neck, as well as some cases of yellow fever in different parts of the City. Of the latter there was one case at our Hotel. We therefore – that is Mayrant & I – set off by the Rail-road at 9 o'clock this morning & returned to Columbia, the weather turning pretty cool in the course of the day. We had met with less game on our trip to Charleston than we had expected – but this we attributed to the weather's not having set in cold enough. We met however with much novelty – particularly in the latter part of the voyage – and were so well pleased with the trip, that we immediately projected another, to be taken towards Christmas. Among other sights on Cooper River, we had witnessed frequent attacks of Hawks – principally Sharp-shinned & Great-footed – on the flocks of Blackbirds that swarmed along the banks. We saw too some birds that I took for Fish Crows, & others that I felt more certain were Great Crow – Blackbirds. Occasionally a Curlew would come in sight – at least so Mayrant called them – I could not tell certainly whether they were of the Long-billed kind, or not.

---

98 The Planters' Hotel was located at the corner of Church and Queen streets in Charleston.

99 Stewart's Hotel was located on Chalmers Street near the Mill's Fireproof Building on Meeting Street.

Sat. 11. Mayrant had heard some stories – true or false – of an Old Buck lying for some time past in Mr. Guignard's[100] Grounds, on the other side of the river, above the Bridge. So we set out very early this morning, & went there on horse-back, crossing the river at Guignard's Ferry, just below the Bridge. Meeting as we got into the main road two boys, bringing a Deer to market, we bought it for five dollars, so as to make sure of our Game, & sent it back to the Ferry, while we went on to our drive. Stopping at the old Stark house, & ordering Cora tied, the boy charged with that duty let her get loose, & in running after her, fell down & broke his leg. This accident detained us until Dr. Gibbes, who was immediately sent for, arrived. We then proceeded to our stands on the road to the Saluda Bridge, old Busby & his son undertaking to drive the cover without dogs. They found nothing there – & Mayrant & I returned, stopping at the old Stark house again & firing our loads of buck-shot at a mark. The day quite warm. Commencing when we first met, & repeating it as often as convenient, Bruno, to revenge old affronts, fell upon Guard & whipped him no less than four times. After the last whipping, which occurred under our horses in the flat as we recrossed the river, Guard, who from hard fare after getting lost at Myer's Plantation has got very poor, & who altho a great fighter, is a very discreet one, plunged into the water from the bow of the flat, swam ashore, & ran away. Bruno had also given two whippings to a large black St. Bernard's puppy of Mayrant's before we crossed the river first, & caused him to desert; & for his further amusement, had given a brief trouncing to a Cur near Bouknight's Tavern. Nothing was killed by any of the part to-day, except a tame Pigeon, run wild, which Bruno treed in a Pine, & Busby junior shot.

Wed. Nov. 22. Having some idea of getting Mayrant's large double barreled Gun from him, walked in the evening with him – some of his children - & Fayette[101] – to fire at marks on the fence round the Rail road Depot, with that gun, his large Blunderbuss, & my double barrel – taking Brant along. His double barrel kicked me too much, & I did not like it as well as I was inclined to before. No shot fired at any game.

---

100 James Sanders Guignard (1780-1856) was the father-in-law of Robert Mayrant.

101 Robert Mayrant and his wife, Frances ('Fayette') Ann Margaret Horry Guignard, were the parents of eight known children, including Robert Pringle, Jr., William Richardson, John Gabriel, Caroline, Frances A., Laura Elizabeth, Anne, and James S. Guignard Mayrant.

Sat. Dec. 23 [1843]. About the 27 Nov. I saw at Baker's a Canvasback Duck (apparently a female) which had been killed in the Congaree Swamp, somewhere towards Gadsden. After a long cessation of sport, caused by my business in the Court of Appeals, & by other affairs of one sort or another, took up the little Blunderbuss, which I have just got from Mayrant – the price for which he obtained it at Glazes', $30, to be advanced by me – & rode with him down to Granby, where we crossed the river in the Nimrod, & came back in two Canoes, giving Bruno a swim. Mayrant's horse getting away, I let him ride Granby back, & mounted myself on Robert Gibbes' horse, taking him up behind me. Evening pleasant. No shot fired.

Sat. [December] 30. Set off with Mayrant on a cruise down the river, for which I had been making preparations for some time. Our intention was to proceed to Charleston by the way of Bull's Bay. A particular account of the voyage, so far as I went, is contained in the "Log-book of the Santee Squadron," which I kept. On this first day, we descended with a full river, from Granby to the Bee Tree Landing, where we encamped. No game obtained, except an English Duck, which I shot under a willow shore, below Threewit's Ferry.

3 shots   1 English Duck (Fem)

Sun. 31. We were joined here in the morning by Paul Chappell & Joel Adams; & in the afternoon, went down to Adams' Landing, encamped on the left Bank, & towards dusk visited Rumph's Pond, on the other side of the river.

1 shot

By me nothing   By R.P.M.   1 English Duck

Mon. 1 Jan. 1844. We took a short hunt in the morning, I paying another unsuccessful visit to Rumph's Lake. Afterward, proceeded down the River to Tucker's Cut-off, & hunted the Old River in company with two Orangburgers whom we found in the Swamp. I got a Ring-neck Duck here, by a very long shot. In the afternoon proceeded on the voyage, & encamped on the right Bank, at a spot distant probably some 15 or 20 miles by water from Adam's Landing.

4 shots

> By me   1 Ringneck Duck (fem)
>
> By R.P.M.   1 Fox Squirrel*,   1 Rusty Blackbird

*I was surprised at the sight of the Fox Squirrel, killed here in the depth of the swamp; but our Orangeburg Gunners told us they were common there.

Tues. 2. Proceeded on the voyage – & encamped at night on the left bank at Thompson's Falls, a short distance below Stark's Saw-mill, & but a few miles from the fork of the Rivers. A little rain.

By R.P.M.   1 Dove

Wed. Jan 3. Sailed early in the morning with a high wind down to the Fork of the Rivers, & spent the day there, Turkey & Duck hunting. Encamped on a Sandbar on the Orangeburg Shore.

4 shots

By me. Nothing	By R.P.M.	By J.A.	By P.C.
	Summer Duck	1 Turkey	1 Cat Squirrel
	2 Doves	(young Gobbler)	

Thurs 4. A pretty fair wind. Made 40 or 50 miles, to Wright's Bluff. Heard the Ivory billed Woodpecker in the Swamp to-day. I had many shots at Ducks rising from the Willow shores, as I sailed down on them with Mayrant in the Lady of the Lake – & severely wounded at least three. The one I got was shot in the water. Vast flocks of Ducks seen passing to some roost in the evening.

11 shots   1 Ringneck Duck (male)

Fri. Jan. 5. Remained at Wrights' Bluff, to hunt Hoover's Pond, which I visited during the day, as well as Scott's Lake & Fort Watson.[102] Saw a flock of about 60 Wild Geese in the Lake & in the Pond. At night, we all went to Hoover's Pond, with Dr. Felder & Mr. Dunn. The expedition, tho a complete failure as to Ducks, resulted in a grand ducking.

3 shots   1 Blue Hawk (male)

Sat. [January] 6. Dropped down the River in the afternoon, 3 or 4 miles, & encamped on the left Bank; naming the place the Turkeyroost Camp, from an unsuccessful attempt upon a Flock of Turkeys at roost close by. Bad weather commencing.

Sun. 7. Another unsuccessful attempt upon the Turkey in the morning – then proceeded down to Dawshee Cove, a distance probably of 15 or 20 miles – & encamped on the left bank, opposite the Cove.

2 shots

Mon. Jan. 8. I paddled with Mayrant by moonlight before dawn up Dawshee Cove – but we were disappointed in our hopes of slaughtering Ducks at roost, very few being there. Proceeded on our Voyage as far as the Canal – probably 15 miles – & encamped opposite its entrance, on the Left Bank.

4 shots

By me,   Nothing   By R.P.M.,   1 Ringneck & 2 Larks.

Tues. 9. Paul Chappell & Joel Adams being tired out, left us here, taking the Canal for Charleston. We went in a drizzling rain but a few miles down, & encamped on the right Bank. I killed a Ringneck in a Creek on the left shore; &

---

102 Fort Watson, a British Revolutionary War fortification constructed on a prehistoric Indian mound, was captured by Francis Marion and Henry 'Light Horse' Lee.

a Black Duck in the river; this last we both shot at several times; but I brought it down from the wing & finally dispatched it. Most abundant signs of Deer & Turkeys in these deep & abandoned Swamps.

7 shots   1 Ringneck Duck
               1 Black Duck

Wed. 10. Villanous weather, from which the place was named the Foulweather Camp. I took a tramp thro the Canebrakes, & came back wet to the skin, with one English Duck, which I had killed in a Lagoon. In the afternoon made about an hour's run, & encamped on the left bank, at the upper end of the Rocky Reach.

6 shots   1 English Duck (Drake)

Thurs. Jan. 11. A deceptive clearing up in the morning. I shot at an Eagle not far from the Camp, & think I wounded it with one barrel. Most of the day spent in duck hunting above the Camp. I followed up a lake called Franklin's, or some such name, for a considerable distance, but got only one Summer Duck, which I shot on the wing. I killed also amongst the Canebrakes, in which they were pretty abundant, two Woodcocks, one on the ground, the other on the wing. Mayrant got eight Ducks. In the afternoon we made about an hour's run, & seeing many Ducks alighting in a pond close to the River on the left Bank, stopped & encamped. I with my Blunderbuss in the dusk killed two English Ducks, which Bruno brought out, tho it was too dark to see them from shore.

10 shots

By me		By R.P.M.	
2 English Ducks		3 English Ducks	
1 Summer Duck		3 Sum. Ducks	
2 Woodcocks		2 Ringnecks	

Fr. 12. Rainy weather kept us at the Duck roost Camp. After an eager pursuit thro wet canebrakes & other swamp obstacles, & firing two shots unsuccessfully, I succeeded in bringing down an Ivorybilled Woodpecker, which gave ample proof of its fierce spirit, & wonderful tenacity of life.

6 shots

By me   1 Ivorybilled Woodpecker (Picus Principalis)

By R.P.M.   1 Sum. Duck
           1 Yellowbellied Woodpecker

Sat. 13. A temporary clearing off. Sailed about 15 miles down the river to Flagger's Ferry.

6 shots

Sun. Jan 14. Our Camp was on the left bank. We hunted on some islands on the other side of the River in the morning, & Mayrant killed a large Otter, which he surprised by stealing marches on him whenever he dived, & which Bruno towed out by the tail. After noon, we set out in a drizzle & ran some 15 or 20 miles down to Cantey's Cove (the Mouth of Mattassee Lake) when we encamped on a cedar grown hill-side on the right bank.

2 shots

By me.   Nothing   By RPM,   1 Otter

Mon. 15. Wretched weather, which kept us at the Cedar Camp two days.

Tues. 16. Dined at Mr. Dubose's. At night, a storm.

Wed. 17. Set off after mid-day with a N.W. gale, & ran about 20 miles, encamping on the right bank, about 4 miles above Lenud's Ferry, at a place which we named the Driftwood Camp.

Thurs. Jan 18. Early in the morning, I killed a Cat Squirrel near the Camp. Afterwards, we made full sail down the River, & ran with a fair wind 40 miles or more, encamping on the right bank of the North Santee, in a Rice plantation[103] of a free negro named Collins, about 2 miles above Hume's Ferry. As we approached the low tract between the Rivers, we saw ducks by thousands – principally Black & English, with Ringnecks & Teal among them. We were unable to do anything with them.

8 shots   1 Cat Squirrel

Fri. 19. A freezing morning. Took a Snipe hunt in the rice fields. Stowed the boats with fire wood for the Saltwater voyage. In the afternoon dropped down & encamped in front of Mr. John Hume's house, on the left bank.

11 shots

By me   1 Snipe   By R.P.M   1 Snipe
          1 Robin

Sat. Jan. 20. Took a hunt down the Rice plantations, in company with two young Gentlemen from Mr. Hume's, Wilson & Howard. First proceeded to some grounds on the left bank, for a Snipe-hunt. I, however, was more engaged with Ducks, & got a fine Buffelhead Drake which I shot as he rose from a Canal. We afterwards crossed the river for more regular Duckhunting. I got but one Ringneck, shot in a submerged Rice-field. At the close of our hunt, I

---

103 The cultivation of rice, first grown in coastal South Carolina in the 1670's, required deep financial pockets and a large number of laborers, the majority of whom were enslaved Africans. Those planters who were successful "were among the wealthiest of the wealthy in the antebellum South. Of the fifty-two South Carolina planters who owned more than three hundred slaves in 1860, thirty-seven (or 71 percent) were Low-country rice planters." Scarborough, William Kauffman. *The Allstons of Chicora Wood*. Baton Rouge: Louisiana State University Press, 2011, 37.

determined to take the Stage at night for Charleston. The principal cause was Bruno's behavior; who had become very much indisposed from confinement on board our boats, & so fierce as to be dangerous to strangers – having already bitten several people. In addition to this, altho it was a great disappointment, to miss the shooting in the Rice plantations & on the sea coast, just as I had got within reach of it. Still I had got quite tired of Mayrant's Company, & was willing enough to be relieved of it. We had agreed exceedingly well for a week or two; but three weeks, with so much bad weather to boot, had proved rather too much for my patience. Accordingly, I returned with Wilson, leaving Mayrant & Howard to take a night hunt together. In passing thro Pleasant Creek on the way, I shot a Marsh Hare swimming across the Channel. Took the Stage at night – went thro Charleston, & got home the following day with Bruno. My expectations of game on the Cruise had been very much disappointed. And whether it were the remains of my last Fall's attack of Grippe still lurking in my system, or that the exposure & nervous exhaustion of the cruise, added to a fatiguing ride on the outside of the Stage, at night, were too much for me; at all events I got sick the day after my return, with a kind of nervous type of tertian,[104] & have not yet, at the expiration of two weeks, recovered my health & strength completely.

21 shots

By me	By R.P.M.	By Howard
1 Buffelhead Drake	3 Bluewing Teal	3 Snipes
1 Ringneck Duck	5 Snipes	
1 Snipe	1 Redtail Hawk	By Wilson
1 Marsh Hare	1 Marsh Hawk	1 Snipe
	1 Rabbit	

---

104 For those South Carolinians who survived to adulthood, there were the ever present 'fevers' to contend with. These included bilious fever, catarrhal fever, "Country Fever," and Dengue fever, as well as "tertian, remittent, intermittent, miasmatic, and malarial" fevers. Joseph Ioor Waring, *A History of Medicine in South Carolina*, 34.

Mon. [March] 4 [1844].[105] A good deal of dry, mild Spring weather lately. The drudgery of the law has not allowed me time to enjoy it in shooting. Walked out ornithologizing this evening, down the Canal, as far as the lower Basin, taking Bruno with me, who has now recovered his health & spirits. Lara took the distemper about the middle of February, & tho rather sick at one time, with a symptom which I do not remember noticing before, viz, his hair coming out, yet seemed to be relieved by a few rose of Tartar Emetic & Jalap, & is now nearly well. Brant took the distemper soon after Lara, & tho not apparently in any danger, remains in rather bad condition. I came across a Covey of Partridges on the Bank of the Canal, near Taylor's cross-fence, but I got only one Bird. My attention was devoted principally to Sparrows, of which I believe I met with three species unknown to me before – But I am not quite sure that I have made them out right. I commenced shooting this evening, by way of experiment, with both eyes open & fixed on the object, in the English sporting style, recommended by Hawker.[106]

9 shots

1 Partridge	3 White throated Sparrows
1 Hermit Thrush	1 Swamp Sparrow (Fr. Palustius)
1 Snow-bird	1 Field Sparrow (Emb. Pusilla)
1 Song Sparrow (Fr. Melodia)	

---

105 An event of significance to the Gregg and Maxcy families not mentioned in Maxcy Gregg's journal was the death of his mother's uncle, Virgil Maxcy, on the 28th of February 1844. A graduate of Brown University, Virgil Maxcy served in both houses of the Maryland Legislature and represented the United States as Ambassador to Belgium. He died on board the *US Princeton*, along with the Secretary of State (Abel P. Upshur), the Secretary of the Navy (Captain Beverly Kennon), and Navy Bureau chief David Gardiner. What had been planned by its captain as an entertaining cruise for 400 of Washington's political elite aboard the *Princeton* down the Potomac River to Mount Vernon and back up to Alexandria, turned into a disaster. On the first part of the cruise both cannons, the 'Oregon' and the 'Peacemaker' (which took a 225-pound ball), were successfully fired by Captain Stockton and his crew. On the return trip, however, the 'Peacemaker' was unintentionally loaded exclusively with powder; when ignited it exploded on deck and cast-iron pieces flew through the air, killing indiscriminately. In addition to those killed, seventeen others were wounded, including Armistead, the body servant to President John Tyler. The president had been drawn from the deck by the daughter of another passenger, who requested of him that he escort her to her cabin. Armistead subsequently died of his injuries.

106 Lieutenant Colonel Peter Hawker (1786-1853) was an English country gentleman, lifelong sportsman, and diarist. His *Instructions to Young Sportsmen* was so widely-read that it passed through nine editions before his death. The first American edition, published in Philadelphia in 1846, was dedicated to Wade Hampton, III.

SUMMARY FROM OCTOBER 1843 TO MARCH 1844

Month	Oct	Nov	Dec	Jan	Mar	Total
Times Out	10	6	3	20	2	41
Shots Fired	50	24	4	105	21	204
Redshouldered Hawk	1					1
Blue Hawk				1		1
Great Horned Owl		1				1
Pinecreeping Warbler					2	2
Whitethroated Sparrow					7	7
Song Sparrow					1	1
Grass Finch					1	1
Snowbird					1	1
Field Sparrow					1	1
Swamp Sparrow					1	1
Ivory billed Woodpecker				1		1
Hermit Thrush					1	1
Robin				1	1	2
Dove	1					1
Partridge	1				1	2
Snipe				2		2
Woodcock				2		2
Telltale		1				1
English Duck			1	3		4
Black Duck				1		1
Bluewing Teal		1				1
Summer Duck	7			1		8
Ringneck Duck	2	1		4		7
Ruddy Duck	1					1

	Oct	Nov	Dec	Jan	Mar	Total
Buffelhead Duck				1		1
Coot	2					2
Didapper	1	1				2
Great Blackbacked Gull	1					1
Ringbill Gull		3				3
Cat Squirrel	1			1		2
Marsh Hare				1		1

31 Species
Individuals, 63

Great Heron from *Birds of America* (1827) by John James Audubon

April - September 1844:
Camden and the Wateree River

Wed. April 24, 1844. About two weeks ago, while at Lexington Court, my old enemy the Grippe paid me a visit in the shape of a sort of chill & fever, which on my return home was routed with Calomel; but I am not sure but the remedy was as bad as the disease,[107] for I have been left in a wretched state of languor, this, together with the heat of the weather, has prevented me from taking that recreation with my gun which I much wanted after a long & close confinement to rascally law-business. Rode this evening down to the Granby Marshes, where the cover has been destroyed since the field has been thrown open to the Cattle & hogs of the place. Returned across Granby Ferry. I have come very near losing poor Brant. After he had been very much reduced by the distemper[108] which he took a little more than two months since, he was attacked with nervous twitchings for which, as well as diarrhea, I treated him with opium – 1 grain at a dose. He however, grew worse & weaker, particularly in the hind parts, in which he was threatened with palsy. I left off the use of the opium and about twelve days since, he lost the use of his hind legs, & has ever since dragged his hind parts on the ground, not being able to rise. I have had him rubbed down the spine regularly with an ointment of red-pepper – & Peter has given him a decoction of Blackberry, or Dewberry root, under which his diarrhea seems to have been checked, & he now appears improving.

3 shots   Nothing killed.

---

107 Treatments for mid-19th century diseases and illnesses varied and included "bloodletting, taking sometimes 72 ounces from a patient," "snake root and musk," potassium citrate, calomel ("to empty bowels"), quinine ("to attack the fever"), "Dover's powders, morphine, and laudanum. Blistering was prescribed fairly often." Calomel was a popular treatment for grippe. Gregg was fortunate that lethargy was his only reaction to the mercury he ingested to treat his influenza. Joseph Ioor Waring, *A History of Medicine in South Carolina*, 20n, 31. Michael C.C. Adams, *Living Hell*, 49.

108 English sportsman and author Lieutenant Colonel Peter Hawker, in *Instructions to Young Sportsmen*, recommended a combination of three grains of opium and five grains of emetic tartar as the prescription to treat distemper.

Thurs. May 9. Yesterday evening I saw a small flock of Ricebirds – there may have been thirty – feeding in Hampton's old fields. The Broom-grass there is now pretty fresh, from the effect of frequent fires since the completion of the Rail-road, & I could see the birds busily gleaning over the ground. This morning I mounted Granby about Sun-rise, & rode down after them, but did not find them, & concluded that they had assumed their Northward journey. At Everett's Pond, on the way back, I discovered a Little Blue Heron, which lit in the Northern Bay of the Pond. Making a long circuit, & charging one barrel with a red cartridge no. 4, I approached with great caution, & getting up behind a Pine Tree within 35 or 40 yards, had the gratification of at last dispatching an Ardea Coerulea in mature plumage, & felt a kind of surprise at my success after the uniform disappointments experienced by me in former attempts. As I was coming down the Hill, this side of Mrs. Fleming's Field, my attention was attracted by a Red-eyed Vireo, singing in a pine tree – the song struck me as uncommon, & to be sure what bird it was, I shot it. It appeared to hang by the toes to a limb, & I had to dislodge it by another shot. Had no dog with me this morning, as one might have been in the way in shooting Rice-birds. Bruno too is lame. I found yesterday morning that he had been shot in his right hind & fore leg, with 6 or 8 pellets, apparently from a distance. Perpetrator of the outrage unknown. Brant about two weeks ago recovered so far as to be able to rise on his hind legs, & has been tottering about since that time, but his improvement seems slow & recovery uncertain. Much nervous twitching still, & a tendency to diarrhoea requiring to be checked by medicine.

3 shots   1 Ardea Coerulea [Blue Heron] (in mature plumage)
               1 Red-eyed Vireo

Sun. 12 May. Poor Brant died at last, with convulsions. He was buried beside Fan in the corner of the garden.

Sat. July 20. The evening before, I had ridden down the Statesburg road[109] to meet Gen. Hopkins, & make arrangements for the duel between Dickinson & Smart[110] – an affair with which I have been very much worried & much of my time taken up for some time five months past. At the Pond by the roadside, eight miles off, & just this side of Mill Creek, I saw a number of Ardeae Coeruleae in Blue, White, & mixed plumage, & amongst them a bird which I took for the white Ibis, in the brown plumage of the young – rump white, as also the belly. One of the birds in mottled plumage puzzled me – I was not quite sure whether it was a Blue Heron or not. So this afternoon mounted Granby again & rode down to the Pond. Before I got there a magnificent thunder cloud rose behind me, tinged on the crest by the rays of the western Sun with red, & other colors of the rain-bow in a manner that I never observed before. The cloud rapidly spread over head & threatened a black storm. At the pond I found the birds as I had observed them the day before. But while I was creeping up with the view of getting a shot at the Ibis, Bruno rushed out & put the whole Pond in confusion.

---

109 The 'Statesburg road,' now Garner's Ferry Road, ran from Columbia to the town of Statesburg in Sumter District.

110 After his duel in Charleston in December of 1835 Maxcy Gregg was solicited several times to perform the duties of second in a duel. In a convoluted case of politics, accusations of lies, and, primarily, hot tempers, Gregg was requested by Louis T. Wigfall to serve as his second in 1840, and in fulfilling those duties, Gregg was sent to James Carroll (serving as second to Preston S. Brooks) to issue the challenge to settle their differences on the field of honor on behalf of Wigfall. Pistol shots were avoided when the parties agreed to allow a Board of Honor to hear both sides and offer recommendations for settling the dispute. In the matter between James P. Dickinson and James Smart, both primaries were acquaintances of Gregg. He and John Smart were known to each other through their mutual participation in the Camden Debating Club. At the fifteenth anniversary celebration of that organization, president John Smart proposed a toast to his friend Maxcy Gregg: "Modest and unassuming, thoroughly educated and well read in his profession [this] distinguished young gentleman is an honor to his native district." "While the table was ringing with cheers of the warmest approbation," another member was moved to add, "Mr. President: there is no compliment I would take more pleasure in responding to than one paid to Col. Maxcy Gregg. From a long and intimate acquaintance with him, begun at college, I have formed the highest opinion of his character. With intellectual powers of the highest order, and such as admirably qualify him for his profession, he unites a heart adorned with all the virtues which are attractive in human nature. Allow me to add to the sentiment which you have just given, that of a resolute, chivalrous spirit. To say that he does not fear an enemy, would be low commendation. He fears nothing under Heaven, but a base reputation." Maxcy Gregg was acquainted with James P. Dickinson through their respective militia organizations. The DeKalb Rifle Guards, captained by James Dickinson, had challenged the Richland Volunteer Rifle Corps, commanded by Captain Gregg, to a friendly shooting contest just a few years before Dickinson's confrontation with John Smart. Both Smart and Dickinson were also attorneys, in practice with each other in Camden, and in the habit of covering each other's professional business during their temporary absences. *The Camden Journal* (Camden, South Carolina), March 16, 1842.

The Ibis, flying off towards the Mill-pond, offered me a long shot, & I missed it with both barrels. The rain began to fall soon after, tho not very hard, & I rode on & took shelter in Gen. Hopkins' mill for half an hour or so until it past over. Then returned home, somewhat disappointed, & eager to try the pursuit again. The weather for some weeks has been hotter than I think it has been since the summer of 1838.

2 shots

Mon. [July] 29. I was prevented from resuming the pursuit of my new acquaintance the Ibis sooner, by my occupation with the duel – which was fought at last on the evening of the 26th in front of Mr. Thos. Whitaker's house, 5 miles this side of Camden[111] – when the parties tho in great practice & supposed to be dead shots, missed each other two rounds & left off. This afternoon I rode down to the 8 mile pond again, where I saw a great many Ardea Coerulea in the Blue & the white plumage, but none in the mottled. Did not at first discover any Ibis – but on approaching the Pond, leading Bruno by a string, I saw one in white Plumage, feeding in Company with a Great White Heron. Getting them in range, I fired – a pretty long shot, & wounded the Ibis – the Heron seemed not to be hurt. Bruno got loose & went to playing the Devil – all the birds were in commotion – my wounded Ibis flew off beyond the Pond – and another, a brown one, passing me quite close, I might have got it with ease. But Bruno whom I had caught & was holding again, jerked my hand. I lost the opportunity of a fair shot – & missed one at a disadvantage. I went in pursuit of my wounded bird, & discovered it standing on the other side of the Pond. I had approached too near without any cover before I saw it – and it flew off, disappearing over a Cornfield behind Mr. Heath's house. I had observed its head & neck to be tinged with ash color. I did not notice any black on its quills. Its bill appeared yellow. My further search was ineffectual. Returning to the Pond, I saw after a while two Brown Ibises flying over in company with several Herons. But got

---

111 Camden was the judicial seat of Kershaw District. Settled in 1759 on the east side of the Wateree River, it was the oldest inland town in the state. The community was occupied by British forces in 1780 during the Revolutionary War. As seconds in a duel, it would have been General Hopkins' and Maxcy Gregg's responsibility to determine where the duel would be fought, which witnesses would be allowed on the field, and the rules of combat that would be followed. South Carolinians most often chose to conduct their duels outside of the state, most often selecting either a Savannah River island at the Georgia state line or near Limestone Springs at the North Carolina state line. Immediately after the contest, the participants could return to South Carolina to elude arrest by authorities from those states where the duel had taken place.

no shot. Missed a Partridge on the wing, with a cartridge designed for Ibises; & lingering a little while longer at the Pond, set off homewards – where I arrived rather late.

3 shots

Tues. Jul. 30. Rode again to the 8 mile Pond in the afternoon, wisely leaving Bruno at home. Found the Pond full of Blue Herons, principally in the white plumage, some in the Blue, but none in the mottled. Discovering an Ibis or two among them, I crept up with great caution, & wading into the Pond along the fence, got at last within shot of two Ibises, & waiting till they were in range, killed both. By my stealthy approach I had got into the midst of the Herons, & might have taken my choice among them at any distance. At the shot, the whole flock rose, including three more Ibises. These were all in brown plumage. I missed with my second barrel one which approached too near perhaps for a cartridge. They circled round some time, unwilling to leave the Pond. While creeping thro the mud before shooting, I had seen at a distance at the margin of the Pond two birds of the size of Telltales, which I could not make out to my satisfaction. Perhaps they were Telltales. I lost sight of them afterwards. I observed that the Ibises in feeding, probed the mud with their bills, snipe-fashion, instead of striking their prey like the Herons. I waded in & got those I had shot. Riding on to Gen. Hopkins' Pond, I found the dam had been broken by a great rain which fell in Sunday the 21st. Here too, among Herons, I saw some Ibises – but none in the white plumage. I have since learnt from Myers, that he has lately seen a flock of them – that is, white ones – at his Pond – remarking them as strange & unknown birds.

2 shots   2 White Ibises (Ibis Alba) in brown Plumage

Wed. Jul. 31. Rode out to the farm in the evening, with Peter & my dogs, after a hog which has been scrambling over the ditch & doing mischief amongst the corn. Did not find it. I shot a Cuckoo in the woods on the Edge of the further field.

1 shot   1 Yellow-billed Cuckoo

Fri. Aug. 2. Weather still very hot, with occasional rains. Walked in the evening as far as the place which I used to distinguish by the name of Catfish Meadow, where I saw a party of 6 or 8 Robins – a family I suppose. I recognized some of them by their spotted breasts as young ones. Some Mockingbirds amused themselves by chasing the robins, as well as some other birds, away from certain trees which they seemed to regard as their own premises. After shooting at Martins & Nighthawks for awhile, my shot gave out & forced me to a premature return.

15 shots   1 Nighthawk

             4 Martins

             1 Redheaded Woodpecker (in greyish plumage of young)

Sat. 3. Walked over the same ground this evening again & met with one of the young Robins. I tried the plan of firing with both eyes open, & found that it came pretty easy to me. The result however this evening, was that I wounded an unusual number of birds – more than I brought down. The last shots I had were too much in the dark for any certainty.

22 shots   3 Nighthawks

             1 Martin

             1 Redheaded Woodpecker (young)

Mon. 5. Walked in the evening as far as the lower end of Randolph's lane. Shot for a while with both eyes open; but becoming discouraged by missing very badly, took to my old way again, & did somewhat better. The only bird I brought down out of 11 shots on the new plan, was a Bee-Martin, which disappeared most mysteriously from the middle of the lane by the time I went to look for it, after an unsuccessful search by Bruno. Before I finished shooting it was too dark to distinguish objects well. My last Nighthawk rather surprised me by falling.

30 shots   8 Nighthawks

             1 Martin

             1 Leatherwinged Bat

Sat. Aug. 17ᵗʰ [1844] The excessive heats have now abated. Rode in the evening as far as Hampton's old fields, shooting a Partridge, on the ground, as I passed Everett's Pond. Saw a large party of Bee Martins, apparently migrating, or preparing to start. They collected in the Clump of Oaks near the old Mill, & from time to time straggled off southward.

4 shots   1 Partridge (killed sitting)

Thurs. 22. Several shooting-matches have been got up lately. I had used my Blunderbuss unsuccessfully at one which took place on the 15ᵗʰ for a pair of Silver cups – the mark being a rolling target at 50 yards, with buck-shot. There being a match to come off this evening for a horse of John Goodwyn's – target stationary – distance 100 yards – I had been out with James Davis the two preceding evenings, firing at marks on the fence of the Rail-road lot, & trying several experiments – with shot put up in bags – Eley's cartridges &c. We rode down for the same purpose this morning, before breakfast, & seeing a Hawk as we past Robin-Marsh, apparently treed by some Bee-Martins & afraid to take to flight, I put in a load of buck-shot, & getting up with the Blunderbuss behind a tree within about 25 yards of the Hawk, brought him down, hitting him with 3 shot. Our practice resulted in a determination to rely principally upon chain-shot, but to try also some of the patent cartridges, tho much too small, being 12 gauge. In the afternoon, one of our loads of chain-shot, fired by Fredr. Green (who, poor little follow, was nearly pushed over by it) threw seven shot into the Target, the diameter of which was about 15 inches. None of us however was successful. The horse was won by John Goodwyn himself, shooting for one of the young Browns. The number of shot that were up in the Target surprised me – I think there were seventy or upwards, besides an Entire patent cartridge which balled. The shots fired were 150, by 30 or 40 Competitors.

1 shot   1 Redshouldered Hawk (in plumage of Winter Falcon)

Fri. Aug. 23. Rode in the evening down to Hampton's old fields. Wounded a little white Crane, far out in the old pond, & missed 3 shots at Barnswallows, which Birds I have observed about now in numbers for a week or so.

7 shots   1 Nighthawk

Mon. 26. Walked in the evening as far as Lark Field & Wade's Field. Shot a Green-heron at Robin Marsh, this side of the Railroad – & a Snipe at Hunting Corner towards the Lower end of the ancient limits of that favorite shooting ground of my schoolboy days. This is the first Snipe I ever remember seeing at this time of year. I have seen also lately some Wax-birds. I think I had seen them here before in every month of the year <u>except</u> August – & possibly July. Near Cat-fish Meadow saw my acquaintances, the resident family of Robins, again – and afterwards had the misfortune to shoot a Mocking-bird,[112] mistaking it for a robin as it flew by me in the twilight. The last Mocking-bird I killed was by mistake for a Robin in the same way – being shot in one of the Granby India trees one evening more than six years ago. I killed also a very small Nighthawk this evening, scarcely over 8 inches long. Saw few of them this evening – & no Martins.

5 shots   1 Green Heron
          1 Mocking-Bird
          1 Snipe
          1 Nighthawk

---

112 The mockingbird was a favorite among birders for its pleasing vocalizations. Charles F. Holden, a supplier of bird food in the 1870s, made an entertaining observation about the ability of the mockingbird to mimic the sounds of other animals. "Who, on passing through the streets of any large city on a bright night in June, has not heard the shrill scream of the eagle, the mourning note of the turtle-dove, the delicate warble of the blue-bird, the cackling of the domestic hen, followed by the quarrelling of a dozen or more grimalkins, each seeming to vie with the other as to the quality of noise when the cry of the katydid, the mellow whistle of the cardinal, the grunt of the maternal porker searching for her juveniles, the creaking of some rusty swing-signboard, the pipe of the canary, and the cry of some lost puppy wailing in the midnight air, and each succeeding the other with such rapidity, that the listener wonders if such a variety can come from so small an object. All this the mocking-bird is capable of." Holden, Charles F. *Holden's Book on Birds*. Boston: Charles Reiche and Brother, Publishers, 1873 (Reproduction by BiblioLife, LLC, n.d.), 42-43.

Tues. 27th Rode in the afternoon to Hampton's Middle Pond. At Everett's Pond on the way, fired at a large white Crane, but believe my cartridge balled. At Hampton's saw a vast congregation of Crows on the railroad embankment beyond the Broken Culvert. I do not know what they were about, unless picking up gravel. Firing at a Dove which passed me, a flock of fifteen Wood Ibises arose from towards the further side of the morass, & lit on two dead trees. I watched them, in their inaccessible retreats, until they put themselves in motion again, & after some circuits, flew off over the opposite woods. I afterwards shot a young Blue Heron, near where I once waded in after a Summer Duck – but Bruno now saved that trouble. After long continued & excessive heat, the weather turned cooler last night.

5 shots   1 Blue Heron (in white Plumage)
             2 Nighthawks

Thurs. Aug. 29th Cool weather. Rode in the afternoon down to Hampton's old fields, in hopes of seeing the Wood Ibises again, in which I was disappointed. Falling in with Henry Chappell & Charles Henry, proceeded in company with them down the Ponds, to take stands in the Bluff-road for the purpose of shooting Summer Ducks. As we were going, I fired a shot from Granby's back at a Sharp-shinned Hawk, apparently pretty large, which flew from the Clump of Trees near the Burnt Mill, but missed. After we arrived at our stands on the Road, vast flocks of Crows past up the Ponds. I shot a Kingfisher & a Nighthawk, both of which fell in the water below the Bridge, from which Bruno brought them out. Shot also at a Humming-bird, but could not tell whether I killed it. A few Summer Ducks past up. I missed one very long shot. Charley Henry thought he shot one, but did not find it. Rode home late by moonlight.

5 shots   1 Kingfisher
             1 Nighthawk

Fri. 30. Rode in the afternoon to Hampton's Middle Ponds, killing a Sparrowhawk on the way, between Everett's & the Wet-weather Ponds, which took two shots to dispatch it, both on the wing, the first being fired from my saddle. Approaching Hampton's Ponds, I saw six Wood Ibises, flying. Then went down the Ponds. I staid awhile at the Broken Culvert, shooting at Chimney & Barnswallows – Then rode below, to the old dam. Killed everything on the wing this evening, except one Dove, which fell in the Swamp, where Bruno couldn't find it – & which I have not counted.

18 shots

    1 Sparrowhawk (fem)

    3 Chimney Swallows

    2 Doves

    1 Barn Swallow

Sat. Aug. 31. Mounted Granby in the evening & set off for Hampton's Ponds; but consumed so much time in the pursuit of a Great Blue Heron at Everett's Pond, that I went no further. I first approached the Bird, which was far out in the water, under cover of the fence on the South side; & firing an excessively long shot, with a green cartridge, triple A appeared to wound it seriously, for flying off low, it lit in a drooping posture at the mouth of the Marsh on the NWest of the Pond. Pursuing & firing two shots at it, it flew to the eastern end of the Pond; where I followed, & firing from the corner of the fence, winged it. The distance this shot was about 55 yards. Bruno now made a charge, & had a long fight with the bird in the water. He might have lost an eye, but for the exhaustion of the Heron, which struck him several times – not thrusting with closed bill, but opening the mandibles, & biting. I afterward found some of Bruno's hair in the serratures near the point. Succeeding at last in getting Bruno away, I dispatched the enemy with a load of small shot; when Bruno had another difficult task in dragging it ashore. Remaining some time about the Pond, I made some bad shooting at Nighthawks. The weather is now getting hot again; it is very dry.

12 shots   1 Great Heron

Sun. [September] 1 [1844]. While riding with Hart in the evening, over his farm, of "Rockwood"[113] we came across a Squirrel up a Hickory tree, near the main road. Hart rode back to the Cabin in which he is at present staying, got his gun, & shot it.

By me.   No shot

By Hart   1 Cat Squirrel

Wed. Sep 4th Rode in the evening down to East Granby, & going out on the rocks, saw a Fish Hawk, which flew about for awhile & then lit on a tree some distance below on the other side of the River. Some Crows attempted to dislodge him, but he seemed to take no notice of them. I got a Canoe at the Ferry & paddled down after him; but before I could get near him, he flew & lit on the opposite of the River. In attempting to cross after him, I ran the Canoe on a mud-bar – the water being now excessively low – & while I was working off, he disappeared. Fired no shot this evening.

Thurs. 5th Rode out in the afternoon for Hampton's old fields. Just the other side of Rocky Branch came across two Cuckoos, one of which I shot from my saddle, with a blue Cartridge No. 5. It flew off, but seeing feathers flying, I followed it 20 or 30 yards in the woods, & found it lying on the ground, wounded. There I fell in with Henry Chappell, with his pack of 4 Pointers. Proceeding in company with him, I fired a long shot, with a Green Cartridge, triple A, at a SparrowHawk on a high Pine near the Rail road, this side of Long Branch. To my surprise, the Bird flew off only wounded to another tree, from which I brought it down with a load of small shot. Arriving at Hampton's Middle Ponds, I was riding up to get a shot at some Doves on a tree in the swamp, when they flew, & firing one barrel, I brought down two. Stationing ourselves on the old dam, we remained

---

113 The Hart Maxcy family maintained its primary residence in Columbia, on the southwest corner of Richland and Marion streets. Hart also managed a plantation, referred to by Maxcy Gregg as 'Rockwood,' but also referred to as 'Ridgewood' and 'Rockford,' located north of Columbia off Monticello Road. In 1913 the property became a tuberculosis asylum, the Ridgewood Tuberculosis Camp, founded by the Daughters of the Holy Cross of Trinity Episcopal Church.

till nearly dark, & saw a good many Doves passing up & down. I think besides what other purposes they may have in visiting this quarter, they resort to the Railroad embankment for gravel. Saw several Night Herons also.

15 shots

By me   5 Doves
         1 Sparrowhawl (fem)
         1 Nighthawk
         1 Yellowbilled cuckoo

By H.C.   4 Doves
          1 Sparrowhawk
          1 Leatherwing Bat

Fri. Sep. 6th Rode in the evening down to Hampton's Burnt Mill again & took a stand for Doves. While there I saw two Wood Ibises make a circuit over the Ponds, high in the air, with a slow flight. Bruno eat up one of the Doves which I sent him to fetch; I gave him a sound whipping, & he behaved better the next time. I shot badly; two of my shots however were at Night Herons, at distances rather too great for loose small shot, both which birds appeared to be wounded. A slight touch of autumn in the weather now.

13 shots   3 Doves

Sat. 7th Rode to Hampton's Middle Mill again this afternoon. Found a covey of Partridges by the side of the Pond above the Rail-road, & got two birds, one not half grown. The broom-straw is so kept down in the old field now by frequent fires, that Partridges are not often to be found there. While at my usual stand below the Dam, saw about a dozen Ducks on the wing.

8 shots

        2 Partridges
        1 Dove

Mon. [September] 16th Rode in the afternoon by Everett's Pond to Hampton's Middle Mill; & finding the stands at the old Dam occupied by Henry Chappell, young Seibels, & a young Elmore, proceeded down the Ponds to the Bridge on the Bluff road, where they afterwards joined me. A good many Summer Ducks past up – I had two shots, but not fair ones. Henry Chappell & Seibels each killed one Duck. Their party had killed several Doves.

5 shots   1 Dove

There was a slight frost on the night of the 29th [of September, 1844] (the Night of the fire above the Court House) & the next night.

The Yellow-billed Cuckoo (Coccyzus americanus)
illustration from *Zoology of New York* (1842–1844) by James Ellsworth De Kay

SUMMARY FROM APRIL TO SEPTEMBER 1844

Month	Ap.	May	July	Aug.	Sept.	Total
Times out	1	1	4	11	6	23
Shots fired	3	3	8	124	41	179
Redshouldered Hawk				1		1
Sparrow Hawk				1	1	2
Nighthawk				17		18
Martin				6		6
Chimney Swallow				3		3
Barn Swallow				1		1
Yellowbilled Cuckoo			1		1	2
Redheaded Woodpecker				2		2
Mocking Bird				1		1
Redeyed Vireo		1				1
Kingsfisher				1		1
Dove				2	10	12
Partridge				1	2	3
Snipe				1		1
White Ibis			2			2
Great Heron				1		1
Blue Heron		1		1		2
Green Heron				1		1
Leatherwing Bat				1		1

Species 19
Individuals 61

October 1844 - September 1845: A River Cruise and Great Flights of Pigeons

Wed. Oct. 9th Rode Buckeye in the evening down to Hampton's burnt Mill, & took my accustomed stand for Doves, two of which, passing in Company, I killed at a shot. Saw a few Summer Ducks, flying by late. Weather, mild.

5 shots   2 Doves

Sun. [November] 3d. Having conveyed my gun to Rockwood the evening before, rode there early this morning, to relieve the tedium of Court, which is now sitting, by a Duck & Squirrel hunt on Crane Creek. After breakfast, we made a rather late start; & accompanied by Jem, Scott, Bruno & Hock, proceeded on foot down a little Branch which heads near the house, to the Creek; & followed the Creek to the River. A vagabond party had been before us however & spoilt our duck shooting; I got only one shot, & that thro thick bushes which gave me no chance. The day proved oppressively warm. On our way back to Hart's house, we gathered a quantity of Hickory nuts.

4 shots   1 Cat Squirrel

      By H.   1 Cat Squirrel

Sun. Nov. 3d After dinner, we rode over to Long Branch, near which I killed a Squirrel, which proved the occasion of a difficulty between Bruno & Scott. Scott got off with a slight rent in his breeches & a great fright. The fall has been very warm; there was a little frost the last two nights of September, & no more until about the end of October. On the 18th of October, in a warm & cloudy afternoon – Thermometer at 80 – I saw several Nighthawks flying about over the Town – not in a straight emigrating line, but backwards & forwards quite at leisure.

2 shots   1 Cat Squirrel

Wed. [December] 25th [1844] Rode out to Rockwood the evening before, to take a Christmas hunt. We set out on foot rather late in the morning, & went over to the Long branch field. In returning, Bruno put up a large Covey of Partridges at the edge of the field on this side of the Branch; but Master & dog we both did badly at the birds. The day quite warm. Jem & Scott with us. We were not out long; & did not go out again in the evening.

13 shots

        1 Partridge   By H.   1 Dove
        4 Doves

Wed. Jan. 1st 1845. Walked a little way out in the evening, by the Grave-yard and towards the Canal.

1 shot

Fri. [January] 10th Rode out to Rockwood in the evening, to take a raccoon hunt[114] with Hart, & Henry Owens. Owens did not come till so late that we had given him out. We started after 8 o'clock, with five dogs. Jem & Wilson

---

114 Milledge Lipscomb Bonham (1854-1943), the son of South Carolina Governor and Civil War general Milledge Luke Bonham (1813-1890), suggested the best way to prepare potatoes and opossum, a dish he favored. "Many people disdain 'possum because they have never eaten it properly cooked. A 'possum should be put up and fed on milk, bread, scraps of meat and potatoes until he has got fat, and has got rid of his wild food. This for the same reason that hogs are penned and fed on corn before they are slaughtered for meat. When the 'possum is killed and cleaned, which is done in the same way used with a young pig, if the weather is cold enough put him on

carried axes, to cut down trees & to keep up our supply of lightwood torches. I took my gun along, to be used whenever practicable. We descended the hills to the west of the Lightning hill Field, and striking the Creek, scrambled along the precipitous bluffs which overhang it, till we got near its mouth. There, the main body of our mongrel pack commenced a furious uproar on the further side, while the veteran of the pack, who was deaf & could not hear the others, gave notice that he had treed something on the hill above us. Leaving Wilson to go to the old dog, we crossed by a new bridge of Scott's, & found the dogs in the edge of a wet marsh, where we soon discovered a Coon on a low tree. As Owens thought he might get away from the pack in the water, he advised that I should shoot him, which I did without difficulty by the torchlight. It proved to be a very large fellow. We then came over to the old deaf dog, & found him at a hollow oak tree, which Wilson was cutting down. After it fell, the Coon was discovered in the upper part of the hollow – and an opening having been made, Jem's dog, Limery went gallantly in, but came out wofully bitten. At last, as the Coon attempted to slip slily out of a hole, Tige seized it, & the other dogs (with the exception of Hock) laying hold instantly, the Coon perished in the unequal struggle. This was towards 11 o'clock. We then recrossed the Creek, and spent the rest of the night in rambling by the picturesque glare of our torches thro the Swamp, without further success. One tree, where Ramrod thought he had a Coon, was cut down; and having made an illumination round the spot, & disposed our forces for a grand scramble, as it fell across the Creek; we were quite disappointed to start no game. We suspected Ramrod after this of lying occasionally by way of encouraging us. At last we came out at the Bridge on the main road, & returned to Rockwood, where Hart & I went to bed after 6 o'clock, while Owens rode home. The night was coldish, & generally a clear starlight, except when once or twice there seemed to be a fog in the swamp.

1 shot

1 Raccoon (He)	Caught by dogs
	1 Raccoon (she)

---

the roof in a dish so that he may freeze; if it is not cold enough for that put him in the ice box for 48 hours. Parboil him lightly, dust him inside and out with a pod of red pepper split open – if he is very fat put a pod of the pepper in the oven with him. Put him in an oven over a good fire and bake or roast him as you prefer. It is a mistake to bake the potatoes with the 'possum, because they come out of the oven sodden with grease. They should be baked separately, peeled and sliced and a half hour before the 'possum is served put in the oven with him. Then they absorb enough of the fat, and the flavor and aroma of the meat. Thus cooked and served with good corn-bread, 'possum is a dish which an Epicurean must not have disdained." Bonham, M.L. (Junior). "A Boy's Memories of War Times and Other Times." Unpublished manuscript, no date; Fairfield County Historical Society Collection, Winnsboro, South Carolina.

Sat. Jan. 11th Having slept late, rode out with Hart towards noon – taking Scott, with Ramrod, Tige, Hock & the old deaf dog. We went over to the woods on Long-Branch, where I shot two squirrels, at both of which Hart had first taken a shot. On our way back, after a short hunt, our dogs started what we took for a fox.

4 shots   2 Cat-Squirrels

Sun. [January] 12th I had left my gun at Rockwood, and was going out there towards noon to-day, but was delayed some time by an accident to Bruno. I had sent him up a stepladder near the smoke-house, for the amusement of Edward Edwards, & in jumping down, he caught his flank, close to the groin, on the sharp point of a small limb which had been trimmed from the apple tree, & cut a long & very ugly gash, but fortunately not piercing much deeper than the skin. I lifted him off of the snag instantly, & as soon as practicable got Peter to sew up the wound, & to fix on with bandages a plaster of tar & grease. In holding him while the wound was sewed up, it gave him so much pain that he gave my thumb a bite without well knowing what he was about. But the poor fellow afterwards seemed fully sensible of the kindness meant to him, & has left the bandages in their place & kept quite quiet on his bed. After attending fully to Bruno, I went out to dinner at Rockwood, and rather late in the evening, walked out Squirrel hunting with Hart, taking Douglas' dog, Ramrod, for Squirrels, & Hock following to hunt rabbits. We did not go more than a quarter or half a mile from the house, in the hollows to the North & West. I missed three shots at two rabbits – and brought down two Doves at a shot, only one of which was found.

4 shots
        1 Dove   By H.   2 Cat Squirrels

Taking the bandage off, some days afterwards, we found that the stitches had broken loose, leaving the flap of skin apparently not likely to unite. Left it however to the operation of nature, & in about a month, it was entirely healed. Some matter however had formed on the inside of the thigh – but after breaking, that healed also.

Mon. Feb. 3 [1845]. This day was fixed upon for commencing a long-deferred cruise down the river, with Mayrant. To avoid all discussion of the subject at home, I took my measures so well that my intention was not known until I was driving from the door with my baggage. We left Granby in the Nimrod about noon, with Stephen & Daniel for a crew, & Guard for a water-dog, instead of Bruno, who had got such a bad character in the last voyage, that I could not have taken him even if his wound had healed. While Mayrant was getting the Boat ready, I saw two Large Gulls flying from Granby Falls down the river. We made but a short run to Geiger's Lightwood Landing opposite Singleton's Quarter – about 7 miles. I landed above the Congaree Neck, after some Ducks, but not getting a shot at them, killed a red-shouldered Hawk. Mayrant afterwards hunted without success down the right bank of the Big Lake. A cold North-Easter which had blown for several days hauled round to the South this morning, and brought up a rain before night. But having a good tent, lent to us from the Arsenal by Capt. Herbert, & plenty of wood, we passed the night very comfortably.

1 shot

By me   1 Redshouldered Hawk

By R.P.M. Nothing

Tues. Feb. 4. A strong North Wester rose this morning & brought clear weather. We strolled a little way down the River bank, without finding any game. Set sail at ½ after 10 o'clock, & ran at a great rate, except where we were obliged to tack, in bends of the river. I landed a mile or two above the mouth of Railford's Creek, & not far below the Bee-tree Landing with the intention of hunting down the Creek & meeting the Nimrod at its mouth. But in consequence of the high water – for a late freshet had left the river still swollen – & of my ignorance of the ground, I was unable to reach the Creek where I wished to, but was obliged, after a very round-about tramp in the swamp, to get directions & proceed to the mouth of the Creek. Mayrant not having arrived, I hunted a little way up the Creek, & returning, met him. The wind had in the mean time risen to a gale, & he had been obliged to scud under bare poles. He reported that he had shot two Ducks which he could not get. I had killed a Cat squirrel, on my way down the Swamp. We ran a mile or two before the gale, & stopped at the head of Barber's Cut off, at 4 o'clock, for the purpose of securing ourselves against the storm. Having pitched our tent, for the sake of shelter, in a sort of mud-hole, where we were obliged to lay a floor of drift-planks to keep ourselves dry, and lashed it all around with guys to trees & an old flat which was stranded at the lower end of the Sand-bar; Mayrant went to the upper-most pond in the old river & killed an English Duck & a Black Duck, and wounded two more which he could not get. As I found a Duck dead at the same place, 36 hours afterwards, which was probably one of these two, I set it down to him here. Mayrant returned to the Camp; & when nearly dark, I went to the same place, & brought down an English Duck & a Black Duck, as they came singly to roost – the latter giving me a stationary mark, as it hovered preparing to descend, to make up for the want of light. Guard brought them out for me. The gale gave our tent some violent shakings this night – but we found that the guys kept it secure.

8 shots

By Me.   1 English Duck (Mallard)
1 Black Duck
1 Cat Squirrel

By R.P.M.   2 English Ducks
1 Black Duck

Wed. Feb. 5th As the gale continued blowing furiously, with an intense degree of cold, & as our shooting ground appeared to be a good one, we concluded to spend the day hunting near our Camp. We made several excursions round the Old River, & to some cuts & lagoons above it – at which last, Mayrant killed two English Ducks. The Ducks seemed to be principally in the river – we saw vast flocks of English & Black Ducks, swimming along the willow shores opposite to us, or flying up stream. Mayrant thought that having gone down to the Coast with the late freshet, they were now on their way back up the Country. I went to the old river in the evening to watch for parties coming to roost, but saw none. On our first walk round the old river in the morning, we started a Wild Cat, unless our eyes deceived both of us. Three Fox Squirrels were killed in the course of the day, in the peninsula between the old river & the Cut-off. All had the crown of the head black, & more or less white on the ears & nose. One of mine was grey on the back & white on the belly – another grey on the back & black on the belly – while one killed by Mayrant was blackish grey above & black below. The water continued to rise with much rapidity, from the late rain, that we had serious apprehensions for our Quarters – but at last, after rising 4 or

5 feet, it slacked this evening, so that we concluded it would be safe to stand our ground. The gale continued, & every now & then a gust would give our Tent a hard jerk this night, as the last – but we confided in our guys, & remained safe.

10 shots

By Me   2 Fox Squirrels (The Squirrels were of both sexes.)

By R.P.M.   2 English Ducks
             1 Fox Squirrel

Thurs. Feb. 6. I went to the old river, very early in the morning, & brought back with me a Duck which had as I supposed been shot by Mayrant, the evening of our arrival at Barber's Cutoff. The Gale abating at length, we struck our tent about 10 o'clock, & crossing the river, both landed to hunt the willow shore for Ducks. Meeting with no success, we set sail, & I landed again on the right bank, some distance below, & walked down till I got opposite to Adam's Quarter, shooting at Ducks several times along the bank, but I had not fair shots – & only winged one Duck, which escaped. I killed a rabbit however, which started before me. Mayrant in the mean time, came along in the boat, landing once on the left bank; & killed two English Ducks. While he stopped at Adam's Quarter, to make some preparations for dinner, I set off for Rumph's Pond, but found myself cut off by high water. Mayrant then took me over in the Boat, & we went to some Ponds & Lagoons on the Richland side, but found no Ducks. Dined on a Duck at Adam's Quarter, and in the afternoon came on a few miles to Tucker's Cut-off – & entering the old river, landed on its right bank & encamped.

11 shots

By Me   1 Rabbit

By R.P.M.   2 English Ducks

Fri. Feb. 7. In the morning, dropped down to the mouth of the old river, 2 or 300 yards from its upper end. Landing on the left bank of this old river, I attempted to hunt up it, but after crossing by hook & crook a number of break overs by which the flood was entering the swamp, I was at last stopped by one which could not be past without imminent risk of a ducking. Killed a Barred

Owl in the Swamp with two shots – and in the old river, as I came back, a Great Heron, with three. Mayrant had fallen in with Miles Jackson,[115] once a Steamboat Captain, under whose guidance we returned to the Upper Entrance of the Old River, and running a little way in, encamped on the left bank. Roasted some Duck for dinner; & in the evening went some distance down the old river in the Nimrod, & took stands on the right bank, for Ducks coming to roost. Mayrant & Jackson got none, tho M. crippled a Summer Duck. I killed an English Duck; one of a pair that lit across the old river; & afterwards, a party of four or more lighting, fired one barrel & saw only one of the Party fly up, & brought that one down with my second barrel. However, when Mayrant & Jackson returned to my stand with the Nimrod, it being quite dark, we were unable to find any of my wounded ducks. It is probable that all scrambled ashore, or hid under the Bank.

12 shots

By Me	1 Barred Owl	By R.P.M.	1 Dove
	1 Great Heron		
	1 Mallard		

Sat. Feb. 8. Morning cold, tho less severe than it has generally been of late. Still, there was a crust of ice over a great part of the old river. Before sun-rise, Jackson took me about a mile down in his canoe, & landed me on the left bank, from which I missed a long shot at some Ducks on the opposite side. Then we took a long tramp thro the Swamp, commencing at the mouth of a Cut which runs from Cedar Creek thro Pinckney's Lake into the old river, & keeping up the right bank of the Cut for awhile, visited a number of Ponds, as well as the Lake, & fired a good many shots at Ducks without effect. The land here belongs to the Misses Pinckneys, & is the same for trespassing on which they brought a suit against Braddy. There are some enormous trees. A Sycamore which we came across, measured I think about 40 feet in circumference just at the surface of the ground, & not less than 25 at the height of 6 feet. Coming at length to the Oak Pond (or one of the Oak Ponds) we discovered a party of English Ducks at one end of it. The approach was beautiful, under cover of a vast fog. I fired & killed two Ducks & winged a third – knocking over two in the water, & bringing down

---

115 Miles Jackson was born in South Carolina around 1808. In 1850, while living on Belville Road, between the Santee and North Edisto rivers, he listed his occupation as 'Millwright'.

another in the flight. My wounded Duck however made off among the trees with which the Pond is filled, Guard's attention being too much occupied with the dead ones to pursue it. We went up the Pond on opposite sides to look after it, and seeing a party of Ducks light in an opening, I fired & crippled one, if not two. But when I sent Guard in, he kept fetching out sticks, instead of looking for the Game, which consequently escaped. At last, Jackson & I undertook to do our own wading. J. who was using my Blunderbuss, shot twice at one of my cripples, the first I think, & finally I despatched it myself. We went on a little further to some other Ponds, & on our return, finding fresh tracks of two Deer in the mud, trailed them for some time, but could not find what had become of them. In the mean time, Mayrant had been hunting about the old river, & killed one English Duck, besides bringing down some more that he could not get. We found him at the mouth of the Cut, embarked with all the baggage. The water having fallen some feet in the last 24 hours, we could not have got out at the upper end of the Old River. Proceeding down to its mouth, Jackson took leave of us in his canoe, & we set sail down stream in the Nimrod. This was at half after 1 o'clock. The neighborhood of Tucker's Old River is according to Jackson, the best hunting grounds in the Congaree Swamp. (Our camp, he thought, was about 4 miles from Gadsden.) The Cut-Off is said to have been opened by one of the Tuckers many years since, who took all his negroes one night, & cut a ditch across the neck in the Pinckney land, for the sake of increasing the Cattle-range on his side of the river. We saw many Robins in different parts of the swamp, but more about here than elsewhere. In our afternoon run, we made many long & wild shots at Ducks rising before our boat from the willow-banks, wounding a few, but not getting any in that way. At one point however, Mayrant manoeuvred so well as to do some execution in a vast flock. We heard them quacking behind a long low point made by a cove on the right bank. An Island lay opposite in the Channel, & unluckily we past to the left of this Island. But as we discovered the Ducks we lowered the mast, worked the boat across to the low point, and pushed softly up, until at last, as the great body of the Ducks, following the example of some straggling flocks, were springing up, at about 90 yards distance, we both discharged our double barrels, and I brought down one Duck and Mayrant, three. We sent Stephen & Daniel scrambling thro the shoal water with Guard after the wounded, which were making off, & paddled the Nimrod round into the Cove to assist in the chase. But two of Mayrant's Ducks escaped, one only of his, together with mine, being secured. Having past

Mucklebush, the Devil's track, the Pocket hole, &c., we encamped at ½ after 5 o'clock on the right bank, just round the point below the whirlpool, & under fort Motte.[116]

22 shots

By Me   4 English Ducks   By R.P.M.   2 English Ducks

                                                3 Robins

By Jackson - Nothing.

Sund. Feb, 9. Made a leisurely start in the morning, & dropping half a mile or so, stopped at the Railroad. A beautiful balmy day. We idled about until the arrival of the passenger Cars, firing a few shots at a mark, placing the Nimrod in charge of the Crew of a Boat which arrived with a load of rice from Belser's plantation, & dining on a Pilau. The Nimrod was to be sent up by Phil Harris's Boat, which was known to be coming up the river. A part of the Bridge was threatening to break thro. However some hasty repairs were made, we past over, & arrived safe in Columbia, with a dozen Ducks. Peter was awaiting our arrival with the horses at the Depot - & we drove up just as Sally Preston's[117] funeral was taking place at the [Trinity] Episcopal church.

Sat. Feb. 22 [1845]. Within the last week, great flights of Pigeons[118] have been reported to be in the Sand-hills, & I have seen some flocks passing over the Town. There is a vast quantity of acorns in the Sandhills. A party of half a dozen students went out to Rose's, 11 miles from Columbia on the Stage-road to Camden, the evening before, for the double purpose of attending a Sandhill

---

116 Fort Motte ('the Farm') was the plantation home, built in 1767, of Rebecca Motte. The site was a strategic position for the British supply route between Camden and Charleston because of its location between the two British-held towns. The 'fort' was held by 165 British soldiers when General Francis Marion and Colonel Henry Lee ordered it burned. Mrs. Motte provided the arrows which fired on her property.

117 Margaret Frances ("Sally") Preston Hampton was the daughter of United States senator William Campbell Preston, and the first wife of Wade Hampton III.

118 In 1813 John James Audubon described a mile-wide migrating flock of passenger pigeons (*Ectopistes migratorius*) that "passed over his head and blocked the sun for three straight days." Once considered "the most numerous bird in the world," the passenger pigeon was extinct by 1914.

Ball, & taking a Pigeon hunt. I should have gone at the same time with Baskin, but did not like to be away all night, on account of the frequent attempts lately made to set fire to the Town. Accordingly, we set off on horseback, about half after 3 o'clock in the morning, arrived before day at Rose's, & after some delay, got breakfast. The alarm was given while we were at the Table, that the Pigeons were coming. Great flocks past, in a general course from N.E. to S.W. some pretty high, but others low enough for a fair chance at them if you could be at the right place. The Students scattered about in the neighborhood of Rose's. Baskin & I rode a little way up the road, & turning to the left into the woods, took stands. Altho many great flocks past, we had few or no fair shots. Baskin with my Blunderbuss got one bird. I did nothing more than draw feathers, tho using cartridges. We got no shots after 8 o'clock, very few flocks passing at a later hour. The morning had been cloudy, with a slight sprinkle, but cleared off into a very warm day. We took a circuit towards the main road, & back in the direction of Columbia. But being encouraged by the sight of two or three very dense flocks flying low down, & searching a place to alight as we supposed, we took a stand among some wild rosemary bushes on a hill, with the hope that some might come in reach of us. None did so however; & towards noon, we commenced looking for the birds along branches, supposing they might repair there for water. Found none & calling by Rose's, discovered that most of our party of Students had gone home, without a bird. A new party however had come out, & they said they had seven Pigeons. Taking the road back to Columbia, we stopped for a snack – and determined to wait for the return of the Pigeons in the afternoon; for we were told that they were seen regularly passing back to their roost, wherever that is. In riding thro the woods, we came across John Boatwright & Heyward Trezevant,[119] who had about 13 pigeons; & in company with them, took stands in the afternoon on a hill about 9 miles from Town. A few flocks past towards evening, pretty high. Perhaps the fusilade they had been exposed to in the morning caused the main body to deviate from their usual route – or as I think more probable, they might have gone to a great distance, & resorted to another roost. The next afternoon, I saw vast flocks passing from

---

Biello, David. "3 Billion to Zero: What Happened to the Passenger Pigeon?" *Scientific American*, June 27, 2014. http://www.scientificamerican.com/article/3-billion-to-zero-what-happened-to-the-passenger-pigeon/ Last viewed June 28, 2014.

119 Daniel Heyward Trezevant (1796-1873)

Lexington towards Camden. I fired this afternoon 3 shots – having fired 6 in the morning. Got home about half after 7, & taking a short time for refreshments, patrolled.[120]

9 shots

By me,   nothing.   By Wm. Baskin,   1 Wild Pigeon

Tues. [March] 4 [1845]. Vast, but irregular flights of Pigeons continue to pass over the Town, from N.E. to S.W. in the morning, & back in the afternoon. They were reported to have a roost in the swamp of Spear's Creek, near Holly Gough's – but that is now contradicted, & they are said to roost four miles beyond Camden. There is said to be a roost also on the Edisto River, at the mouth of Black Creek. Weather very warm. Got up long before light this morning, & rode in my Father's Buggy with Mayrant out on the Asylum Road[121] to way-lay the morning flight of Birds. We saw none till nearly 7 o'clock. Then, having taken a stand in the old field near Mr. Hassel's & on the right of the road, several small flocks past us flying from S.W. to N.E & up the Branch – at a reasonable height for Cartridge. In firing at a flock, I saw a bird fall dead, which I thought was brought down by me – Mayrant saw a bird fall broken-winged, not far off – but neither saw the bird marked down by the other, or supposed that more than one had fallen. I got my bird – and not long afterwards, Cora brought Mayrant his – and as I think each got the bird killed by himself, I set them down so. Somewhat later, we saw some flocks of moderate size, flying from N.E. to S.W. as usual in the morning. Where were the others going, & where were they coming from? Had they been belated the night before, & were they now returning to

---

120 Columbia was, at this time, without an official police force and it was the responsibility of the various militias to patrol the town and maintain order.

121 The State Lunatic Asylum, designed by architect Robert Mills, was begun on December 21, 1822, with the laying of the cornerstone. Constructed of brick and stone with a copper roof, it was characteristic of Mills' trademark fire-resistant, yet visually pleasing, Greek Revival Style of architecture. When it opened in 1828 the mental hospital was "the fourth such institution in the entire country." Robert Mills, a native of Charleston, designed numerous public and private buildings throughout South Carolina (including the Jonathan Maxcy Monument on the University of South Carolina's Horseshoe), as well as monuments in Baltimore and Philadelphia. Perhaps his best-known design, however, is the Washington Monument on the National Mall in the District of Columbia. The road which ran in front of the Lunatic Asylum is now Bull Street. Graydon, Nell S. *Tales of Columbia*. Columbia, South Carolina: The R.L. Bryan Company, 1967, 28.

the general roost? Somewhat disappointed, we returned a little after 8 o'clock. A very cloudy morning – which possibly caused the Pigeons not to leave their roost.

6 shots   1 Wild Pigeon (fem.)

    By Mayrant   1 Wild Pigeon (Cock)

Tues. March 4 evening. Rode back on horseback with Mayrant after dinner to the horse-Pond in Lexington, beyond which we took a stand for Pigeons. A good many flocks past, tho nothing like the multitude frequently seen of late. They were mostly high up. We undoubtedly wounded many more than we got. While I marked down one which I shot from a flock distant I think about 120 yards from me, & which came to the ground about 200 yards off so much disabled that Bruno easily caught it, Mayrant saw another fall the other side of the Pond, that I did not observe, & never got. Evening cloudy, with glimpses of sun-shine, & quite warm. We started a pair of English Ducks out of the Pond on our arrival – & as we were coming back, a small Duck of some kind which seemed to have lain perdue. A singular accident happened to me – I missed my purse, containing eighty odd dollars, from my pocket, & concluded that I must have dropped it after taking it out to pay toll at the Bridge. But I found it hanging to the saddle on Buckeye, the end containing silver being fastened between the saddle & the blanket & beneath the pummel, in a manner which made it very difficult to account for its catching there.

5 shots
    By me   1 Wild Pigeon (cock)

    By R.P.M. 1 wild Pigeon (hen)

Wed. March 12th. Rode in the evening out on the Asylum Road, & round the headwaters of the Branch which crosses the road this side of Mr. Hassel's, being the main tributary of Smith's Branch. Not a single Pigeon to be seen. Cloudy & dark.

Fri. 14. The Pigeons, after an interval of several days, reappeared this morning, passing over the Town in vast numbers; & about half after 3 o'clock in the afternoon, commenced returning. A little later, I rode Buckeye out & took a stand a little way beyond Mrs. Fleming's field. A great number of gunners were popping away at different stations. I was rather beyond the line of march pursued by the Birds. They were flying at great heights - & altho in immense numbers, yet generally in somewhat open order. Two or three times, from some cause or other, flocks descended low. But few were brought down by all the numerous gunners. The Pigeons seemed this morning to fly principally over the Corporate limits of the Town – few passing south of Hayne's old negro settlement, or north of Butchertown.[122] The weather, after a continuance of warm days, now turning cooler.

6 shots

Tues. 18. A great many Pigeons having past over in the morning, I rode with Mayrant in the afternoon, to take a stand near the Coogler place on the road to the Broad River Bridge, where they were reported to be in the habit of flying low on their return. After waiting a good while without seeing any, we took to pursuing some Doves about the fields. I had nothing but cartridges for long shooting with me; & tho I wounded some Doves, got none. One that Mayrant despatched was first very badly wounded by me. Towards Sun-set, one flock of Pigeons past over, at a great height. I afterwards heard that the great body past this evening higher up, near Frost's. The weather having turned pretty cold, we saw piles of wood laid in the orchard at Coogler's, to make fires to keep off frost.

6 shots

By me.   Nothing   By R.P.M.   2 Doves

Sat. Mar. 22[d] [1845]. Rode out to Rockwood in the evening, to take a raccoon-hunt with Hart & Henry Owens. The latter did not disappoint us as he had done two weeks before, when I rode with my gun to Rockwood & after waiting an hour or so, came home again. To-night I did not take my gun with me, but used

---

122 Butchertown and Cottontown were just north of the town limits of Upper Boundary (Elmwood) Street.

Hart's. We set out a little after 8 o'clock, in a bright moon shine, & after going down some distance thro Roach's fields, the Dogs treed a raccoon in the edge of the Creek Swamp. The tree was a very large one – an Elm, Owens said. As we went up to it, several Turkeys flew from it – at least Owens said so, & I suppose he was right, tho I was surprised at their roosting on a bare tree. Following one which he pointed out to me on a pine where it had lit, I got a flying shot as it took the alarm & flew off. After about an hour's work with the axe, the tree fell with a tremendous crash, & the dogs caught a Coon – a she-one, & rather small. We then went on, crossed the Creek on a log, & proceeded to the river bank, near its mouth; but except a Turkey that was disturbed, & a few rabbits that some of the dogs would occasionally run, came across no more game. So we returned, crossing the Creek at Scott's Bridge, & getting back just at midnight. On the way, we thought we saw an Owl on a dead pine in a field of Roach's – but I did not get a shot. Our force to-night consisted of Wilson, with his axe – Ramrod, Tige, Limmery, & Hock – Jem not being well, & the old deaf dog disappearing before we started. I remained for the night at Rockwood.

1 shot
    Caught by the Dogs. 1 Coon (female)

Sat. Ap. 5, 1845. Rode out to Rockwood in the evening for a Coon hunt. The Party was composed of Hart, Henry Owens, myself, Wilson, Scott, & five dogs. Starting a little after 8 o'clock, we hunted some distance down the Creek; then crossing, came up on the other side, & returning by the Bridge got back to Rockwood at half after 1 o'clock. One Coon was treed in the swamp, but the tree being very hard, we did not attempt to cut it down. A huge Possum was caught by the Dogs in a field of Broomstraw on the others side of the Swamp. Night dark – weather warm. I carried Hart's gun, but had no shot.

Sunday, April 6: Getting up late in the morning, walked with Hart towards the Lightening-hill field. Limery treed a Squirrel, & Hart went back & got his gun, with which after several shots I brought the Squirrel down.

5 shots   1 Cat Squirrel

Sat. Ap. 19. The Circuit being over, took a cruise down the River with Mayrant, a more particular account of which is contained in a separate Journal which I kept on the voyage. One of our principal objects was Turkey hunting; but the Spring being very forward & warm, it proved too late, & we found that the gobling season was over. For our Crew, we had Stephen, & Jem Macomb, with Guard for a retriever. Capt. Herbert had lent us a tent from the Arsenal. We embarked in the Nimrod at East Granby about noon, & ran by evening as far as Savanna Hunt, & encamped on a Sand bar just above the mouth of it. Summer Ducks were the principal game seen on the river. I wounded a Coot & Mayrant brought down a Florida Cormorant, which evinced great toughness & tenacity of life.

12 shots

By me   1 Summer Duck

By R.P.M.   1 Rabbit
           1 Cormorant (Phalacrococrax Floridanus)

Sun. 20. Two or three English Ducks were seen this morning & the evening before; stragglers belated, or prevented from migrating by some accident. Before striking our tent, I shot a Blue-wing Teal, close to the shore below the Sand bar. In the middle of the day, we landed below the Bee Tree, & dined on some fish which we got from two negroes who were fishing there. An accident occurring early in the afternoon prevented us proceeding further down than Taylor's Ferry. The Nimrod was nearly capsized by the awkwardness of a negro whom we were taking on board, & who laid hold of the mast when he lost

his balance. Mayrant fell overboard in deep water with his gun, which there was much difficulty afterwards in fishing up. No material damage was done, however; & after putting things to rights, we camped at the spot. The shots which we made at Ducks to day, as generally on the voyage, were at very long distances, which accounts for the small number killed.

6 shots

By Me	By R.P.M.
1 Bluewing Teal	1 Summer Duck

Mon. Ap. 21. Made a long run today, & having a moon-light evening, did not stop till 9 o'clock, when we encamped below Stark's Mill, on the right bank. In the afternoon, I shot a musk-rat swimming; but greatly to my regret, lost it among some roots under the Bank. I also wounded badly a Gray Fox Squirrel, coming to drink at a Sand-bar.

10 shots

By Me

    1 Blue-wing Teal

By R.P.M.

    1 Summer Duck

By Jem Macomb 2 Doves

Tues. 22. Dropping down in the morning to the Fork, landed on the upper Bank of the Wateree Old River, & having set out our Gill-net & fishing poles, & leaving Macomb & Stephen with the baggage, took a long tramp thro the Swamp. I shot a Mississippi Kite from a high tree on the Bank of the Wateree, & a Blue Heron at a Cypress Lagoon. We also killed some Cat Squirrels; & I killed, with sticks, two Copper-belly snakes. Our net caught a Gar, a Fat-fish & a Gizzard Shad. To avoid mosquitoes, we crossed the River, & encamped on the Sand bar at the head of the Santee, where we kept up our quarters about three days, making excursions on the river & in the Swamp, & subsisting pretty well on the fish caught by our net & lines.

5 shots

By Me

    1 Mississippi Kite
    1 Ardea Caerulea (mature)
    2 Cat Squirrels

By R.P.M.

    2 Cat Squirrels

Wed. 23: The fish taken to-day were a Redhorse, a Mudfish, two Cat, two Carp, & a Bream. An enormous Gar was entangled in the net, but broke out with his mouth fastened up. His length appeared to be 5 feet. In the forenoon, I hunted with Mayrant thro the Swamp on the Sumter side, where altho we found abundance of Turkey tracks, we got no game but Squirrels. I shot a Hooded Warbler, & killed with a stick a Chicken Snake. In the afternoon, a short thunder shower came up.

8 shots

By Me   By R.P.M.

3 Cat Squirrels   1 Cat Squirrel

1 Hooded Warbler (Minodioctes Mitratus - male)

Thurs. Ap. 24. Three Cat fish & an Eel were taken this morning from the lines set out the night before. Nothing found in the net, which we suspected had been robbed by some runaway, or other vagabond. Mayrant & I afterwards went over to Manigault's Island, where we were for a long time entangled in the Canebrakes; & where we found little game. Mayrant, besides two Squirrels, shot a Chicken Snake & a Copper belly. This afternoon, a Hawk was seen sailing over the river & Swamp, about as large as the Redtail, broadwinged, & of a very dark color. Mayrant mentioned that on former excursions down the river in the past winter, he had killed two of the kind. Is it the "Butes Bachmanii"[123] seen, but never obtained by Audubon?

No shot by me.   By R.P.M.   Cat Squirrels

Fri. 25. Fish taken to-day, three Red horse, two Catfish, & an Eel. The day so hot that we did not hunt. While lying at the Camp, two Bald Eagles came in sight, apparently a male & female, playing in the air. Also, a dark colored, broad-winged Hawk, like the one seen the day before. In the course of our Cruise, a few Fish-hawks, & several Swallowtails & Mississippi Kites were seen. I was surprised, however, considering the season of the year, how few waterbirds, either of the Swimming or Wading tribe, were met with. We saw very few Snakes with the exception of those already mentioned. The only poisonous ones were one or two Moccasins. Sturgeon were very abundant in the river, making their

---

123 Most likely named for Audubon's friend, the Reverend John Bachman, a Lutheran minister and naturalist. A native of New York, Reverend Bachman moved to Charleston where he developed a friendship with John James Audubon. Two of Audubon's sons married daughters of Bachman. William K. Bachman, the son of the Reverend Bachman, was a witness to Maxcy Gregg's 1861 Last Will and Testament.

leaps out of the water. This afternoon, we broke up our Camp, which from the quantity of fish & offal strewed about during our stay, had been named "Camp Carrion," & by very hard work at the oars, ascended the river to Stark's lumber-landing, a distance of about five miles. From this point across to the railroad is only a quarter of a mile, over land. But having no means of conveying our baggage across, we concluded to work up the river the next day. We saw this afternoon one Turkey fly across the river – the only one seen on the voyage.

Sat. [April] 26. With half a day's terrible labor, in a broiling sun, worked up stream to the railroad, a distance of about 6 miles. Cooled awhile, & took the cars for home. We were disappointed on our expectations of game on this cruise. We met with little but Summer Ducks. And of them, many of the females had broods of Ducklings following them in the water. Such we always spared, tho we took many chases after the young, but always unsuccessfully. The old ones sometimes feigned lameness, to draw off Guard, or ourselves; but the Ducklings of the smallest size scampered out of the way with wonderful agility.

4 shots

By Me, Nothing By R.P.M. 1 Ringneck Duck

Mon. [August] 4 [1845]. The summer has been remarkable for the greatest continuous heat, & the greatest drought within memory. There were some days as hot in 1838, but not a continuance of such weather; and the drought in the fall of 1839 was not so excessive. Early in July, I crossed the dry bed of Cane Creek on the Winnsboro road, as well as of Smith's Branch. This evening, I walked with Mayrant & Baskin to Dr. Fisher's Pond, which in consequence of a late rain is full, tho last week it was lower than I ever knew it to be reduced by dry weather. Edward Leverett[124] accompanied us on the pony; we mustered five puppies in the party, together with old Guard. I took Ranger, who was so much frightened,

---

124 Charles Edward Leverett, Jr. (1833-1861), was the son of Mary Bull Maxcy and the Reverend Charles Edward Leverett. Mary Maxcy Leverett and Cornelia Maxcy Gregg were first cousins, and were frequent correspondents and visitors to each other's homes (the Leverett family lived in the Beaufort area). Edward was, at this time, twelve years old.

it being his second appearance in public, that I had to make Dennis[125] carry him frequently in his arms. At last he seemed to acquire courage amongst the pack of Dogs, Children & Shooters in which he found himself, & began to fetch birds a little, being his first attempt in that way.

17 shots

By Me	By R.P.M.	By W. Baskin
3 Nighthawks	about 5 Nighthawks	1 Nighthawk
5 Martins	1 Large Beetle	1 L.W. Bat

Wed. Aug. 6. Walked to the old field this side of Randolph's in the evening. Found Randolph's lane shut up by Brown's field. Bruno & Ranger with me; the latter learns rapidly to fetch birds; watches them falling and runs to find them.

29 shots

1 Dove
2 Nighthawks
9 Martins

Thurs. [August] 7 [1845]. Walked in the evening with Mayrant & Baskin as far as the old field to the west of Levy's Spring. Had several children along, but no dog besides Ranger, who is acquiring confidence abroad, & whose proficiency is quite satisfactory.

20 shots

By Me	By R.P.M.	By WB
3 Nighthawks	8 Nighthawks	3 Nighthawks
11 Martins	4 Martins	
1 Leatherwing Bat		

Between W.B. & myself   1 Nighthawk

---

125 Dennis, a slave of James Gregg, was about fourteen years old at this time. Mr. Gregg also owned Dennis' mother (Hester) and sister (Harriet).

Thurs. 14. Walked in the evening to Dr. Fisher's Pond, taking Bruno, Ranger & Dennis with me. Ranger took to fetching out of the water readily, having Bruno's example to encourage him in swimming. Martins appear to be diminishing in numbers. I brought down a Yellowhammer from a high tree in Calico Branch, by a long shot with a Cartridge of no. 8.

9 shots

    1 Yellowhammer

    1 Martin

Sun. 17. Being at Rockwood in the evening, but without my gun, rode out with Hart after Squirrels, which are doing mischief in his Corn. He shot at two, but did not kill either.

Thurs. Aug. 21. Walked in the evening down to Dr. Fisher's Pond, where Ranger, with Bruno's example before him, acquitted himself very creditably in fetching out of the water. Edward Leverette came down after me on the Pony, & took a few shots with my gun. Baskin also joined me.

9 shots

By Me,

1 Barn Swallow

1 Lesser Yellowlegs

1 Spotted Sandpiper

By E.L.

2 Bee Martins

1 Bluebird

Fri. 22. Rode in the evening with Edward Leverette, to Everett's Pond, which now seems to be much farther gone than it was in the great drought of 1839. Besides several Herons, Great, White and Green, there were in the Pond a few Wood Ibises, which took the alarm very quickly & flew off. After manoeuvring awhile to approach the larger Herons, without success, I gave Edward L. a shot at a Green Heron & a Dove, both of which he wounded. A Thunder Storm was brewing, which after our return broke loose with every grateful violence.

Thurs. Sep. 26. After a summer of unexampled heat, the weather has lately become pleasantly cool. It had much moderated by the time I went over to attend the Brigade Encampment, which commenced on the 15th. At the end of that week there came a northeast rain, since which fire has been requisite in the morning. Rode this evening to Hampton's Burnt Mill, where from a stand I had taken, I shot a Night Heron flying up the Ponds. Bruno & Ranger with me.

4 shots

    1 Night Heron (in immature plumage)

    1 Dove

Fri. 27. Set off to walk down to Fisher's Pond in the evening, to meet Baskin & try Ranger at some Partridges – but Ranger taking fright on the way & running back, I returned for him & took Bruno along to keep up his courage. Rode Granby down, Edward Leverette accompanying me on the Pony. Dismounting, walked with Baskin round the Pond, having to go some Distance up Rice Branch before we could cross it. Found no Partridges.

3 shots   1 Pileated Woodpecker

By Baskin,   1 Crow, not got.

Summary from April to Sept. 1845

Month	Ap.	Aug.	Sep.	Total
Times out	10	7	2	19
Shots fired	50	84	7	141
Mississippi Kite	1			1
Nighthawk		8		8
Purple Martin		26		26
Barn Swallow		1		1
Hooded Warbler	1			1
Pileated Woodpecker			1	1
Yellowhammer		1		1
Dove		1		1
Night Heron		1	1	
Blue Heron	1			1
Lesser Yellowlegs		1		1
Spotted Sandpiper		1		1
Summer Duck	1			1
Bluewing Teal	2			2
Cat Squirrel	6			6
Leatherwing Bat		1		1

16 Species
Individuals, 55

"Shooting Wild Pigeons In Iowa"
from *Frank Leslie's Illustrated Newspaper* September 1867

November 1845 - December 1846:
A Near Fatal Accident and a German Bird Dealer

Nov. 14, 1845. Mayrant was about to make a short cruise down the River, and I agreed to accompany him as far as Threewits' Ferry, not having more time to spare. Accordingly, we embarked in the Nimrod at Granby, a little after mid-day, taking with us Charles Henry, William Macomb, Stephen, & Guard. Mayrant spoke of having lately seen seventy Turkeys on the Sand bar above the mouth of Gill's Creek. Charles Henry & I took a tramp thro the adjoining woods in search of them, but found no signs of Turkeys. Afterwards, I took another tramp with Mayrant thro the Swamp & cotton wood thicket at the head of the Big Lake, with no better success. I fired this day but one shot, at a Dove, which I brought down, but did not get & do not count. We encamped for the night under our sail, on the Bank of the River near the Big Lake.

1 shot

Sat. Nov. 15. Early in the morning, we all three went to the Big Lake, & hunted round it, but there were very few Ducks there, and so got no shot. Embarked about 9 o'clock. In a cove above the mouth of Tom's Creek, we got within shot of a Great Heron, which I killed from the Bow of the Boat. I landed & hunted for some distance up Tom's Creek, but found no Ducks. Before I went up the Creek, I had winged a Summer Duck in the River, but it escaped. Peter was to come down on the Lexington side, with Granby, & meet me at Threewits' Ferry. We landed on the Richland side, to wait his arrival, & I went with Charles Henry to the Green-Hill Lake, where we shot at some Ducks, but got nothing. Peter not coming, Mayrant & C.H. reembarked at 2 o'clock, & I took the road afoot, on the Lexington side, to meet Peter. After I had become quite weary, & foot-sore, & towards 5 o'clock, I met him hurrying along at a great rate, between Congaree Creek & Haugabook Swamp. His unfortunate love of the bottle had overcome

111

him on the road. I was very unsuccessful in shooting to-day, making most of my shots at long distances. Besides my Crane, I got nothing but a Cat Squirrel, at Haugabook Swamp, at the Bridge.

14 shots

1 Great Heron

1 Cat squirrel

My shooting was now to be interrupted for a long time, by an accident which came near being fatal. Returning Thursday evening, 27th Nov. from a Muster of the Lower Battalion at Myer's Hill, I was attacked with the Measles.[126] Taking it merely for a bad cold, I sent for Dr. Clifton the next day, who gave me some medicine. Having to get up in the night (that is, early on the 29th) I fainted & fell into the fire, burning my head, neck & right hand very dangerously. I came to with the pain & started up, probably just in time to save my life. About two months of close confinement & great suffering followed, during which I was nursed day & night by my mother, with a mother's devotion. For many weeks afterwards it was necessary for me to undergo much pain & constraint, in restoring partially, by mechanical means, such as springs & bandages, the flexibility of the fingers, & preventing distortion of the neck. To recover an imperfect use of the hand, such as I now have, required a long time. And in addition to this cause of interruption in my sporting pursuits, came the Mexican War,[127] which kept me in a state of feverish anxiety for nearly a year before I

126 Typically a childhood disease, measles was the cause of fourteen deaths in Charleston in 1821. Other leading causes of death among children and infants in that year included "Worm Fever" (from which there were twenty-five cases), teething (18), "Convulsions" (42), and, leading the statistics, diarrhea (95). It is no wonder that the mortality rate among children during the antebellum period was high. Infants were often given their first 'medical treatment' as newborns when their umbilical "stump" was dressed "with dirty cobwebs" to aid in healing. Joseph Ioor Waring, *A History of Medicine in South Carolina*, 60, 62n.

127 The United States recognized the independent Republic of Texas in 1837. It was not until 1845, however, that Texas became the twenty-eighth state of the Union. When negotiations between the United States and the Mexican government over the precise boundary between the two countries failed, President James K. Polk ordered Brigadier General Zachary Taylor and half of the United States Army's troops to advance from Corpus Christi to the Rio Grande River. The Mexican government remained obstinate to negotiations. Brigadier General Taylor's troops repelled enemy forces at Palo Alto on the 8th of May and at Resaca de Palma the following day. Declaring these hostilities to be acts of war, President Polk presented his case to Congress that the Mexican army had been the attacking force. Two days later, on the 13th of May, Congress

obtained a commission, & occupied for a great part of that time in efforts to get into the service, & the correspondence and solicitation which became necessary with that object.

While confined by the above accident, I had the misfortune to lose my poor friend, William Baskin, who died 8 Jan, 1846, and Dr. Clifton, who died 25 [or 28] Jan.

Towards the end of January, I was able to walk out, with my hand in a sling & my neck wrapped up. I so far recovered in February, as to be able to attend Court early in March & use my pen with my right hand, tho very awkwardly.

There was much cold & stormy weather while I was laid up, and not for the most affectionate nursing, which I had, it would be a very gloomy period to remember.

Sunday, [March] 8 [1846]. Rode Granby to Rockwood, where I dined, & in the afternoon, walked with Hart across the Lightning hill field. The Dogs treed a Fox-Squirrel, at which Hart commenced throwing stones. After he had succeeded in driving it out of the nest in which it was lying, I went to the house for his gun, & mounting Granby, gallopped back with it. I found him with his coat off, still pelting the squirrel. Firing from my left shoulder, I brought the Squirrel down. It was very heavy – gray, with black crown & white nose. Afterwards, from the top of a high tree nearby, firing again from my left shoulder, I killed a Sparrowhawk.

2 shots

  1 Fox Squirrel
  1 Sparrowhawk

---

declared war against Mexico. Among the troops of volunteers raised to serve in the Mexican-American War were the Palmetto Regiment of South Carolina. Commanded by former governor Pierce Mason Butler, the regiment's lieutenant colonel was thirty-two year old Camden lawyer and duelist James P. Dickinson.

Summary from October 1845 to March 1846

Month	Nov.	March	Total
Times out	2	1	3
Shots fired	15	2	17
Sparrowhawk		1	1
Great Heron	1		1
Fox Squirrel		1	1
Cat Squirrel	1		1

Species
Individuals, 4

Sat. Ap. 18, 1846. Rode to Rockwood in the evening, for the purpose of going out Turkey hunting with Hart, very early the next morning. On the main road, near Rockwood, firing from my left shoulder, without dismounting, I killed a Dove.

1 shot   1 Dove

Sun. 19: We set off at half after 4 in the morning, and crossing the Lightning Hill field, took stands by the fence on its west side. After we had been there for some time, a Turkey flew by us, not approaching the field, but passing it. I fired just as the Turkey was lighting amongst the bushes on a ridge, when it rose again & flew off. I had fired from my right shoulder, & found my crippled hand a great impediment. We heard some more Turkeys gobble, but did not see any. Striking down towards the Creek, northwards, the Dogs treed a rabbit in a little hollow tree on the edge of the Swamp. Hart screwed it out. On our way back to breakfast, the Dogs treed some Squirrels, one of which Hart shot; and firing three times, I crippled another, so that it was caught by the dogs.

4 shots

     By Me,   1 Cat Squirrel   By H.M.   1 Cat Squirrel

               Screwed from a Tree   1 Rabbit

Sun. 19. Same day. Sometime after breakfast, we walked over to the Long-Branch field. The Dogs treed something on some very high Pines by the Branch, but we could not see anything, except some knots & bunches of pine straw, the character of which we ascertained with my little "Waldstein" spy-glass. I missed a Rabbit running – and tho I had begun to shoot from the Right shoulder, felt apprehensive of shooting badly for a long time.

1 shot

Same day. In the evening, we rode to the Lightning Hill field. Hart not carrying his gun. No game seen, nor any Turkey tracks except an old one.

Tues. Aug. 11: Walked in the evening to the Brickyard. Found my crippled hand so far restored, so to enable me to shoot on the wing with facility. Mayrant was to accompany me, but was prevented by business. Ranger shows the great loss he suffered in his education in consequence of my accident. He needs to be trained anew to the simple matter of fetching birds.

7 shots   5 Nighthawks

Sat. [September] 5 [1846]. Riding to Rockwood without my gun this evening, I saw in a little pond formed in the road near Dr. Roach's by much rain which has fallen lately, a Blue wing Teal, seeming very tame, & unwilling to fly off. Getting Hart's gun, I returned and killed it. It appeared a young bird, but poor – probably separated by some accident from its Companions.

1 shot   1 Blue wing Teal

Wed.16: Rode in the evening to Hampton's Middle Mill, & took a stand for Night Herons, but got no shot. The weather beginning to grow a little cooler, after much excessive heat. I think I brought down a Dove, but Bruno did not find it.

2 shots   1 Nighthawk

Fri.18. Rode in the evening, to the same place, but did not fire a shot.

Mon. 21. Walked in the evening, down the Canal, as far as the Lower Basin, in search of some wading waterfowl that I heard Bill DeSaussure speak of last year, as having been shot by his brother about this season. Found nothing. The walk very difficult, from weeds & Beggar's lice. Towards dusk as I returned, Bruno found a Covey of Partridges on the hillside North East of Holmes' Lake, & I got two – about half grown, or somewhat further advanced.

2 shots   2 Partridges

Summary from April to Septr. 1846

Month	Ap.	Aug.	Sept.	Total
Times out	4	1	4	9
Shots fired	6	7	5	18
Nighthawk		5	1	6
Dove	1			1
Partridge			2	2
Bluewing Teal			1	1
Cat Squirrel	1			1

5 Species

Individuals, 11

Sun. Nov. 15, 1846. Having ridden out to Rockwood with my gun the evening before, went Squirrel hunting with Hart this morning, before breakfast. Set out about Sun rise, & returned about 10 o'clock. We hunted back of the Garden, & at no great distance from it. With the aid of Limery & Hock, we treed three Rabbits, besides a few Squirrels. The first of the Rabbits escaped in some hole among the roots of a tree, while we were vainly smoking a hollow up the trunk. The second was screwed out of a hollow hickory. The third could not be found, altho Jem was at the trouble of cutting open the log at which the Dogs barked.

2 shots

By me,	1 Cat Squirrel	By Hart,	2 Cat Squirrels
	Screwed out of a tree,		1 Rabbit

Same day. After breakfast we set out again, followed by Jem, Wilson & Harry, all carrying old public arms – besides little negroes. We hunted round the Eastern fields till between 2 & 3 o'clock. A Fox Squirrel, which was treed up a very high pine near Long Branch, took 9 or 10 shots from Hart & myself & Jem, to bring him down. Jem, however, using a rifle, did no damage. My Little Spy-glass was of much service in discovering some Squirrels, which otherwise would have escaped.

11 shots

By Me.   4 Cat Squirrels
          3 Cowpen Blackbirds

By Hart, 1 Fox Squirrel
          The Fox Sq. was mostly gray - nose & ears, white
          5 Cat Squirrels

By the negroes,   1 Cat Squirrel (which they cut down a tree to get at.)

Tues. Nov. 17. I rode out to Rockwood in the evening to meet Henry Owens & John Pearson for a Coon hunt. Having met, set off about 7 o'clock, (carrying no guns) accompanied by Jem, Ben, Scott, Hock Limery, the black puppy Rolla, & 5 or 6 dogs of Owens & Pearson. Owens' dogs had taken a surfeit of carrion, & hunted badly. We went to the Creek by the old Buffalo trail, down the Creek to the place where Scott's Bridge stood before it was washed away, up the Creek for some distance on the other side, then across again; and finally we returned by the Long ridge running up to the northern end of the Lightning Hill field. Owens wished to keep the party out all night. Hart insisted on coming home, for which I also voted, as we met with no sport. By a sort of compromise, we got back about 2 o'clock in the morning; and then Owens kept us up for an hour & a half longer, as he would neither go to bed nor go home. At last he & Pearson mounted their horses & set off with their Dogs for another hunt, promising to come back for us if they treed a Coon – but we heard no more of them. This night completely disgusted Hart with Owens & Coon-hunting.

Sun. Nov. 22.   Rode out to Rockwood in the morning for a Squirrel-hunt. Weather singularly capricious. At first, cold, with bright sunshine – then clouds rapidly formed with a South West wind, which veered to East, when there was a Storm threatening & a slight sprinkle of rain. The Sun struggled all day with the clouds – in the afternoon there was thunder, a high wind rose from the West – and at last the day ended clear & cold. I used Hart's brass-mounted rifle – he, his shot-gun. In using this old rifle, the interval between the flash of the pan & the explosion of the charge, seemed so long to me, accustomed as I have long been to percussion arms, that I could not keep my aim steady – the day also was rather dark for the rifle sights – & I suppose I made pretty wild shooting. I touched but one Squirrel, whose tail I shaved near the root, giving him a very odd appearance as he dragged his brush after him. He escaped however, altho badly wounded by Hart. This was in the Hollow near the gate of the Lightning Hill field, where Hart considers the Squirrels as very difficult to be shot. One of my shots was fired thro a nest.

8 shots

      By Me, nothing   By Hart,   3 Cat Squirrels

This was my last day's shooting this winter.

In Dec. 1846, near Christmas, I bought from a German Bird Dealer & gave to Julia, a Starling & two Goldfinches. The Starling was frozen to death in Julia's study on the morning of the 8th of Jan. 1847, which struck one as a remarkable circumstance considering the Northern origin of the Bird. A warm South West wind had brought up rain, which cleared off, with a high North Wester on the 7th Jan., producing intense cold. The Thermometer in the open air at 5 o'clock on the morning of the 8th was at 17 (Fahr).

One Goldfinch, Cinderella, afterwards died. The other, Bluebeard, has lately (I write 12 Nov. 1848) been transferred to Mr. & Mrs. Hassell,[128] who say he is not a Goldfinch, but a Thistlefinch.

(Mem. 4 March 1849: This Bird has since been stolen from Mrs. Hassell.)

Mem. 23 Dec. 1846. Birds brought to Columbia for sale by a German, named Reiche,[129] about 200 in number, principally canaries at 12.25 apiece but including also the following:

2. Two Nightingales, price $10 a piece

3. A Blackbird (Turdus Merula) $15

4. A Thrush $15

5. A Starling $4

6. Several Goldfinches $1.50 a piece

7. A Bullfinch sick $1

8. Some Brown Linnets $2

9. Some Yellow Linnets

10. Some Chaffinches (Lussifiula) [Fringilla] $1.50

11. Some Siskins (Znevivja) $1.50

12. A hybrid or two

---

128 The von Hassells, Swedish emigrants, ran a girls' school out of their home near the Gregg family residence.

129 Reiche, the German bird dealer from whom Maxcy Gregg purchased the birds for his sister Julia, was Charles Reiche who began importing canaries from Germany, first through New Orleans in 1842 and through Charleston the following year. Charles and his brother, Henry Reiche, expanded their successful business into large game animals which they sold to zoos around the world. Animals native to the United States, such as buffalo, elk, caribou, and grizzly bears, were highly sought after in European menageries. Once established, the brothers ran their business from 55 Chatham Street, New York City. According to the Reiche brothers the most common cause of death among birds was cold weather, "occasioned by either hanging a bird in a draught of air, [or] near a loose-fitting window." Charles F. Holden, *Holden's Book on Birds*, 21.

SUMMARY FROM OCTOBER 1846 TO SEPTR. 1847

Month	Novr.	June	Total
Times out	4	1	5
Shots fired	21	1	22
Cowpen Blackbird	3		3
Cat Squirrel	5		5

2 Species
Individuals, 8

Bullock's Oriole, Baltimore Oriole, Mexican Goldfinch, Varied Thrush and Common Water Thrush from *Birds of America* (1827) by John James Audubon (1785 - 1851)

JANUARY 1847 - AUGUST 1848: THE MEXICAN WAR

Memoranda of Sporting Incidents & Observations in My Mexican Excursion from scattered notes &c. commenced 4 March 1849

For the remainder of the winter of 1846-47 my thoughts were constantly running on the war, and from the time the ten Regiment Bill[130] was introduced in Congress, I was looking out for letters from Washington, or news of the proceedings of Congress, by every evening's mail; and I did not shoot any more.

On Sunday, the 28th of March, I returned from Winnsboro Court. The day was very pleasant. I was on horse-back; and my sporting feelings were revived by sights on the road; one of which was of a Redtailed Hawk with a Squirrel in his Talons. The burden was too heavy to be carried far at a flight; but tho I pursued him from tree to tree, the Hawk would never abandon his prey. At this time, I had nearly despaired of obtaining a Commission; but this evening, I received from the Post Office my appointment[131]

---

130 In January of 1847 the United States Senate began debating the issue of whether the Ten Regiment Bill, enacted to raise a second levy of troops for duty in Mexico, would pertain to regular active duty or volunteer forces. The Senate rejected the volunteer system on the 28th of January. A proviso to the Bill would have left it to the President, James K. Polk, to appoint officers to the regiments raised by the Bill, a condition objected to by Senator John C. Calhoun and others. The proviso was removed from the Bill, thereby delaying the appointments of officers since the Senate, which was responsible for military appointments and promotions, was scheduled to recess on the 3rd of March. This delay, noted a South Carolina newspaper, was bound to be a "sore disappointment to the many young men here who are waiting for commissions." As he wrote of his frustration in his Sporting Journal, Maxcy Gregg was among those disappointed by the delay. *The Edgefield Advertiser*, February 17, 1847.

131 After returning from Winnsboro and receiving his commission on the 28th of March 1847, Gregg wrote to the Adjutant General's office accepting his appointment and returning the required Oath of Allegiance. Gregg also requested copies of Army Regulations, Ordnance Regulations, and the manual on cavalry tactics, "without which," the new major explained, his "want of experience in Military matters must cause me serious embarrassment in discharging the duties of the service." Although he was "keenly interested in military science and studied all that

123

of Major in the 12th Infantry,[132] and immediately entered on my duties in the Recruiting service. After a few excursions[133] into Lexington, Edgefield & Kershaw, I went to Charleston on the 6th of May – remained there till the 27th, with the exception of three days spent in an excursion to Walterboro – then

---

books could teach concerning the art and practices of war," Maxcy Gregg's actual experience in military tactics to this point was limited to his State militia duty. Letters Received by the Office of the Adjutant General, 1822-1860, Publication Number M567, Roll 0343, National Archives and Records Administration (NARA). Neill Webster Macaulay, "Maxcy Gregg, Lawyer, Soldier and Savant," SCCRRMM.

132 Major Gregg also promptly reported by mail and requested instructions of his superior officer, Milledge Luke Bonham, lieutenant colonel of the 12th Infantry, who was at that time in New Orleans awaiting reinforcements before making the final leg of his journey to Vera Cruz. Bonham had personal reasons for serving his country and his state in the Mexican War. Maxcy Gregg, indeed all South Carolinians, would have been well aware of the fate of James Butler Bonham, the brother of M.L. Bonham and between whom there was "a very strong tie of brotherly affection." James Bonham was among the group of Texas patriots killed while entrenched within the walls of the Alamo in 1836. He had been a school friend of William Barret Travis, and while practicing law in Edgefield James Bonham determined, against the advice of his younger brother, to abandon his profession and join his friend in San Antonio. Once the Texans were settled in the old Alamo mission Travis sent his trusted friend to ride out and enlist reinforcements from Gonzales. Meeting up with another South Carolina acquaintance, Samuel A. Maverick, they rode in search of support. When they returned to San Antonio they found the fort surrounded by the troops of Santa Anna and in the ninth day of a siege. Maverick, "by his own manly statement afterwards, considered the case hopeless, refused to seek an entrance and tried to persuade Bonham to retire to Gonzales." Unwilling to abandon his friend William Travis, "by means of preconcerted signals, [Bonham], alone, made his way through the lines of the enemy, and into the Fort, and lost his life" with the other revolutionaries. *The Anderson Intelligencer*, November 11, 1896. *The Newberry Herald and News* (Newberry, South Carolina), April 11, 1889.

133 Until Major Gregg received a response from Bonham and the Adjutant General's office, he thought it best to undertake the task of recruiting and drilling. He set out from Columbia during the afternoon of the 29th of March and travelled to Charleston Harbor where he reported for duty at Fort Moultrie. There he was met by two companies of North Carolina recruits, Company I under the command of Captain William J. Clark, and Company G, captained by Walter P. Richardson. These North Carolinians were the first to be ready for embarkation to the seat of the war. Gregg hoped the transportation of the troops would take place by the 10th of June and that he would be allowed to accompany them. Indications are that the Office of the Adjutant General supported his plan to sail for New Orleans, from which place he could continue to supervise the recruiting of his regiment, but by the 9th of April he had received conflicting orders. Lieutenant Colonel Bonham wanted Gregg to recruit from his base at Fort Moultrie until the other companies were full and ready to sail. Plans for transporting the two North Carolina companies were progressing by the 22nd of May when Lieutenant Colonel Bonham issued orders for Major Gregg to submit requisitions to the Charleston Quartermaster and Commissary departments for chartering a vessel to Vera Cruz and for obtaining supplies in adequate numbers for the troops' subsistence until they reached New Orleans.

went to Sullivan's Island, & staid there till the embarkation of a Detachment of Troops for Mexico, on the 19th June. Sunday, the 20th came back to Charleston; came up to Columbia in the 22d and remained at home till the 10th July.[134] One day while out at Rockwood, the 27th June, I fired a shot with Hart's gun at a Redtail Hawk on a dead pine in front of the house, but only wounded it. On the afternoon of the 10th July, paid a last visit at my Grandmother's – and to my poor Friend Pemberton, who was on his death bed, & survived but two days longer. On Sunday, the 11th July, I went down to Charleston, taking my Double barreled Gun with me this time in a case given to me by Mayrant. The next day I went over to Sullivan's Island, where I staid at Lee's Tavern till the 2d Septr, my principal occupation being the study of Spanish. Then, as the number of recruits assembled for those unlucky companies, D & A of the 12th was at last becoming more respectable,[135] I moved into Fort Moultrie, where I joined a Mess of the Lieutenants of those Companies, & of K, 13th Inf – &

---

134 On a previous visit with his family in Columbia in April a number of his peers from the legal profession hosted a dinner there in his honor. This visit in June and early July, however, was for the benefit of his family. On the 10th of July he visited Susannah Hopkins Maxcy, his maternal grandmother, who was now in her seventy-eighth year. Before leaving Columbia he placed the ring he always wore on the finger of his mother. He also presented his family with his photographic likeness, a relatively new scientific product, of himself in his uniform. The double-breasted, fourteen-button Army frockcoat, worn by senior grade officers, was a bit ill-fitting on Gregg's 140-pound frame. The standing collar was hidden by his full goatee which showed signs of gray, and his receding hairline was obvious. The most noticeable features were his piercing blue eyes and thin, wide lips. On close inspection scarring on his right ear from the burns he had recently suffered were visible. The thirty-two year old wore his hat pinned up on the left side by a non-standard issue cockade to which was attached a pendant featuring the Palmetto tree, emblem of South Carolina.

135 Gregg experienced some embarrassment over the poor recruiting from his native state. This disappointing showing was due principally to "indifference to the service, arising from political causes" in South Carolina, as well as Carolinians' "general distaste for the regular service, a want of proper military ideas, & a preference for the volunteering system." Young men of his state had no doubt heard from friends already in service with Colonel Pierce Mason Butler's Palmetto Regiment, and potential recruits were hesitant to enlist "at the commencement of the sickly season, & at a time when engagements have been made for employment in agriculture during the summer." Major Gregg reported all of these concerns to the Adjutant General in Washington, concluding that "these causes, & others, all acting together, have rendered the recruiting service a task of peculiar difficulty" in South Carolina. Major Gregg assured Washington, though, that he and his junior officers were making every effort to recruit. In mid-July Gregg was finally able to dispatch the two North Carolina companies on the first leg of their transfer to Mexico. The South Carolina companies continued recruiting in Alabama and North Carolina with disappointing results. Gregg then sought, and received, permission to recruit from New York City and Philadelphia. By mid-September, as Major General Scott's troops were recovering from the battles of Contreras, Churubusco, and Chapultepec, and were at the gates of Mexico City,

remained until our embarkation the 16th Oct. The weather till the latter part of September was excessively wet – the wettest summer I think that I have ever known. This, together with my constant occupation in drilling the Troops from the commencement of September, prevented my using my gun while on Sullivan's Island. Indeed there would have been little to shoot, except a few Longbilled Curlews, a few Ground Doves, Minute Terns, Gulls & some few of the smaller waders. One Sunday not long before our embarkation[136] – I think it was the 10th of October, I walked with Peter Gaillard by the Back Beach to Truesdell's Oyster plantation near the N.E. end of the Island. We saw a Bald Eagle perched on the narrow summit of one of those abrupt & wild-looking Sand hills which have been tossed up by the winds in the interior of the Island, and I got quite near enough to have shot it if I had had a gun.

23 Oct. 1847: At Sea, in the Gulf Stream, South of Florida, a Falcon alighted on the Maintop-yard. I felt confident that it was the Falco Peregrinus. I was fearful of cutting the rigging with a cartridge, tho Capt. Williams told me to fire at the bird where it was – so had a rope shaken to frighten him, & as he flew, brought him down, but he fell in the water & was soon left far behind. This must have been fifty miles, as I think, from any of the Florida Keys, & a hundred or more from the coast of Cuba.

Gregg reported to the Adjutant General's office that he anticipated he and the South Carolina companies would be ready to sail for Mexico by the first of October. Letters Received by the Office of the Adjutant General, NARA.

136 Finally, on the 16th of October, Major Gregg reported that his recruiters had returned to Fort Moultrie from New York and Pennsylvania. He, the two South Carolina companies, and Company K of the Thirteenth Infantry, boarded a transport ship and on the 19th they set sail for Vera Cruz. Gregg's detachment from the Twelfth Infantry included 2nd Lieutenant (and acting Adjutant) Ornsby Blanding, 1st Lieutenant John J. Martin, 2nd Lieutenants Abner M. Perrin and John D. Otterson of Company A, and Captain Oliver P. Hamilton and 2nd Lieutenant Christopher R.P. Butler of Company D. The Thirteenth Infantry was officered by recently promoted Major Edward Manigault, acting Commissary Lieutenant Thom, and from Company K, Captain H.E.W. Clark, 1st Lieutenant R.S. Hayward, and 2nd Lieutenant E.J. Dummett. Among the noncommissioned officers, musicians, and privates there were eighty-seven men of Company E, 12th Infantry; ninety-five of Company A, 13th Infantry; seventy-five of Company K, 13th Infantry; and miscellaneous others, bringing the total to two hundred, sixty-four passengers. Major Gregg and his troops arrived in Mexico well after General Santa Anna had surrendered his army.

We had embarked in the fine ship Orphan, on the 16th of October, but not been able to get out of Charleston Harbor until the 19th. Then with fair winds we made a most favorable passage, reaching Vera Cruz[137] in eleven days. Soon after commencing the voyage, a pair of warblers were observed on board – continuing in the Ship for a day or two. They probably landed at Abaco when we were approaching the Hole in the Wall.

1 shot   1 Peregrine Falcon?

Sunday, October 24: The wind having become light, we were sailing more slowly than usual this afternoon, S.W. of the Tortugas, when a Booby approached the Ship, & in hopes of bringing it down on Deck, I fired, but only wounded it. After alighting in the water at some distance, it returned leg broken, and circled round the ship for some time. I attempted to bring it down on board, but in falling it missed the Stern-boat & was lost. This day, & the day before, saw a few Frigate Birds – and some other sea birds not known to me. On a Sand-bank near the Tortugas Light-House, there seemed to be a vast assemblage of Sea-fowl.

2 shots   1 Booby Gannet (Sula Fusca)

Mon. 25th. Becalmed to-day. An Egret (Ardea Alba) approached the Ship this morning, but tho apparently weary, was afraid to alight.

Tues. 26th. Renewed our Course with a fine breeze to-day. One or two small birds, warblers or Sparrows, approached the Ship; and a Booby or two & a few Sea-birds unknown to me were seen.

Thurs. 28th. A Great Heron seen to-day, or the day before, within about 40 miles of some of the Islands on the Campeche Banks.

---

137 Vera Cruz was the port of entry into Mexico for Major General Winfield Scott and his nearly 12,000-man army on the 9th of March 1847.

Fri, 29th. This morning, a Sparrow Hawk alighted in the rigging. I had him frightened, and after missing two shots on the wing, brought him down with a third, but he missed the side of the vessel, & fell into the water. I suppose this was 160 or 180 miles from land. In the afternoon, a Dove, very weary, alighted two or three times in the rigging, & went off. I took it at the time for the Carolina Turtle, tho I observed a difference, the tail being shorter & rounder. Afterwards, when I became acquainted with the Mexican Turtle (which I take for the "Texan Turtle Dove["] – Columba Trudeani – Audubon) I concluded that this bird belonged to that species. Three or four times within the last few days, a large Bird had been seen, which I took for a Gannet.

3 shots   1 Sparrow-hawk

We anchored in the harbor of Vera Cruz on the 30th Oct. The next day, Sunday, the 31st, we landed, & marched to the Beach near the little river Bergara where we encamped. One of the first birds I saw in Mexico was the Pelican – many of which frequent the harbor & the neighboring Coast. I had no opportunity of examining one in my hands, but I take them to be the "Brown Pelican – Pelecanus Fuscus." There was something strange to me in their first appearance, heightening the foreign aspect of everything around.

Not many fish were seen during our voyage. Occasionally the Flying Fish would be seen skimming over the waves. One fell on deck one day.

Our encampment on the Beach at Bergara, at the foot of the low, burning Sand-hills, was very uncomfortable. The water, whether obtained from the little stream, or by sinking shallow wells in the sand, was vile, & produced diarrhoea. A Norther drove a shower of dust before it, threatened to blow down the tents and to overflow the Camp. A land-wind rendered the heat suffocating, & brought swarms of flies. The roar of the surf made it difficult to drill on the only hard ground to be found, and the heat & sickness threw greater obstacles in the way. Unity of command was wanting among the many detachments of raw levies brought together. All were anxious to march into the Interior, and becoming unwell & out of humor myself, I suffered my gun, which had rusted in the Sea air, to be idle in its case, & never used it, altho there would have been an opportunity of shooting many new birds, of brilliant plumage.

I think it was about the 10th of November that vast flocks of Geese began to pass over Southward, often low enough to be shot. The flights continued for several days. I think there were both Canada Geese & Hutchins Geese, with one or more other kinds. Some individuals, tho not whole flocks, were white.

These I suppose were old Snow Geese. One afternoon I rode out with Lieut. Mumford a mile or so on the Jalapa road to try & shoot geese. He had a musket, loaded with Ball & Buckshot. I had only my dueling Pistols in my holsters, with balls. He missed one or two shots, I think. I did not fire, but ascertained the bad condition of my arms by snapping once.

Frigate Pelicans were often to be seen soaring on high; & Fish Hawks taking fish along the shore. One day I was surprised by the sight of a large dark looking bird, sailing overhead, with a broad patch of white on the wings. This I afterwards found was the Quebranthuesos – which I take to be the Caracara Eagle – abundant in the Interior.

On the 17th of November, I shifted my Camp to the grassy plain on the margin of the ponds to the South of Vera Cruz, where I joined the command of Lt. Col. Johnston, under whom I was to march to Mexico. About these ponds there might be good sport, but I did not shoot.

On the 27th of November in the afternoon, my Battalion commenced the march, moving as far as the Bergara, & encamping on the further side.

Sunday, the 28th, I marched about 12 miles, & encamped on the further side of the San Juan River, Lt. Col. Calhoun being encamped on this side. As we escaped with our wagons from the difficulties of the heavy sand over which the road runs for the first few miles, & emerged from the thickets of the Sand hills into the open country near Santa Fe, the view was charming – extending over undulating prairies, interspersed with thickets of Acacia or other thorny trees. Just beyond Santa Fe, I saw for the first time walking on the ground, a Quebrantahuesos – with which I was afterwards to become familiar. I had seen one on the wing before, as mentioned above. Here, too, a wild Goose was seen, alighted in the road. I dismounted, & going after it with my Pistols, fired several shots at it – three or four I think. At each shot, it only removed a short distance along the road before us. One or two musket shots were also fired at it by [John D.] Otterson, but it escaped all, & at last went off. This evening I first saw Parrots in Mexico – two, if not three, species. The change from a sickly & uncomfortable Camp to the march was exhilarating in its effect.

3 or 4 shots (Pistol)

Monday, the 29th I remained in Camp for Col. Johnston to overtake me.

Tues. 30th. We marched to Paso de Ovejas – 11 miles. I think it was near the place on the road, marked "Cuesta de la Calcra" this day, that I saw several large birds flying up a hollow, or watercourse, which I took for Wood Ibises. I had left my Mahogany gun-case at Vera Cruz, as unfit for roughing it on the road, & made Ned Glover carry my Gun, hung over his shoulders, on my Gray Mexican Pony. And during the halt at the San Juan, I had put my gun in order for shooting. So to-day, a large dark colored Hawk, sailing over, soon after I had seen the Ibises (or whatever they were) I brought it down. But it fell into a tangled thicket of all kinds of briars & spiky Mexican Plants, & Ned could not get it. I promised a reward to a Camp follower if he would get it & bring it after me, but I never heard any more of it. It was a Hawk that I do not think I had ever seen before, unless it might be the same that I saw in the Spring of 1845 at the junction of the Congaree & Wateree, & took for the Buteo Bachmanii.

1 shot

Thurs. 2 Dec. On the march from the Puente Nacional[138] to the Pla[y]a del Rio to-day, a cold rain commenced falling. I was at the head of my Battalion, at some distance from the other troops, when a fluttering of wings was heard in the woods on the road side which some of us at first took for Young Turkeys. Getting my gun out of its wooden case, I pursued, & firing at a single bird in a tree, brought it down. It was a very fine, Pheasant-like Bird, which I some time afterwards found goes by the name of "Chachalaca." I have been unable to identify it with any species mentioned in any of my books. It is mentioned

---

138 Nearly a year before Gregg's arrival in Mexico, Brigadier General Franklin Pierce and Colonel M.L. Bonham had led their troops in an attack by 500 Mexicans from breastworks above the National Bridge. In the face of an enfilading fire and a barricade blocking their route across the bridge, the future president saw that his artillery was useless. His only recourse was to "cross under the plunging fire of the enemy's escopetas." Ordering an advance, Colonel Bonham led the attack under a withering fire in which his horse was shot and Pierce received a ball "through the rim of [his] hat in very disagreeable proximity to [his] face." The Americans advanced over the barricades and in "less than ten minutes the enemy were in flight in every direction, and the American flag waved upon the high bluff which they had occupied." Milledge Luke Bonham Papers, SCL, UCS.

by Clavigero.[139] See his History of Mexico (Spanish translation), Vol. 1, p. 31. According to Col. M'Call, it is the "Penelope Poliocephala" of Wagler. See "Proceedings of Acad. Nat, Sci. – Phil" – June 1851, p. 222. See description in little Green Journal.

1 shot   1 Chachalaca (Penelope Poliocephala?)

Frid. 3. I think it was on the march to Encero to-day that I saw a long contest in the air between a Raven & a Quebrantahuesos. At first the Raven had the advantage, & kept uppermost, forcing his antagonist sometimes to alight on the ground. But after awhile, by manoeuvring & power of wing, the Quebrantahuesos rose above the Raven, & continued to worry him as long as I was in sight.

I did not fire my gun again on the march to Mexico. In most of the Country over which the road passes on the table-land of the interior. I think that from the scarcity of cover, trees, & water, game must be scarce. Our last day's march, from Ayotla to Mexico, was Monday, the 20th Dec. This day we saw countless Ducks of different kinds, in the water, on both sides of the road, connected with Lake Xochimilco & Lake Tezcuco.[140] On my return in June following, the places where these multitudes of Ducks had been swimming, had been left dry by the subsidence of the water.

While in the city of Mexico, from the 20th December 1847 to the 6th of March 1848, I did not shoot at all. From debilitating attacks of a kind of typhoid fever, I was for the greater part of the time too weak to undergo fatigue or exposure. But when our Regiment was ordered to Cuernavaca, I cleaned up my gun, hoping for some sport in that quarter, in which I was to be much disappointed by sickness. We marched Tuesday, the 7th of March, and arrived at Cuernavaca on the 10th.

─────────────

139 In addition to the study of the Spanish language Maxcy Gregg was able to obtain a copy of *The History of Mexico Collected from Spanish and Mexican Historians, From Manuscript, and Ancient Paintings of the Indians* by Francesco Saverio Clavigero so that he could read up on the history of Mexico and that country's natural environment. The author of the book, "the Abbe Clavigero," was a native of Vera Cruz, though of Spanish descent. He spent years studying the natural resources of Mexico and learning the language and traditions of its indigenous people. Clavigero, Francesco Saverio. *The History of Mexico Collected from Spanish and Mexican Historians, From Manuscript, and Ancient Paintings of the Indians* (Volume One). Philadelphia: Thomas Dobsun, publisher, 1817 (Reproduction by BiblioBazaar, no publication information), viii.

140 Lakes Xochimilco and Tezcuco were two of three lakes at Buena Vista which broke the approach to Mexico City. The third was Lake Chalcothe.

Thursday, March 16. Riding early in the morning with Lt. Col. Seymour two or three miles down the Acapulco road, I shot with a Ball from my Pistol, a Quebrantahuesos, which offered a tempting mark, perched on a thorny Tree by the roadside. Being only winged, I had a hard race to catch it. When caught, it offered none of the resistance which Hawks usually do, showing, as it seemed to me, a nature much more Vulturine than Falconine. See description in green-covered Journal.

1 shot (Pistol)   1 Quebrantahuesos (Polybeous Brasilinesis?)

Fri. 17. Rode with Bonham[141] & Seymour early in the morning, down the Acapulco road, taking my gun with me. Saw a rabbit, looking very much like our common rabbit, but could not get a shot. Saw also some of the Mexican Turtle Doves which I had noticed before as different from the Carolina Turtle, & killed one. Killed also a Flycatcher, which may have been the Muscicapa Crinita – but I could not satisfy myself about it. See Green Journal.

6 shots

          1 Mexican Turtle Dove (Columba Trudeani?)
          1 Flycatcher (of uncertain species)

Sun. 19. Rode with my gun early in the morning on the lower road to within a little way of the Hacienda of Atlacomulco. Came across a Covey of Mexican Partridges, but missed the only shot I got. Afterwards, killed two Carolina Turtles, for comparison with the Mexican bird killed two days before. Just as I had loaded after shooting the Doves, a Fox, or an animal much like one, jumped a stone fence, & ran along the edge of a field I was in. I fired both barrels at him, with small shot, but apparently missed.

5 shots   2 Carolina Turtle Doves

---

141 Milledge Luke Bonham (1813-1890) graduated from South Carolina College with second honors in 1834 and was admitted to the South Carolina bar in 1837, two years before Maxcy Gregg. He was elected to the South Carolina House of Representatives where he served from 1840 to 1844. In March of 1847 Bonham was commissioned lieutenant colonel of the Twelfth Infantry, but was promptly promoted to colonel when Louis D. Wilson of North Carolina declined the command position.

Sunday, March 26th. Returning in the afternoon with a party of Officers from a visit to the Hacienda of Altacomulco, I came across a Covey of Mexican Partridges (Codornizes) at the same place as mentioned above, & killed one. See particulars & description in Green Journal.

2 shots   1 Mexican Partridge (or rather Quail) - Ortyz Californica?

Saturday, April 1. Rode with a large party of Officers to the old extinct Volcano of "La Herradiera" taking my gun with me, but found no game.

Sun. Ap. 2. Rode in the afternoon with Bonham & Col. Margucilio, to see some beautiful waterfalls. On our return, I stopped to shoot at some Nighthawks, to satisfy myself of the species. Satisfied that it is the same bird with that of the United States. They are common – tho not numerous – at Cuernavaca.

5 shots   1 Nighthawk

Sun. Ap. 23 (or perhaps the 16th). Riding out in the morning, on the Altacomulco road, missed a Quebrantahuesos with a Pistol loaded with Ball.

1 shot (Pistol)

Thurs. 4 [May]. Riding in the morning in the Potrero of Acapanzingo with Capt. Mower & Lt. Coleman discovered three Deer across a deep Bananca, & dismounting, pursued them a long way with my Pistols. The heat and fatigue were excessive – but fortunately produced a favorable effect, in checking a Dysentery under which I had been suffering for many weeks. The Deer appeared to me the same as the Common American Deer – Cervus Virginianus.

Tues. May 9. Set off for the City of Mexico,[142] to recruit my health, accompanied by a small escort, & rode to the village of Ajusco. I saw a Chachalaca run across the road, some distance this side of the Cruz del Marques – but could not get a shot. Saw several Robins, as I had seen several in crossing the same Sierra before. Saw also, for the first time in Mexico, our Bluebird, or a bird very much like it – & several Alpine Larks. Many of the latter I saw the next day & afterwards, in the "Potreros" or Pastures round the city of Mexico. But perhaps these Larks may be the "Western Shore Lark" "Alauda Rufa" described in Audubon's 7th vol. of Na. Birds, Miniature Edition.

Wed. May 10. Rode to Mexico this forenoon. In descending the mountains, a Chachalaca ran across the road before me. I dismounted from Chester, & missed a disadvantageous shot. In riding over the valley to-day, I saw & heard amongst other numerous small birds the Maryland Yellowthroat.

1 shot

---

142 By the time Gregg reached Mexico City the Mexican army had surrendered and General Scott had established an American Army of Occupation. A number of officers established an informal club, a "drinking and dining society," which became known as the Aztec Club. The first officers elected included John Quitman, President, and Captain John B. Magruder, Second Vice President. A constitution was adopted along with a $20 membership fee. Maxcy Gregg was quick to join the club, whose membership read like a Who's Who of the Civil War, and included Pierre Gustave Toutant Beauregard, Barnard E. Bee, Milledge Luke Bonham, Jefferson Davis, Richard S. Ewell, Adley H. Gladden, Ulysses S. Grant, Joseph Hooker, Benjamin Huger, Joseph E. Johnston, Phillip Kearny, Robert E. Lee, James Longstreet, George B. McClellan, Samuel McGowan, George G. Meade, Roswell S. Ripley, Winfield Scott, Philip H. Sheridan, and William T. Sherman. Pryor, Elizabeth Brown. *Reading the Man: A Portrait of Robert E. Lee Through His Private Letters*. New York: Penguin Books, 2007, 171.

While at Cuernavaca, amongst other Birds, I noticed the following:

1. Wax Birds – tho not during the latter part of my stay.

2. Catesby's Razor billed Blackbird – common also near Vera Cruz.

3. A species of Oriole, very brilliant, black & yellow, improperly called by the Mexicans "Calandria" common also about Vera Cruz.

4. The Barn Swallow – very common, as also about the City of Mexico.

5. A bird very much like the Chimney Swallow, but of much greater size – in the habit of flying high up – seen also elsewhere in Mexico.

6. Sparrow hawk.

7. Red bird.

8. Blue Grosbeak – pretty common.

9. The Large, dark colored white throated Wren, with a shrill voice, which climbs about the walls of houses – common also in the City of Mexico.

10. Raven – very common.

11. Carion Crow – most abundant.

12. Turkey Buzzard – rather scarce.

Another bird which I often noticed near the City of Mexico, was a kind of sparrow, nearly the size & color of the Catbird, which it greatly resembles at a little distance.

We commenced our march from the City of Mexico, Saturday, 3 June, and were overtaken by the rainy season on the 6th when we arrived at Puebla.[143] After that, we had rain every day until we reached Jalapa, the 12th.

Mon. June 5. Being in advance of the Column, between San Martin & our last halting place at Rio Frio, I saw a Chachalaca running, in the fields, and fired both barrels, the second loaded with buckshot, but missed. The Bird would not fly.

2 shots

---

143 Puebla, nearly 186 miles northwest of Vera Cruz and 93 miles southeast of Mexico City, was the second largest city in Mexico, with a population of around 80,000.

Thurs. 15. We remained in Camp on the Rio Zedeno, near Jalapa, for eight or nine days. Some fine weather, tho many showers of rain during the latter part of the time. This morning, I set out on horseback, with my gun, to visit the Hill of Macultapec, between our Camp & the Town. I found the stone walls very much in my way, in getting across the fields, & had to make my man Porter pull down three or four. One of these was at the end of a long lane, which stopped without outlet in the middle of a field – and for pulling this down, I was soundly rated by an old woman who came out after me. Saw no game. Had a grand view from Macultepec, being able to make out the line of breakers as far as Vera Cruz. The haze did not allow me to distinguish the Town or Shipping.

Sat. June 17. Walked with my gun up the River Zedeno in the morning, but found no game. The Forest growth looked less strange to me in its general character, here, than either on the coast or in the Interior. I do not now remember any of the Trees of the United States as occurring in Mexico, except the Sweet Gum & the Sycamore, seen here, and the Balsam Pine (if my eye did not deceive me) at the Rio Frio. Note: 12 Feb. 1854. The Grand Cypresses at the foot at Chapultapec, are evergreen. I am not quite sure whether they are the same as our Cypress.

From our Camp on the Zedeno, we moved down to Encero, where for five or six days we had a very wet time of it. Our new Camp, from the Brow of the Hill, overlooked Santa Anna's Country House – between the Camp & the House, lies an artificial Pond. In this Pond was a flock of some small species of wild Duck. I could not satisfy myself as to the species. I think the birds were an old pair with their young. Here also I saw a Curious Wader, about the size of a Snipe or Woodcock, but longer & more slender – purple colored, & remarkable for the habit of stretching its wings perpendicularly over its back on alighting & displaying a conspicuous patch of yellow in them. I had seen the same bird about the Pond South of Vera Cruz, in November preceding.

Tues. 27. Resumed the march for the Coast this morning. In passing over the extensive grassy slope this side of Encero, I saw a pair of birds fly up which I took for the Virginia Partridge – if I was not mistaken, it was the only time the bird was seen by me in Mexico. Encamped at Plan del Rio.

Wed. 28. Marched to the National Bridge. A few miles this side of Plan del Rio, I killed a Troupial, which I should take for the Common Troupial (Icterus Vulgaris, Audubon, vol. vii, p. 357) were it not that Audubon describes that bird as having the head black; while according to my notes (see little blue journal, or "Register 1848") the head was orange. The extent of wing also given by Audubon, is much less than in my bird. Many of the pendulous nests of this bird, two feet long, were seen on the road in this part of the Tierra Caliente.

l shot   1 Troupial (Icterus Vulgaris?)

Arriving at the National Bridge in the heat of the day, I took a fever; getting better in the afternoon, I found my horse Chester was taken violently ill. He had been poor & out of condition for some months. His attack now may have been of Bots. He appeared in excessive pain – lay down – staggered wildly about – nothing could be done for him, and before dark, he was lying in his last struggle as I supposed, in Santa Anna's yard. But marching long before light the next morning, I found that tho lying in the same spot, he was still breathing. So I asked a Quartermaster whom I succeeded in rousing from his sleep – Captain _____ to look after him, and left the poor fellow to his fate. I was supplied with a Mexican Pony for the remainder of the march, by Parker, a Contractor attached to the Army.

Thurs. June 29. Marched to the River San Juan. At Paso de Ovejas, where we arrived early in the morning, some flocks of small Parrots, or Parakeets, were screaming & darting about. I killed three of these. (I think they were eating mulberries, but whether the tree was the same as our Red Mulberry, I cannot tell – perhaps it was a European Black Mulberry.) I tried to-day to get a chance to kill some of the larger Parrots, of which I think there are two species seen by me, if not more – but I did not succeed. I killed also, while halting at Paso de Ovejas, a pair of Mexican Ground Doves or "Tortolitas" (I think I have also heard the name of "Coco" given to them) but I am not satisfied whether they are a different species from our Ground Dove or not. I am rather inclined to think they are – and that besides the Mexican bird, so common throughout the Country, I have seen near the Coast our own bird. Within a few miles of the San Juan I killed a Hawk, which puzzles me as much as the little Doves. I cannot tell whether it was the Red-shouldered, or a species somewhat smaller, & slightly different. See Descriptions of the three preceding Birds in little blue Journal.

4 shots   3 Little Parrots (Psittacus _____)
           2 Mexican Ground Doves (Columba _____)
           1 Red-shouldered Hawk?

From our Camp on the San Juan, we marched about midnight, & arrived on the Beach at Bergara soon after Sunrise. In passing thro the Sandhills this side of Santa Fe, before day, we perceived from some distance a very strong odor, which Bonham pronounced that of a Pole-Cat. On the Beach at Bergara, the heat became excessive very soon after Sunrise, and after moving about for a while, laying off the Camp of Bonham's Brigade,[144] I was attacked with a fever, became very faint, and had to lie down under the shade of a wagon.

We remained on the Beach from the 30th of June until the 6th of July. The heat and the danger of fever compelled me to spend nearly the whole of the day under my Tent, with the Wall looped up for the circulation of air – and I never used my gun.

On the 6th day of July the last Detachment of our Regiment, under Lt. Col. Seymour, embarked; and that night, Bonham, Linn & myself spent in Vera Cruz. The next morning, July 7th, we embarked on the Steamer James L. Day,[145] which carried some troops of the old line – the 3rd Infantry, I think. We made the passage to New Orleans in four days, arriving on the 11th. We were not discharged from service until the 25th having been obliged to wait for the arrival of our Regiment in Sailing Vessels, and until all the Muster-rolls were completed, & the Companies mustered out of service. A part of this time I passed at Carrollton, near which the Regiment was encamped, and where I had another slight brush of fever.

---

144 Bonham's Brigade (the brigade of Brigadier General Franklin Pierce until he returned to the United States after the surrender of Santa Anna) was part of the 3rd Division commanded by Major General Gideon J. Pillow. The brigade included the 9th, 15th, and 12th Infantry Regiments.

145 The *James L. Day*, under various captains, made several trips in 1846, 1847, and 1848 to and from Vera Cruz transporting American troops.

On the 26th of July, I left New Orleans and arrived at Mobile early the next morning in a Steamer. Here, by a Steam-boat trick, we were retained for a day, & Bonham overtook the rest of our party. Two days voyage by a Steamboat took us to Montgomery, Bonham stopping on the way. I passed one night in Montgomery – took the railroad for West Point the next morning, 31st July – had a disagreeable night's ride by Stage to Griffin, on one of the Georgia railroads – and sleeping the next night at Augusta, arrived at home on Wednesday, the 3d of August, after an absence of a year and twenty-three days.[146]

It was full time to leave New Orleans when I did, as cases of yellow fever were fast breaking out. In Vera Cruz, too, we were under the impression that the Vomito[147] was just beginning to prevail when we came through; tho I have since understood that there had in reality been much of it in the Town for months before, but from a well-founded policy, as little as possible had been said about it.

---

146 Among those who gave their lives in the Mexican War was Gregg's friend, Lieutenant Colonel James P. Dickenson who was wounded in the ankle during the battle of Churubusco on the 20th of August 1847. Although in itself not a life-threatening wound, infection set in and "his impatient spirit took its flight." Dickenson's body was temporarily buried near Mexico City until January of 1848 when it was exhumed, placed in a lead coffin, and transported home. Funeral services were held at a Dickinson Family cemetery near Camden on the 22nd of January 1848. Claiborne, J.F.H. *Life and Correspondence of John A. Quitman, Major-General, U.S.A., and Governor of the State of Mississippi* (Volume II). New York: Harper & Brothers, 1860 (Reproduction by Dalton House/ Forgotten Books, London, 2015), 316.

147 Yellow fever was referred to by the Mexicans as *vómito* or *vómito negro*. Its symptoms included "excruciating headaches, high fever, constipation, pain in the joints, and vomiting of blood from internal bleeding." Meyer, Jack Allen. *South Carolina in the Mexican War: A History of the Palmetto Regiment of Volunteers 1846-1917*. Columbia: The South Carolina Department of Archives and History, 1996, 47n.

"Maxcy Gregg", Carte-de-Visite (full-length portrait), circa Late 19th Century, Ed McCrady Military Papers from the collections of the South Carolina Historical Society.

September 1848 - March 1849: Rockwood

Thurs. 14 Sept. 1848.[148] Rode to Granby in the evening, with R.P. Mayrant, to look for Ducks coming on. Saw none. I did not shoot. Weather this Fall very dry.

Mon. [November] 6 [1848]. Rode out in the afternoon, & at Fisher's Pond, overtook Mayrant, who had killed one Duck and winged two others, but found himself too unwieldy, from his fat,[149] to go out after them in the little batteau. This I navigated with some difficulty through the snags, & enabled Mayrant to kill one of the wounded Ducks in the Southern edge of the Pond. The Dead bird I got from the shallow on the opposite side. The other wounded one escaped. They were, I think, Widgeon. We rode on to Granby – several Summer Ducks passed down the river, at which Mayrant made some long shots. One that he fired at appeared to fall, far down the Stream and in the Dusk. I made a trip after it in a canoe, without success.

1 shot

Tues. Nov. 7. Rode early in the morning with Mr. Hassell in his Buggy to his farm, taking Bruno with us. A cold & bright day, which we spent till the latter part of the afternoon, in rambling about within a moderate compass. Mr. H.

---

148 After his return from serving in the Mexican War Maxcy Gregg often used the military system of writing the date – day/month/year.

149 Although he was overweight and fifty-two years old in 1861, Robert P. Mayrant enlisted as a private in Colonel Maxcy Gregg's six-month regiment of volunteers. When the regiment was reorganized in August of that year after its term of service had expired, Private Mayrant re-enlisted. In December of that year, however, as the seriousness of the war was becoming evident and physical stamina was required of all troops, Mayrant was discharged from the Confederate States Army due to "his age and excessive obesity." Compiled Service Record, Robert P. Mayrant, NARA.

killed three Partridges at a shot, upon the rising of the only Covey that we found. Also, a Rabbit, bearing on its side a vast dark-colored Larva (or wolf). Bruno discovered symptoms of old age, becoming very tired.

6 shots

By Me, 1 Robin   By B.J. Von H.,   3 Partridges
                                      1 Dove
                                      2 Redwing Blackbirds
                                      1 Rabbit

Sat. 25. Walked in the evening to Everett's Pond, carrying one of my long Pistols in a sling. I had come across a Covey of Partridges a few evenings before, by the water's edge, on the south side, but did not find them again. Firing two shots at a mark, 15 yards off, found the pellets struck very scattering. Perhaps the load of powder was too heavy.

Sun. Nov. 26. Rode to Rockwood towards the middle of the day, carrying a Pistol. Hart was out Calf-hunting. After his return, & after dinner, I walked with him, over to the Long Branch fields. I fired one shot at a Rusty Blackbird, with my Pistol, & tore feathers. Afterwards missed some Doves, a long shot, with Hart's gun. Hart killed a Dove & a Partridge – at the latter of which I should have had a fair shot, sitting on a fence rail, but after springing the trigger, the Pistol went off without my pulling it, as it had done before – something being out of order about the trigger spring.

2 shots   By me,   nothing   By Hart,   1 Dove
                                          1 Partridge

Sun. Dec. 3. Rode to Rockwood in the morning, and walked with Hart to Long Branch, carrying his Double Gun, only one barrel of which was in serviceable order. He carried my little single-barreled shot-gun. A sunny day – the weather becoming mild, after some severe cold. I killed a Sparrow-hawk in the Long Branch field – then having spent some time in driving some Cattle out of it, we went on to Free Mary's, where I got first two Doves at a shot, & then another. As we were about leaving this field, we flushed some Partridges, which we followed in the woods for some time unsuccessfully. As we came back, our attention was attracted by a Congregation of little Birds, mostly Bluebirds, but including several small warblers of other species, darting about a particular spot, & chattering vociferously. Observing closely, we saw that they were descending by reliefs to a small Dogwood Tree, & eating the berries which were on it. They seemed to be in a great frolic, which continued for some time.

6 shots   By me,   3 Doves   By Hart,   nothing

1 Sparrowhawk

Sun. Dec. 31. Having ridden out to Rockwood, walked to the Long Branch field with Hart. The children,[150] attended by several little negroes, accompanying us as usual. I missed one shot at a Sparrow, with my little single-barrel. Hart killed two white-throated Sparrow for Mary, whose health is bad.

1 shot   By me, nothing

By Hart,   2 White-throated Sparrows

Sun. [January] 14 [1849]. Drove out to Rockwood with my mother in the morning. Hart & I took a short walk, to the Longbranch Field, but did not fire a shot. Children following part of the way, with little negroes, as usual.

This winter has been mostly very warm, summer weather prevailing through the greater part of December. There were 10 or 12 days of cold weather in the beginning of this month, on one of which there fell a snow, but not enough to cover the whole of the ground. To-day, turning Summer weather again.

---

150 In 1848 the children of Hart and Mary Manning Maxcy included four year old Martha, two year old Jonathan, and one year old Ashley. A fourth child, Susan, was born in 1848 or 1849.

Tues. [February] 6. Having discovered a few evenings before, a roosting place of a Covey of Partridges on the Bank of the Canal just below Taylor's Bridges, walked down there this evening with Bruno, but could not find the Birds. On the way back, thro Brown's Field, pursued for some time a very large flock of Larks, but very wild, missing 3 shots.

Sun. 18. A very cold day – some flakes of snow fell in the morning. Walked as far as Hampton's Burnt Mill, carrying one of my Duelling Pistols in a sling. Missed a shot at a Goldfinch at Long Branch, – afterwards killed a Yellowhammer by the rail road near Hampton's Pond. Blistered my heels with my old Bootees, a heavy pair which I had taken with me to Mexico – have since given them to Peter.

The Robins have made their appearance about town within the last week, & are now abundant – tho much harassed.

Monday morning, the 19th the Thermometer out doors fell to 15 degrees – the greatest cold this winter.

2 shots   1 Yellowhammer

Sat. Feb. 24. Walked with a Pistol down the Canal, as far as Taylor's Bridge.

Thurs. [March] 1. Walked in the evening down to the Brickyard, where I made a few pretty shots on the wing, bringing down on Dove particularly, at the distance as I think of 45 yards, when I had to fire at a glimpse through the opening between two Trees. Shot a Rabbit in the bed of the Canal below the Brick Bridge, which behaved curiously. It was wounded in the back of the head, and lower part of the back, and seemed to be at the same time partially palsied, and, tho not touched in the eyes, blinded – floundering round in short circles in the mud when I attempted to secure it with a stick, & hiding in the grass & weeds. At last it came out by me on dry land, & a very slight blow despatched it. Gave the rabbit to a little son of O.Z. Bates, who came along with his Father.

Bates had a red horse taken in a Gill net in the river in which he said he had found also the remains of a large shad, & Cat-fish, mostly devoured, probably by an Otter.

9 shots

1 Dove	1 Yellowhammer
2 Robins	1 Rabbit

Sat. March 3. Walked in the evening over some of my old school-boy shooting grounds, & to the Brickyard and the River. My first shot was in Lark field, at a Lark on the wing, which I brought down at a very long distance. Afterwards, I missed some long shots at Doves. Finally, killed, with a cartridge, a Cat Squirrel, in the top of a slender tree some distance below the Brickyard. Weather now warm – evening very smoky, hazy & dark. This whole winter has been remarkable for frequent & sudden changes of weather – most of the weather has been warm, but with many intervals of cold, felt the more severely from their short continuance.

8 shots

1 Lark
1 Cat Squirrel

Mon. March 19. Walked in the evening to the Brickyard. A flock of Doves now frequents the grounds in that neighborhood, feeding I think on grass seed. Where the Yellowhammer Trees used to stand, by creeping in the gulley through which the Stream now runs, I got within 20 yards of this flock, feeding on the ground, & so thick that I expected to do great execution – but I only killed three, & did not use my second barrel. Then, brought down a Yellowhammer, flying, by the Spreading Sweet Gum close by. Afterwards, by crawling in the little Ditch between the Grave-yard and Lark Field, I got another shot, at a greater distance – tore great quantities of feathers, having loaded with a cartridge of No. 7 shot, but got only two Doves, both of which flew off to some distance, and one required a second shot to dispatch it. Found a single Snipe at the Brickyard, & missed two shots. Put up also a Covey of Partridges in the Brickyard, below the Causeway, & pursued them across the Canal unsuccessfully. Killed a Rabbit near Cow-drown Hole, while searching for the Partridges. Had no Dog with me – Bruno's temper is so savage now in his old age, that I am always rather fearful of his doing some mischief. The weather for the last week has been quite warm, the leaves coming out rapidly. The Robins seem to have disappeared in this warm weather.

13 shots

     5 Doves

     1 Yellowhammer

     1 Rabbit

Fri., Mar. 23. Rode in the afternoon to Granby. In passing Lark Field, saw a flock of Doves feeding as usual of late on the ground. Crawled up on the West side, & got a long shot, but only tore feathers. So gave up the pursuit. At the more easterly of the Granby Marshes, Bruno put up two Pectoral Sandpipers, which at the time I mistook for Snipes, tho with some doubt on the subject. (The same mistake had happened to me some years before, on finding some Pectoral Sandpipers in some of the little marshes near Cayce's house.) Afterwards, I saw the Birds again on the ground – they had returned without my perceiving it. Fired at them – both flew off. One came down dead at a little distance. I thought the other came down also in the direction of the Larger Marsh, but could not find it. The Bird I brought home with me differed in one particular from Audubon's description – the second primarily being almost as long as the first, instead of a great deal shorter. River quite high now.

5 shots   1 Pectoral Sandpiper

Besides the unseasonable warmth of the Weather for most of this winter, there has been an excessive drought, commencing last Summer. The water in my Father's well is now lower, I believe, & muddier, than even after the dry summer & fall of 1839, when about January following, it almost failed. Reed's spring is also much reduced in the volume of water.

SUMMARY FROM SEPTEMBER 1848 TO MARCH 1849

Month	Sep.	Nov.	Dec.	Jan.	Feb.	March	Total
Times out	1	4	2	1	3	4	15
Shots fired	0	9	7	0	5	35	56
Sparrowhawk			1				1
Robin		1				2	3
Lark						1	1
Yellowhammer					1	2	3
Dove			3			6	9
Pectoral Sandpiper						1	1
Cat Squirrel						1	1
Rabbit						2	2

8 Species
Individuals, 21

Purple Martin from *Birds of America* (1827) by John James Audubon

April 1849 - November 1854:
The Loss of Hunting Companions and Uncle Maxcy

Sun. 1 Ap. 1849. Returning on horse-back from Winnsboro Court to-day, I carried a Pistol in a sling under my Coat; but met with nothing to shoot on the road. Stopped & dined at Rockwood.   On Sunday, the 15th while I was at Sumterville,[151] attending Court, a Snow fell, to the depth of two or three inches on the roofs of houses & other places where it was not melted. The appearance of the young foliage of the Trees, covered with Snow, was very singular. The young leaves through the woods were mostly scorched or killed, either by the snow, or more probably by two or three hard frosts which followed it. The Upland willows, scrubs, & Post Oaks, which I thought more hardy, suffered particularly. The Persimmons suffered most, having all their leaves blackened & killed. Before the Snow, the weather had begun to be oppressively warm.

While attending Court at Camden, the first week in this month, I discovered a Hawk's Nest on a pine Tree in the swamp near the Grave yard at the Southern extremity of the Town. I saw the Bird several times, & frightened it from the nest where it was setting. I took it for the Red-shoulder, in the plumage of the Winter Hawk – but I am not sure but it may have been the Red-tail.

Thurs. 15 Nov. 1849. Walked in the evening to the Grave yard, to try one of my Duelling Pistols with the cartridges which I got Geareley to import. Their execution at 25 yards was very irregular and unsatisfactory. I'd not fire at anything but a mark. Turning to come home, in the Dusk, I heard the note of a bird which I did not recognize among some Fields. It was too dark to see it. I supposed it to be some other kind of Plover.

---

151 The town of Sumterville became 'Sumter' in 1855.

Fri. 16. Walked with my Gun in the evening, after the bird which had excited my curiosity the day before. Found, in the neighborhood of a flock of Kildees, & killed a Golden Plover, which I took for my bird. It had lost a leg, by some old hurt; half way between the foot & knee – & was quite poor, & lousy. Meeting afterwards with Glaze, the Fisherman, who had killed three Summer Ducks on the River, he told me he had shot at the same one-legged bird & torn feathers, on his way out; that he saw some others at the same time amongst the Kildees; that there had been a great many in the old fields a few weeks since; and that they came, more or less, every fall. He called them "Chewinkers" & spoke of others seen in company with them, larger, & some with long bills, like Snipes. These Long-billed birds, however, he did not suppose to be of a different species. He spoke also something about Curlews. On the whole, I suspected him of some invention & amplification, having so rarely seen the Golden Plover myself, & never having killed any but those four which I got 30 Nov 1838. He spoke of having, once, together with Chauncey Hall, killed 20 or 30. Tho I suppose it likely he may confound the Bartram Snipe, & possibly some other bird, with this, under the mane of "Chewinker." I thought that "Chewicker" was a name of the Kildee.

1 shot   1 Golden Plover (Charad. Pluv. or Marmoratus)

Tues. Nov. 20. Walked in the evening, with my Gun over the old fields from the neighborhood of the Grave yard to Upper Boundary Street[152] in search of Golden Plovers, but found none. I had been in the middle of the day over a portion of the same ground, trying my Rifled Pistol at a mark on Kinsler's high fence, without seeing any of these Birds. Just before going out this evening, I killed with my Blunderbuss, charged expressly for the purpose, a large Yellow Cat, formerly wounded by me. This makes the sixth Cat that I have shot in the garden since September, including two Kittens, besides wounding a large Grey Cat, a Stranger, the other day. The Cats had become such an annoyance from the number frequenting the garden, that it was necessary, greatly to Leah's[153] displeasure, to thin them off.

---

152 Upper Boundary Street became Elmwood Avenue around 1872.

153 Leah, Peter's wife, was enslaved to James Gregg from as early as early as 1833. She was around 52 years old in 1850.

Wed. 21. Walked in the evening to Fisher's Pond, near which Mayrant tells me he has sometimes seen Golden Plovers. Did not find any. Then to Robin Marsh. While I was sitting down in the South East Corner of the Railroad Lot, a little after Sunset, a Mottled Owl alit on a low branch of a pine sapling near me, which I killed.

1 shot   1 Little Screech Owl (in adult plumage)

Thurs. Nov. 22. Walked in the evening with my Gun as far as Robin-Marsh.

Thurs. [December] 6. Walked in the evening to Robin Marsh, taking my Gun as a pretext for strolling about there, but fired no shot.

Sun. Feb. 10, 1850. Walked in the evening, thro the Farm, taking Ranger & Blanco with me, & having my longest rifle Pistol slung under my coat. There were a good many Crows about the stacks of oats, which flew into the woods as I past. Getting a rest on a Hickory bush, I brought one down from the top of an oak, at a distance of about 40 yards (allowing for the height of his perch). I had a very fair aim, and do not wish to regard it as a chance shot, but I doubt whether I could do it again. *This Crow was one-eyed – the pupil & Iris of the other having become white & hard from some accident or disease.

I had intended to resume fully the use of my gun this winter, but another pursuit occupying from the latter part of November, very much of my time, & other circumstances, amongst them, unfavorable weather, have prevented it. The winter has generally been quite warm, with a great deal of rain. The severest weather has been within the last week, the Thermometer falling for four mornings to 26, 22 & as low as 18 Degrees. It is now mild again. One cause of my not shooting more has been Granby's stiffness in the knees, incapacitating him for a gallop.

Notwithstanding the mildness of the winter, the Robins came into the Town early, first appearing about the 23d of Dec. It seems to me that the same was the case in the very warm winter of 1827-1828.

Mr. Hassell, having a Puppy given to him by John Singleton, which was banished from the yard by Mrs. H. for killing poultry, gave him to me. He was sent over to me the 22nd Jan., being then 4 or 5 months old. His former name, Fun, given to him by the School-girls, I discarded, rechristening him Blanco. He has the appearance of a Setter, tho I do not know whether he is full blooded. He looks something like my old Fan.

Bruno, about the beginning of last October, had fallen into a very low state of health, becoming very poor, & so weak that taking him out to walk, he could barely follow me, & I had to lift him over all fences. He was often to be seen grazing the ground, & eating the dirt. There was a strong suspicion that he was starved, altho I could hardly believe either that Leah would have taken that mode of revenging the death of the Cats, or that she could have prevented him from getting enough to eat among the other Dogs. I fed him well – he immediately improved, & gradually recovered his flesh & strength – altho his strength, & especially his activity, are now very much impaired by old age.

1 shot (with Rifle Pistol)   1 Crow

Thursday, February. A cold day, following several others. Walked out in the morning, accompanied by Ranger & Blanco, & taking a Rifle Pistol. Went to Everett's & the Wetweather Ponds. Missed five shots, the last at a Crow; the others at a Dove, Redheaded woodpecker, & Robin.

Fri. 23 Aug. 1850. About 3 o'clock in the afternoon, being informed by Dennis that a bird which he called a Crane had lit on an India Tree by the Woodhouse, went out with my gun & shot it. Found it to be a White Ibis, in the plumage described by Audubon as that succeeding the first moult, brown above & white beneath. Dennis said it had lit there but a few minutes before. The negroes were all collected in the yard, looking at it, but it seemed quite undisturbed. I did not discover any indication of sickness or accidental hurt causing its unusual visit.

1 shot   1 White Ibis

This Summer, in which I scarcely touched my gun, I lost my old Companion Bruno. He died about the 29 May, two days after I had left home for the first meeting of the Southern Convention of Nashville.[154] I had first noticed the decline of his strength in a day's shooting with Mr. Hassell at his place, 7 Nov. 1848. He recovered for a while from the extreme weakness into which he fell in the Autumn of 1849, but the heavy weight of old age was on him, and unexpectedly he was one day found dead in his retreat, either under the house or under the kitchen.

Lara also fell into a state of decrepitude, & was found dead on the 7 August.

In the afternoon of Friday, 23 Aug., there came a great rain, succeeding a drought of ten days. Rocky Branch rose & carried away my Father's bridge at Turkey Point. A great Freshet in the Rivers followed. Broad River, at the Railroad Bridge, 28 miles above Columbia, was within 18 inches of the Great May Freshet of 1840. At the Columbia Bridge the difference was greater – 4 or 5 feet. Duration of Freshet short.

In the afternoon of Saturday, 24 Aug., there came an outrageous storm,[155] which made great havock among the trees in Columbia, especially the old India Trees. There was some rain, but a great deal more wind – at first, I think, from the South, but when it did the mischief, it was from the West. It reached the height of its fury about 8 o'clock P.M. after which it moderated. Five of our India Trees in the Street & yard were blown up by the roots. Three of the Spanish Mulberries were blown down; four other India Trees much broken. Many

---

154 Maxcy Gregg was a delegate from Richland District representing South Carolina at the Southern Congress Convention held at Nashville, Tennessee, June 3-11, 1850. Other South Carolina delegates included R.F.W. Allston, James Chesnut, Jr., Langdon Cheves, James H. Hammond, David F. Jamison, Francis W. Pickens, and Robert Barnwell Rhett. The Nashville Convention was attended by a total of 176 delegates from nine southern states. Gregg was among those secessionists who were willing for South Carolina to leave the Union on her own, but the extremists from Georgia and South Carolina who voted for immediate secession were overruled by the more moderate cooperationist faction which wanted to wait for other states to join the exodus. Little was accomplished at the Convention except for the decision to meet again in Nashville in November where nearly fifty delegates attended, representing seven Southern states. Maxcy Gregg was among the full slate of sixteen delegates from South Carolina. The delegates failed to win support for secession, but passed a resolution affirming the constitutionality of a state to secede. The second Convention also denounced the Compromise of 1850.

155 This hurricane in August of 1850, which lasted nearly twelve hours, combined heavy rain, wind, thunder and lightning and resulted in a great deal of damage to trees and corn crops throughout the state. Rivers and creeks rose to unprecedented levels, flooding lowlands and washing away bridges.

other of the larger Trees – Mulberries & Cherries – were shaken, & more or less loosened in the ground. A new Hay-shed of my Father, at Turkey Point, was blown down. Our fence was broken in several places by the falling Trees; the two India Trees near the corner falling over on the fence by my gate. From the newspapers, it appears that the storm was felt at Charleston, tho not so violent there. It is described as very violent at Raleigh, N.C., and at Montgomery, Al. The wind is generally represented as commencing from the eastward (on the 23d) and ending West.

On the 15th of June, on my journey back from Nashville, I saw, at a Country House in the valley of Battle Creek, Tennessee, a Sand Hill Crane – in the brown plumage. It had been wing-broken, & went about the yard tame.

Mon. 21 Oct. 1850. Walked in the afternoon over the old fields towards the river, looking for Golden Plovers, but found none. Went to Young's Mill, where I fell in with Robert Gibbes, waiting for Ducks. Staid a while & saw a few Ducks, mostly Teal, I think – but none came within shot. Then down to the Brickyard & home. A light frost fell this morning, the first of the season, tho I did not see it myself.

1 shot   1 Kildee

16 Dec. 1850. My excellent old Horse Granby, died. Supposed cause, Bots.[156] He was probably 20 years of age. I had had him since the 24th of July 1837.

Sunday, 9 March 1851. On one of my walks, discovered the nest of a pair of Red-shouldered Hawks, on a tall Pine near the Western end of Everett's Pond.

---

156 Bots is a disease of the digestive system of horses and other mammals caused by the infestation of botfly larvae in the stomach.

Sunday, 16 March. Visited the place again, and found one of the birds sitting very closely on the nest.

Two or three more visits were made up to 8 or 10 April, and an old bird always seen with my glass, sitting close on the nest.

15 April 1851. A Pointer Puppy, apparently 3 or 4 weeks old, was given to me by Paul Chappell. Contrary to my request & expectation, it was a bitch. Named her Jezebel – and afterwards gave her to Jonathan.

Sunday, 27 Ap. Walking out in the morning, found that there were young in the nest. The old Bird, getting a glimpse of me as she was about to make a second visit to the nest with some food in her beak, turned off, & would not go to the nest for an hour & a half, during which time I remained as well concealed as I could in the neighborhood. She was soaring over head [a] great part of the time. While soaring, she made an occasional swoop at a Black Vulture, as it sailed nearer than she liked to her premises. I do not think her mate was about at all. Once I saw two other Red-shoulders soaring at the same time with my Bird – but I think it was another pair.

My further observation of this family of Hawks was prevented by my engagements in the political campaign of 1851[157] – which opened brilliantly with the Meeting of Delegates from the Southern Rights Association in Charleston,

---

157 Following the Nashville conventions Maxcy Gregg and other extremists continued to campaign for public support in the fight for the secession of South Carolina. Gregg served as the Manager of the Secession Party and spoke frequently at political gatherings. At one such meeting in March of 1851 he presented a resolution suggesting "the absolute necessity of secession." At another public meeting held at the South Carolina College a large audience gathered to hear a dozen speakers, representing both Cooperationists and Secessionists, "ventilate themselves." When the engaged orators failed to arrive at the venue, Maxcy Gregg, although showing "some uneasiness and annoyance at the non-appearance of the wordy combatants," apologized to the audience, then spoke for nearly two hours. Purvis, Edith Anthony. *The Gallant Gladden: The Life and Times of General A.H. Gladden.* Columbia, South Carolina: Palmetto Bookworks, 1996, 185. Julian A. Selby, *Memorabilia and Anecdotal Reminiscences*, 36.

4 May,[158] & gave me constant & engrossing occupation, with the failure of the Secession Movement,[159] from the mortifying result of the election of 13 & 14 Oct. 1851.

May 1851. Got a blooded horse at the Encampment, near Camden, from Satterwhite, reputed as 5 years old, 21 April preceding. Named him Camden.[160] Price $200

21 June 1851. Camden gave me a very high fall near the South West corner of the College wall. Afterwards, rode him with a Martingale,[161] & had a saddle made on purpose, with padded rolls down the skirts, to secure me in the seat against his vaults & capers.

---

158 Maxcy Gregg was a conspicuous delegate at the meeting of district organizations to the Southern Rights Association conference in Charleston in early May of 1851 where he addressed the assemblage and submitted resolutions. Convinced that Northern abolitionists would continue to infringe on their rights "until abolition became an accomplished fact," it appeared likely that South Carolina would leave the Union. Since the regional representatives did not actually represent South Carolina, however, the resolutions passed by the delegates held little sway. Proposals for yet another meeting, the Convention of the People of South Carolina, were offered, with plans to meet in April of 1852. Maxcy Gregg attended this convention as a delegate and served on the Committee of Twenty-one. South Carolina failed to gather support from other Southern states. In paraphrasing a statement by the Richmond *Whig* regarding South Carolina's "uncompromising aggressiveness" toward secession, historian David Duncan Wallace noted that "of all the States, [South Carolina] would lose most by the dissolution of the Union, whereas if she were towed a thousand miles out to sea, the Union would not miss her." Schultz, Harold S. *Nationalism and Sectionalism in South Carolina, 1852-1860*. Durham: Duke University Press, 1950, 29. Wallace, David Duncan. *The History of South Carolina*. New York: The American Historical Society, Incorporated, 1934, 118.

159 Gregg considered the secession movement a failure because the elections of delegates to the upcoming Convention of the People of South Carolina resulted in the selection of a majority of Cooperationists.

160 Maxcy Gregg was in the habit of naming his horses for the towns in which he purchased them. During the Civil War he rode a horse named 'Richmond,' most likely bought in the Virginia capital in the spring of 1861.

161 A martingale is a training device which prohibits the horse from raising or lowering its head more than a few inches.

Monday, 26 Jan. 1852. After a very long interval, took up my gun to-day to get some Doves for my Father, now seeming convalescent from a late attack of Jaundice.[162] Walked early in the morning to the Farm where, about the Western Field, planted last summer with corn & peas, a good many Doves are to be found, but extremely shy. Kept after them for several hours, getting only three. I shot so unsuccessfully, sometimes tearing a quantity of feathers without getting my birds, that I began to suspect my New cartridges (Blue No. 7 & 8) of being of inferior make, and my powder of having lost its strength from the length of time it had been in the flash. Perhaps, however, my being so long out of practice, had more to do with my missing. Coming back, I found a very large flock of Goldfinches feeding on fennel seed near the site of Fred Hood's old house. Trying to see how many I could get at a shot, I killed only three, as they always settled rather scattering.

On my first arrival at the Farm, I had a glimpse, as I thought, of a Peregrine Falcon, in chase of some Doves. Afterwards saw a Cooper's Hawk, which possibly in the imperfect view I had, I might have mistaken for the other.

There has been much excessively cold weather this winter, with an absence of rain. The coldest was on the morning of the 20th of January, when my Thermometer in the open air stood at 8 Degrees. It had stood at 60 on the 18th – fallen rapidly to 30 by the morning of the 19th and continued descending all that day. For about six days, it scarcely rose to 30 Degrees. By this morning, (the 26th) the temperature had moderated. The weather being dark & rainy looking. Twice before (once in December & once in Jan) there were severe spells of cold, when the Thermometer got as low as 14. On the night of the 19th, before midnight, the Aurora Borealis was seen (tho I did not learn about it till the next day). The color was ruddy. This makes the third appearance of the Northern lights since last Fall. The first time was on the morning of the 7th of September, when I happened to get sight of it a little before day-break. It then extended from about 15 degrees West to 30 degrees East of North, rising 30 degrees or more towards the Zenith in several distinct streamers. The light was white, and at times quite bright so much so as to obscure the Smaller Stars behind it; but varying in intensity, and sometimes fading very suddenly. It did not entirely disappear until the day-light advanced upon it. The next appearance was about the 29th of Sep., directly after dark in the evening. The color was then ruddy, or bloody, & it came at a most unlucky time for the Secession Party, as there were

---

162 After retiring due to deafness in December of 1845 from his seat in the General Assembly, in which he had served for twenty-four years, James Gregg focused on his legal career. In January of 1852 he "suffered a paralytic attack…from which he never recovered." Maximilian LaBorde, *History of the South Carolina College*, 68.

many parts of the State where it added to the panic among the ignorant classes which resulted in the defeat of the Secession Party in the Election for Deputies to a Southern Congress. I happened to be engaged in doors, so that I did not see it until it was beginning to fade.

The day before this day's shooting, (Sunday, 25 Jan.) having walked to Everett's Pond, I had an opportunity of watching closely with my Glass (the French one) a Marsh Hawk (in a state of plumage intermediate between the rusty & reddish colors of the young, and the bluish back & white breast of the old bird) which came to the Pond to bathe. The shallow water at the edge of the Pond, having been frozen to the bottom, the ice was beginning to melt on the surface. In deep water it had entirely melted. Still it was a cool day for bathing. The Hawk, after perching for a while on a snag in the edge of the Pond, jumped in, & remained in the water a long time – plunging his head under, throwing the water over his body, & after standing still awhile, repeating the bath. Having finished to his satisfaction, he came out, shook himself a little, and then flew off into the woods.

12 shots

3 Doves
3 Goldfinches

Wed. 28 Jan. Walked to the farm in the evening, after the Doves, but did not get a shot at one. Fired once at a Crow, & once at a Solitary Partridge, perhaps the sole survivor of the old covey. I saw a Peregrine Falcon, which, perching in a large Oak, I was able to make out satisfactorily with my glass from across the field. I made a circuit to approach the Bird under cover of the woods, with good prospects of success. But before I could get up, the Hawk darted off along the edge of the woods with surprising velocity, not frightened I think, but either in pursuit of some game, or moving from restlessness.

2 shots

Wed. [February] 4. The day after I was out last, my Father had an attack of an alarming character, completely prostrating him, and attended by a slight paralytic affection of the right leg, & arm, which latter, however, was of short duration. As he had by this time recovered sufficiently to need some birds for his diet, I walked out in the evening, to the Farm, where I was able to get at a single Dove, which, however, required two shots to despatch it, making a flight badly wounded after the first shot, and falling as it passed me before my second barrel. The morning is the best time for these Doves and if I had a Companion, to pursue them about the field, leaving me in ambush in the Ditch within shot of the Persimmon Trees to the Western side, there would be a chance of doing some execution among them.

2 shots   1 Dove

Fri. [February] 20 [1852]. Walked in the evening as far as the Brickyard, but saw very few Doves, of which I was in search, and no robins, although the latter have appeared in the Town within the last week or two. Fired mostly long shots with Cartridges. Once, shooting through a crack in Kinsler's high fence at three old field Larks on the ground, thought I had winged two, but if so, one escaped my search; the other set off for a long race, and I gave him to some little German-looking girls whom I set after him to catch him. The Dove – one of two that I had in range – was killed at 80 yards, near where the clump of Locust used to stand. I found that the Brick Bridge was a capital stand for Crows flying from up the river. By concealing myself behind the Parapet, I might have got many more shots, if I had chosen. I brought down three out of five that I shot at [and] wounded a fourth. The weather since the beginning of this month has been rather mild, but continues excessively dry. There has scarcely any rain fallen since Christmas, & not much in the part of the winter before Christmas.

13 shots

1 Dove   1 Lark   3 Crows

Sat 6. Killed a Robin in the Garden.

Tues. 6 July 1852. The Martins, in a great swarm, took a fancy to roost in the Spanish Mulberry Trees in the yard this morning, & I found some difficulty in dislodging them by shooting. I brought down, as well as I could ascertain in the dark, 38, of which 22 fell at one discharge of the Blunderbuss, which I used as well as my Double barrel, one barrel of which would not go off. But I understood that a dozen more were picked up the next morning by some little negroes in Wm. English's yard, so I count fifty at least as slaughtered.

Some weeks since – on the 11th of June, riding in the Farm in the evening, I started a Turkey Hen, with a brood of about 4 Poults. She flew from the side of the Ditch, in the Eastern most line of the Farm, across the corn-field, followed by her young, which though very small, made out to fly very well. Afterwards, I started her several times in the Pine woods, to which she had betaken herself, first from one tall Pine, & then from another. I had no gun, and if I had had one, should probably have spared her – a piece of forbearance of which I should not have been capable in my younger days.

4 shots   50 Martins

Wed. July 7. Another obstinate invasion of the Martins in the dusk of the evening, only repelled by repeatedly firing among them with my two guns.

6 shots   15 Martins

Thurs. 8: The Martins came back again. Thirteen fell to a double shot by the kitchen – and twenty-one to one barrel, from one of the large Mulberries in the Garden. I count only those found at the time. A number of children, black & white, from the neighborhood, repair to the gate to receive the game.

4 shots   34 Martins

Fri. 9. This evening, the Martins sought lodgings in the same Mulberry Tree in the Garden, & were only driven off for the night after bringing down 3, 7, & 14, at three shots.

3 shots   24 Martins

Wed. 28. For some time, the Martins have not been so obstinate in coming to our Trees to roost, Peter having been able to frighten them off, by shouting at them; and they have betaken themselves with more pertinacity to Loma's trees (next to the College) notwithstanding the shots fired at them there. This evening, however, a swarm settled in the Large Spanish Mulberry in the Garden, nearest to the front fence; and I had to fire a shot to dislodge them, which brought down twenty-three. These fell (all except one or two quite dead) at such long intervals, & the flock of birds left the Tree so slowly, by detachments, that it seemed to me that many of the dead birds must have been sustained on their perches for some time by their living companions, who did not fly off at once. Long afterwards, I heard the Flock circling about by moonlight – and two or three shots were fired at Loma's.

1 shot   23 Martins

14 Oct. 1852. In gallopping up the road to Rockwood, by Frank's farm, Camden stumbled & fell down, not hurting me, but suffering some bruises himself. His feet had grown out too long.

9 Oct. 1852. Received as a present from Joel Belton Adams, a Pointer, named Rake, about a year old. Changed his name to Lark.

Sunday, 17 Oct. 1852. At Rockwood. Walked out rather late in the morning to the Long-Branch field. Saw a few Doves, & found one Covey of Partridges. I got but one shot, and brought down a Bird which fell in a thicket of Briars & weeds where I could not find it. Having no dog but Hock, we were unable to do anything more with this covey. Ashley[163] was with us. Weather warm. We returned to dinner.

---

163 Ashley Maxcy was the five-year-old son of Mary and Hart Maxcy, and Maxcy Gregg's first cousin.

On the 5th of October our family moved out to Rockwood,[164] leaving me in Town until the adjournment of Court. I moved out on the 8th.

On the morning of the 11th, early, being at the front door, & seeing Jezebel shaking and snapping at something in the woods near by, I went & found that she had caught a Ground Mole (Sealops Aquaticus) probably by scratching it out of its burrow as it moved along. I took it away from her, and the little animal being strong & tough, recovered from its towzling, and seemed not much hurt. I kept it in an old Powder Canister, and the next morning, let it loose in the woods, where it quickly descended to a safe distance beneath the surface.

2 shots

Oct. 1852. After our removal to Rockwood, Jezebel, having bad habits, of coming into the house, snatching meat from the table, sucking eggs &c., was given away, to young Rives.

Fri. 22 Ap. 1853. Walked in the evening with Hart to look at a Hawk's nest, to which we were guided by Henry. It was in the top of a tall but slender pine, on a steep hillside near Crane Creek. We did not see the Hawks, nor any sign of young in the nest, tho I fired a Cartridge at it. Lately some of the negroes had cut down a large pine on a neighboring ridge, on which was a Hawk's nest, & got four young ones which I did not see. I found in the ruins of the nest a rabbit's leg, & conjecture therefore that the Hawks were Red-tails, though query – could red-shouldered Hawks carry Rabbits to their nest?

Near Sumterville, about the 12th of this month, I saw in a shallow Pond two Ducks which were strange to me, but which from an attentive examination with my small spy glass & a comparison of Audubon's plates, I take to have been a pair of Shovellers, male & female. At another time, saw on the wing high in the air a Bird which I took for an Anhinga. I had seen a similar Bird near the same place before some two or three years since.

---

164 Maxcy Gregg's father, "after a long life of service to his community," died on the 24th of October 1852. James Gregg was one of the first to be buried at the newly established Elmwood Cemetery in Columbia, after a eulogy delivered by Dr. Benjamin Morgan Palmer at First Presbyterian Church. This move by the family from the sprawling home on Senate Street to the country home of Hart Maxcy was no doubt due in part to the reduced financial circumstances of the family following the death of James Gregg and his outstanding debts. It now fell entirely to Maxcy to provide for his mother and his two adult sisters. Maximilian LaBorde, *History of the South Carolina College*, 68.

Tues. Dec. 6. A flock of Wild Turkeys, probably including some tame ones ran wild, have been frequently seen about Rockwood this Fall, some having been seen one or two mornings since in the South part of the Cotton-field on the Lightning Hill, where they are now sowing wheat. Hart & I went out & watched for them from daylight till 8 o'clock this morning, but they did not show themselves.

Went again early in the morning with Hart to the wheat-patch to watch for Turkeys, but saw none. A North East Storm coming up, came back about 8 o'clock in a drizzle.

Thurs. [February] 2 [1854]: Rabbits have been doing mischief in the garden at Rockwood lately. Steel traps, of the kind used for Rats, have been set for them, as well as one or two box-traps. The steel traps have been often sprung, and rabbit hair found in them, but the animals had always escaped. They seemed to avoid going into the box-traps. To-night having had the holes in the fence stopped up about 9 o'clock, Hart & I went into the garden with our guns, & a torch carried by Paul, but no rabbits were to be found.

Wild Pigeons have been seen occasionally since the early part of December, sometimes in large flocks.

A yellow-bellied Woodpecker has for a long time frequented the Tall Hickory in front of my window. I noticed him before Christmas, & while sick with a cold, had an opportunity of observing that he often spent the whole day, or nearly the whole day, in active pursuit of his prey on the Tree. Once or twice I saw two birds together, but I thought one was the steady visitor. How many thousand insects, eggs, or larvae, must have existed on one Tree, to afford a constant supply of food to a Woodpecker for many weeks?

Sun. Feb. 5. On my way to Town, not far from Rockwood, yesterday morning, I found[165] a Rabbit in its form. It allowed me to ride nearly over it. I darted my stick at it, but missed by an inch or two. The Rabbit made a little bound & stopped – then went off someway further, but in no hurry. When I first distinguished its

---

165 Gregg initially wrote that he had "*discovered* a Rabbit in its form," but changed it to "*found* a Rabbit in its form," making a technical distinction between the two verbs.

feathers, its eyes were open & I thought it was looking at me. Do any hares sleep with their eyes open? Or do they easily wake at the slightest noise, so that on being approached in their forms, their eyes are always seen open? This morning I loaded my Rifle pistols, & walked to the place with Jonathan & Ashley, but the Rabbit was not there. In the afternoon, I took the pistols again, & went with Jonathan & Ashley, Martha & Susan, to look at some other forms, known to the boys, in fence corners on the road-side along Hart's corn-field. Did not find any Rabbits, and shot at a mark awhile, letting the boys fire some shots.

Tues. Feb. 7. Having seen my rabbit in his form as I rode by yesterday morning, I went to the place soon after Sunrise this morning with my gun, taking Jonathan & Ashley along. The rabbit was away. Observed the hole made by the ferule of my stick the other day, barely missing the form.

Fri. 10. Went early this morning, with Ashley, to look for the rabbit again, but did not find him in his form. Afterwards shot a Yellow-hammer, back of the North Orchard.

1 shot   1 Yellowhammer

Sun. 12. Walked in the evening back of the Stable with Jonathan & Ashley, in search of a rabbit with whose form Jonathan had become acquainted. The Rabbit was not in the form. Missed a Dove on the wing, in the Cotton-field.

1 shot

After supper, went with Hart through the Orchard to look for Rabbits. Amongst other pieces of mischief, they are barking fig bushes. The moon being full, though the weather rather cloudy, there was light enough to shoot. A Cat, watching by a Hay-stack, had rather a narrow escape, though being on the look out for cats, I suspected what it was, & did not fire. Saw no rabbits.

Wild Pigeons are now brought to market in Columbia in some quantity. I have been told they all are brought from Lexington.

Tues. Feb. 14: The nest of a Great Horned Owl was discovered to-day, in the Top of a Pine tree near the Long-Branch field. Only one Old Bird was seen, sitting close on the nest, where Hart shot it. The tree was then cut down, & two young ones were found. Hart thought there were more in the nest, but the top of the tree was so broken & crushed in the fall, that some of the young may have escaped the search amongst the confused mass. I saw at night the two young, which had been found. One of them was dead, the other still alive. I should suppose they could hardly have been hatched more than one or two weeks, being very ungainly in figure, & covered with white down. But there was a great difference in size, one being twice as large as the other, & its rudimentary plumage further advanced; its wings also much longer. The largest might be something over the weight of a Partridge. Are the young of the Great Horned Owl hatched at different periods as related by Audubon of the Barn Owl? The Old Bird measured about 22 inches in length, & at least four feet, six inches in extent of Wing.

Weight of the largest young one, 7 ounces; smaller, 4 ounces.

The hind quarters of 2 rabbits were found in the nest. The owl, commanding a view of the rice-patch from the nest, had a good opportunity of watching for game while sitting.

Sun. Feb. 19: Pleasant having reported that an Owl had been hooting near the chicken-coop, just before day-break, or at cock-crowing for the last three days, I went out at 5 o'clock this morning to watch for him. The moon, shining dimly through a cloudy veil, would have given an uncertain light to shoot. I stayed till broad day, but the Owl did not come. Pleasant asserts that the Owl was in the habit of imitating the voice of the chickens, & making sounds something like their own in reply to them. Is there any foundation for this? Or is it a mere fancy?

Fri. Feb. 24: Having yesterday morning, on my way to Town, seen a Rabbit occupying the form which I thought had been deserted, I walked to the place this morning with Jonny & Ashley, but again found the form empty. Then, at Jonny's urgent entreaty, shot a Hermit Thrush.

Within the last week, the Robin season has commenced in Town.

1 shot   1 Dove

Sat. 25: Walked with the boys again after the rabbit, but with no better success than before. While waiting for the boys to dress, I shot a Dove in the garden, which has lately been ploughed.

In riding to Town afterwards, I saw a small flock of Wild Pigeons passing over. They have ceased to be brought plentifully to market.

Tues. Feb. 28: Having again seen the rabbit in the old place on my way to Town the morning before, went after him with the boys this morning, & saw that he was in his form. I approached softly behind an old field Pine, desiring to see if he slept with his eyes open. He proved, however, too wide awake – for before I got quite to the tree, which was within four or five steps of him, he bounded off through a thicket of little pine saplings, allowing me but a bad chance for a shot. I missed him with one barrel, & snapped with the other, the cap having fallen off of the tube. When crossing the road to Dr. Roach's North field, I saw across it, & as I supposed, just at the other side, what I took, for a very black-looking Hawk, perched on a dead Pine. Going round, found that it was a Turkey Buzzard, at such greater distance, and having gone so far, fired both barrels at him, but only stung him with the small shot. Before going after the Rabbit, I had missed a shot at some Doves, across the Garden.

4 shots

On Sunday, 19 March, riding in to Town by the Asylum road, I saw a Loggerhead impale a Lizard on a splinter of the top rail of a fence. It is the first time I have ever seen the bird do it; nor have I ever before found Lizards or Grasshoppers impaled. The Lizard, when I got up, was not quite dead. It was spitted through the back of the head. It was of the dark brown, rather dirty-looking species. Returning by the same road in the evening, I could not see the Lizard, but I did not find, or recognize, the right place.

Tues. [May] 9. Having lately seen a few Rice Birds frequenting the hollows between Cotton Town & Butcher Town, I walked with my gun this evening to Hart's wheat field (on the Lightning Hill) to see if any of the birds were there, taking Jonathan with me. Saw none. The wheat not yet in the milky state, and I should think would not yet suit the Rice birds. Saw a small Hawk, which seemed to me different from the Sparrow Hawk or any other that I know – tail very long – wings rather short, but very sharp. At times it looked like a Dove, both in the flapping of its wings, and in sailing. It was very shy & I could not get at it. Afterwards, near the house, I missed a shot at a Leather-winged Bat.

Some time after this – on the 24 May – I heard of a bird, which from the description, I supposed to be a Ground-Dove, being killed in Dr. Roach's wheat field, where it was in company with a flock of Rice-birds.

1 shot

Oct or Nov 1854. After removal into Columbia,[166] Lark disappeared. Suspect he was stolen by a man named Moore.

---

166 Maxcy, his two unmarried sisters, his mother, and several slaves, moved back to Columbia to a one-and-a-half-story (with basement kitchen) residence on Richland Street. The house, built around 1841, was purchased by Maxcy's two sisters, who had received an inheritance from their paternal bachelor uncle, Elias Gregg, following his death in 1854. Maxcy cut a 'scuttle door' in the roof of the house and installed his telescope as an observatory. The Gregg home was located just a block and a half from Hart Maxcy's town home at the corner of Richland and Marion streets.

The Gregg House on Richland Street (between Bull and Pickens Streets)
showing Maxcy Gregg's rooftop astronomical observatory.
Bird's Eye View of the City of Columbia, South Carolina, 1872.

February 1855 - August 1858: Granby Revisited and A Fishing Excursion on the Edisto River

Sunday, 18 Feb. 1855. Took a walk across the Broad River & Saluda Bridges, & back by the Congaree Bridge. Carried one of my duelling Pistols, with which, charged with mustard seed shot, I killed by the River, near the Columbia Bridges, a Wren, which I take for Troglodytes Hyemalis, & a Finch, which I take for Fringilla Melodia.

2 shots (with Pistol)

>> 1 Winter Wren?
>> 1 Song Sparrow?

Sat. 26 Dec. 1857. Resumed my gun after a very long interval. From December 1854 until about last August, it had stood in the corner of my room loaded with buckshot (for Burglars) without having ever been fired. When I took it up for the purpose of cleaning it, it went off perfectly clear – having had Starkey's Water-proof central fire caps in the tubes.

There had been a Christmas storm. This was a bright, cold day. Set off at 8 o'clock, with Col. William Wallace,[167] & rode up the River, going first into Lorick's & Powell's grounds (formerly Pemberton's and Scott's) and then beyond Crane Creek (by the main road) and into Frost's Plantation, and as far as his Mill on the River. We found but three Coveys of Partridges the whole day, & saw little or nothing else to shoot. Our luck was bad and we brought home but a single Bird, killed by me. Wallace killed one Bird, as we inferred from the dog coming back with feathers in his mouth, after one of Wallace's shots. But the Bird could not be found. We had an old white Pointer of James P. Adams, named Joe, who must have been a good dog when young, but is now feeble & broken down. When

---

167 William Wallace, born around 1825, was a planter and lawyer in Columbia in 1860.

we found our first covey, we refrained from firing into the flock on the ground, which we might have done with great effect. The Birds afterwards did not give us fair play in the bushes, & we repented of our magnanimity.

About sunset, being in the Fork between Crane Creek & the River, we looked for the Buffalo-trail ford, but the water was too high to venture. We then had a most fatiguing ride through the edge of the Creek Swamp in getting out to the main road. Fortunately, it was a bright moonlight, or we could not have got along through the tangled growth of bushes, briars & vines. Reached home after 7 o'clock. I have not been so tired for many years. Made an appointment with Wallace for next Saturday, to shoot towards Granby.

By me 6 shots

    1 Partridge   By Wm. Wallace,   9 shots

Sat. 2 Jan. 1858. Col. Wallace could not go to-day, & I prepared to go alone, intending to ride in the Carriage to the Columbia Bridge, & from there walk to the grounds about Granby. But from fair weather, it changed by morning to rainy; and waiting till 10 o'clock, when I concluded that it was not likely to rain hard, I set off afoot, and went round by Wallace's Branch, & down Smith's Branch to the River – there down to Kinsler's Brick-yard. Got home about dark, pretty tired. There were a few slight showers while I was out, but I did not get wet. Had Dash with me, who being untrained, could not render much service. But if Partridges had been about, he might have found & flushed them; and I saw but two, which he put up in the latter part of the afternoon, in the field lying East of the Canal and to the South of the old Gum Spring. I did not see a single Dove, Robin, Oldfield Lark, or Blackbird all day; nor a Rabbit. The birds I killed were all shot on the wing; the Kildees in the Marsh between Mr. Wallace's & Butcher Town; the Yellow-hammer near the site of Davis' old Mill. Was the scarcity of all sort of common Birds this day, & the last time I was out, accidental? Or have they been so thinned or driven off, by an increasing number of Gunners, with the increased population of the Town? My last shot was at a Sparrowhawk, which I missed.

4 shots

    1 Partridge

    1 Kildee

    1 Yellowhammer

Thurs. 14 Jan. Late in the afternoon of a rainy day, Pleasant called me from the dining-room to show me a Partridge, running across the yard. Loading my gun, & going out to look for it, I found it perched on one of the big-gate posts, from which it went up into one of the oak trees in front, where after some hesitation & shifting of position to avoid having the bird in range with some neighboring house, I killed it, a sitting shot.

1 shot   1 Partridge

Sun. 17 Jan. After a long continuance of rainy weather – three storms, I think, running together – a fine, fair day. Walked towards the middle of the day to the River, & up the canal to Broad river Bridge, carrying a dueling-Pistol with me.

2 shots (Pistol)   1 Ruby crowned Wren

Tues. 20. There is now little left to mark the site of the old Town of Granby. All the Houses are gone. The old oaks & Cedars about Mrs. Hane's House & most of the India trees have been cut down. And the little grave-yards of the Hane & Seibels families are close pressed by the Cotton-field, the soil where the houses & gardens once were being fresh and rich. Aleck Taylor, who is now the owner of the Old Town, has thrown within his fence the little Marshes which used once to be my favorite Snipe grounds, but which for many years, from being thrown open to cattle, had become bare of cover. The cover is now thick, and a high growth of broom-straw adjoins the marshes. Riding down here two days ago, without a gun about Sunset, I found a vast multitude of Old field Larks preparing to roost in the broom-straw. This evening I rode down with my gun, leaving Dash at home, as I thought he would be in my way in shooting the Larks. Arriving about an hour before Sunset, I found that the Larks had not yet betaken themselves to the broom-straw. After a while, they began to come, but I did not see near so many as the other evening. Besides two Larks that I got, I brought down one certainly, & perhaps three, which from the lateness of the hour I could not find in the thick broomstraw. I saw this evening a Marsh Hawk fly at a redtailed Hawk, & make him take to a tree. I had seen the last evening I was here, a Marsh Hawk flying at two Redtailed Hawks, & treeing them both. I do not remember ever to have seen such a thing before, the redtail

& red-shouldered Hawks being powerful enough to rob the Marsh Hawk of game caught by it on the ground, as I once saw happen with a Partridge. In coming back through Cayce's lane, I saw a Bird pitch over into a little marsh on the left of the road, and heard a singular note, more like the harsh sound of some insect, than the voice of a Bird. I dismounted & went in pursuit, but the light was insufficient, and I saw no more of the Bird, though I heard the note again. It left me puzzled. My first idea on seeing the Bird alight, was that it might be a Snipe. The lateness of the hour, & perhaps the size of the Bird seemed to make it more likely that it was a Woodcock. But I have no recollection of ever hearing such a note from either of these birds, or from any other.

12 shots   2 Oldfield Larks

Mem. 23 May 1858.

A very serious cold, the first symptom of which being a strange sensation in the chest, I noticed while out on the afternoon's shooting mentioned above, prevented me from using my gun again last winter. I was laid up for about three weeks. The disease did not quite rise to Typhoid Pneumonia, but came very near it. I could not trace the attack to any particular cause.

Tues. 18 May 1858. Set off for a fishing excursion down the North Edisto River, with a party composed of Genl. Jones,[168] Govr. Adams,[169] John P. – Jeremy – & Randolph Adams, John Hopkins, Geo. Addison & Major Carwile of Edgefield,

---

168 In the mid-1830s James Jones served as an officer during the Seminole War. For many years before the Civil War Jones served as Adjutant General and as Quartermaster General of South Carolina Militia, and he was Chairman of the Visiting Committee of the Citadel Academy. His last position before the bombardment of Fort Sumter was as superintendent of the construction of the state's new capitol building in Columbia. He was appointed commander, with the rank of colonel, of the Fourteenth South Carolina Infantry on the 9th of September 1861, a regiment which (later under the command of Samuel McGowan) was assigned to Gregg's brigade in the early months of 1861.

169 James H. Adams (1812-1861), Gregg's "highly esteemed friend," served South Carolina as its governor from 1854 to 1856. A Yale graduate, Adams was one of the state's leading proponents for the revival of the African slave-trade, a stance which "shocked public sensibility." The former governor was a delegate to the South Carolina Convention in December of 1860 and signed the Ordinance of Secession. He died shortly after returning from Washington, DC where he had traveled as a representative of the state in a failed attempt to negotiate with President James

Gen. Jamison[170] & a Mr. Hall – and Wm. Glaze as Quartermaster & Commissary. Some several negroes & a white attendant of Genl. Jones, Antonio, completed the Party. Proceeding by the Railroad to Rowe's Pump, about 9 miles below Orangeburg, we were conveyed thence to Rowe's Bridge, with our baggage, by Mr. Murray Robinson, who was expected to join the Party, but did not do so. We pitched our tents the other side of the River, near Rowe's Bridge – and at this point Genl. Jamison, with Hall, joined the rest, having paddled down from Orangeburg Court House in a Bateau, & caught a good String of fish on the way. In the course of the afternoon, soon after our tents were up, there came a thunder shower, with a gust of wind, & some hail. I had my gun with me, being the only one that was carried in the Party. Glaze had a small rifle – the "Volcanic" and a Colt's six shooting Pistol, both of which were used for shooting at marks. I did not fire my gun the first day at anything but a mark – nor did I fish.

Wed. 19 May. This day was spent at the Camp & in the vicinity, some of the Party fishing in different directions, others, with the servants, being occupied in repairing & caulking the fleet, which consisted of a Flat, for the baggage, & five Bateaus, which would conveniently carry three persons in each. I did very little fishing, & caught nothing. In the morning, I missed a shot at a Chimney-Swallow. In the evening, I walked a mile or two from the camp – & fired some shots at nighthawks & a Kildee. A plentiful supply of fish was procured, principally Trout & Red-bellied Perch. In the afternoon a Thundershower. After night, Addison & Carwile left us.

While walking out in the evening, I saw at a distance a Red-tailed Hawk pursued by a Bee-Martin; and through my spy-glass, thought that I perceived pretty clearly that the Bee Martin actually alighted & remained for a few moments in on the Hawk's back.

9 shots

Buchanan for the transfer of Fort Sumter. Last Will and Testament of Maxcy Gregg, 1862; Series S108093, Reel 0023, Frame 00707, SCDAH. Johnson, Allen, editor. *Dictionary of American Biography* (Volume 1). New York: Charles Scribner's Sons, 1928, 72.

170 David Flavel Jamison (1810-1864) was elected president of the Secession Convention. Jamison was a close friend of the prolific South Carolina author William Gilmore Simms, and it is quite possible that this fishing excursion served as the inspiration for one of the early scenes in Simms' 1863 novel *Paddy McGann; or The Demon of the Stump*.

Thurs. 20. After breakfast this morning, the fleet proceeded down the River, Glaze taking charge of the flat, the rest being divided among the bateaux. Clear, bright weather. We landed at a field in Mr. Jenning's Plantation, where instead of pitching the tents, we took shelter in an open log-hut built for a corn-crib. The distance, by water, from Rowe's Bridge, was guessed to be towards 18 miles – the River being so very crooked, that it probably makes 3 or 4 miles by its course, for one in a straight line.

I accompanied Genl. Jones in a bateau paddled by Antonio; Jones in the bow, I in the middle. We <u>bobbed</u> for trout, occasionally stopping to fish with worms for bait, & a lead sunk to the bottom for Red-bellied Perch. Jones' position in the bow being the most advantageous for bobbing, & I being but a tyro, he had some success, I none. All I did was to hook a Jack, which I raised out of the water & held with sufficient address to let him flit off. A very abundant supply of fish, however, was taken by the Party.

This morning, while in the bateau, I saw a small Hawk – probably a Sparrow Hawk, though I am not entirely certain – flying with something in his talons, pursued by a small bird, the species of which I did not distinguish. My conclusion was that the Hawk had taken the Mate – or more probably, from its size, one of the young, of the bird by which he was pursued.

In the afternoon, a party of eight wood Ibises were seen flying.

In the evening we were visited by Mr. Jennings, who took supper with us. Being on the look-out for Swallow-tailed Hawks (none of which, however, I saw during the whole excursion) I enquired of Jennings, & was informed by him that although he had never seen a nest, yet from seeing the Birds frequent the vicinity in the Summer months, he was convinced that they sometimes have nests in the Swamp. He had not, however, noticed any of the Birds this Summer. He promised to keep a look out for them, and to try to get me the nest & eggs (for Dr. T.M. Brewer). I authorized him for the purpose to offer a reward to the negroes in the neighborhood.

Mr. Jennings informed me that he had seen the Swallow-tailed Hawk catch fish; affirming that he had seen fish of a pretty large size taken; I think he named 3 or 4 pounds as his conjecture with regard to the weight of the largest. He could not say certainly whether the Hawks dived beneath the surface of the water in their plunges. Genl. Jones told me that he also had seen these Hawks catch fish. Both he & Mr. Jennings are acquainted with the Fish-Hawk, but Genl. Jones has only known it for five or six years, & before that time always heard the name of Fish Hawk applied to the Swallow-tailed Hawk in Edgefield

174

District, where these last are seen about Mill ponds. Many years ago, William Manning, in Telfair County, told me that he had seen the Swallow-tailed Hawks dive for fish (See my Journal for May 1840, p. 23). I had heretofore looked upon this statement with doubt, supposing that Manning might in some way have confounded the Swallow-tails & the Fish Hawks. But I shall now communicate the fact, as well vouched, to Dr. Brewer.

Fri. May 21. Last day of the voyage. Before proceeding down the river, a Fox Squirrel was discovered in a clump of large Trees left on the River Bank in the Field, a little above the Camp. Several shots were fired at him; one, or perhaps two, by me, with my gun. Glaze at last brought him down with his 'Volcanic' Rifle.

I discovered a 'Hair-worm' (Gordius) in a ditch. Mr. Jennings, who had visited us again, insisted that the common account of the change of a hair into a living animal is correct; and I saw that Genl. Jones, though more cautious in belief, rather inclined the same way. But the eye-piece of my Field Glass, used as a Microscope, exhibited the creature plainly, as flat in shape, like a tape.

Our run to-day was down to the Railroad Bridge, a little below the junction of the North & South Edistos. With the bob I caught 3 Trout – about one-pounders. Genl. Jones caught 4, one of which went over 4 pounds, the rest about the size of mine. Five of our small Trout, which were towed through the water by a string tied to a nail, were lost by the breaking of the nail; greatly, as I could perceive, to the silent chagrin of the General. He also took some Jack Fish with the bob; & some Perch & Cat (the latter of two kinds – one with broader head & even tail – the other with smaller head & tail more forked) with the lead line & worms. I also caught two Cat-fish.

It was roughly estimated that about 200 fish of all kinds were taken by the party this last day; and perhaps an average of 100 or more on each of the preceding days.

During the whole cruise, I did not get sight of an Alligator, for which game I carried one barrel loaded with a Cartridge of Buckshot. Two or three were reported as seen by some members of the Party.

About midnight Friday night we got on board the railroad train from Augusta, with our baggage; & proceeding by Branchville,[171] the different members of the Party were dropped at their respective destinations. Fell in with Genl. Bonham, on his way from Edgefield back to Washington.[172] Genl. Jones, Glaze & myself got to Columbia about 6 o'clock Saturday morning, and I proceeded, darkening my bedroom, to take a long nap.

I heard the statement made while on this excursion, that it is only the female Trout which grow to a large size, the males being smaller. Some say the males do not exceed the size of a pound or two. And the same rule, as to the superior size of the Females, was said to apply to other Fish; perhaps to the most.

Mem. 15 Aug [1858]. Towards the end of June last, two young Hawks, not fully fledged, were brought home by Hart's boys from Rockwood. They were taken from a nest containing a third young one, said to be larger, which escaped. I took them for Young Coopers Hawks. The accounts given of the Old Birds seen about the nest, were confused, but seemed to point to the Red-shouldered Hawk. If that was the Species, the young Birds had the wings very short; the wings & tails being in the proportions of the Coopers Hawk. After some weeks, the larger of the two – supposed to be the female – escaped & flew off, first killing & eating one of a Crowd of Mocking-Birds which beset it. The other survivor got into Hart's well, & was drowned yesterday.

Mem. 23 Feb. 1852. Weighed by Fisher & Heintsch's[173] scales, in winter clothing, 157 pounds. My weight when in college was from 130 to 135 pounds. After my journey to the mountains, towards the end of 1837, it rose to about 140 pounds. It generally was rather below & never much exceeded this till after my return from my Mexican Campaign, when in full health, it was still about 140 pounds.

---

171 The town of Branchville served as the junction of the South Carolina Railroad (which ran between Augusta, Georgia and Charleston) and the Columbia Railroad.

172 Milledge Luke Bonham was serving, at this time, in the United States House of Representatives.

173 Fisher & Heinitsh were druggists; their store was located at 100 Richardson (Main) Street, Columbia.

8 June 1853. Weighed by Fisher & Heintsch's scales, 161 pounds, of which 8 lbs. weight of clothing (coat & pants)

I think my weight after this increased to 164 or 165 lbs, - but I am not quite sure.

24 Aug. 1854. Weighed by Fisher & Heintsch's scales, 155 lbs, having been somewhat reduced lately by a fever.

3 Sept. 1855. Weighed by Fisher & Heintsch's scales, 139 lbs. (in summer clothing – very light coat). Health good. In the Spring preceding, had some slight recurrence of chill & fever.

18 Dec. 1855. Weighed by F & H scales, in winter clothing, 146 lbs.

19 Ap. 1856. (not full winter clothing) 153 ½ lbs.

5 Aug. [1856]. Weighed by F & H scales (thin summer clothing, about 5 lbs.), 148

15 Feb. 1858. (in winter clothing – after sickness – Typhoid Catarrah) 146 ¾

3 July 1860. (in thin summer clothing – after ill health of preceding winter and Spring) 137

"Maxcy Gregg", Carte-de-Visite (seated portrait), circa Late 19th Century
Ed McCrady Military Papers from the collections of the South Carolina Historical Society.

Duck Hunting in December, engraving by George Hunt, based on design by Francis Calcraft Turner (ca 1782-1846)

Grave Marker of Maxcy Gregg, Elmwood Cemetery, Columbia, SC

Grave Marker of Pleasant Goode.
Trinity Episcopal Cathedral, Columbia, SC

Jonathan Maxcy first president
of South Carolina College and
Grandfather of Maxcy Gregg

Great-Grandfather of Maxcy Gregg, Esek Hopkins
of Rhode Island, commander in chief of the
American navy/ eng'd by J.C. Buttre, N.Y. United
States, 1877

Birth place of Maxcy Gregg on Senate St.

1518 Richland Street, the Gregg Family Home, 1854-1863

General Maxcy Gregg died in this house following his wound at Fredericksburg. Stonewall Jackson used this home as his headquarters prior to the Battle of Chancellorsville

South Carolina Ordinance of Secession, with Maxcy Gregg's signature

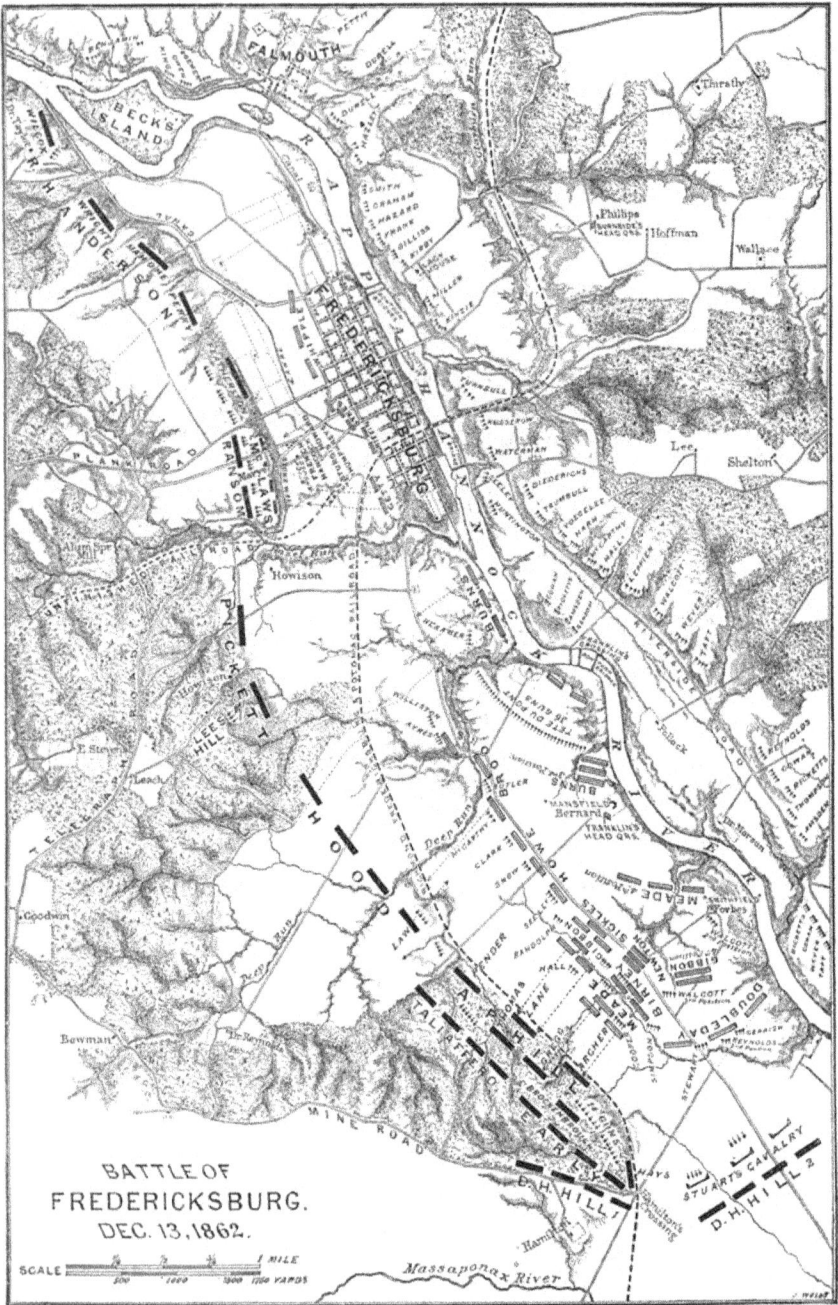

Battle of Fredericksburg. Dec. 13, 1862.
Wells, J. (1862) Battle of Fredericksburg. [S.l] [Map] Retrieved from
the Library of Congress, https://www.loc.gov/item/99439203/.

BIBLIOGRAPHY

BOOKS

Adams, Michael C.C. *Living Hell: The Dark Side of the Civil War.* Baltimore, Maryland: Johns Hopkins University Press, 2014.

Brown, Varina D. *A Colonel at Gettysburg and Spotsylvania.* Columbia, South Carolina: The State Company, 1931.

Buell, Thomas B. *The Warrior Generals: Combat Leadership in the Civil War.* New York: Three Rivers Press, 1997.

Carson, James Petigru. *Life, Letters and Speeches of James Louis Petigru, The Union Man of South Carolina.* Washington, D.C.: H.L. & J.B. McQueen, Inc., 1920.

Childs, Arney R., editor. *The Guignard Family of South Carolina, 1795-1930.* Columbia: University of South Carolina Press, 1957.

Claiborne, J.F.H. *Life and Correspondence of John A. Quitman, Major-General, U.S.A., and Governor of the State of Mississippi* (Volume II). New York: Harper & Brothers, 1860 (Reproduction by Dalton House/Forgotten Books, London, 2015).

Clavigero, Francesco Saverio. *The History of Mexico Collected from Spanish and Mexican Historians, From Manuscript, and Ancient Paintings of the Indians* (Volume One). Philadelphia: Thomas Dobsun, Publisher, 1817 (Reproduction by BiblioBazaar, no publication information).

The Columbia City Directory. Columbia, South Carolina: Steam-Power Press of R.W. Gibbes, 1859.

The Columbia City Directory. Columbia, South Carolina: Steam-Power Press of R.W. Gibbes, 1860.

Cooper, Edward S. *Louis Trezevant Wigfall: The Disintegration of the Union and Collapse of the Confederacy.* Teaneck, New Jersey: Fairleigh Dickinson University Press, 2012.

Cyclopedia of Eminent and Representative Men of the Carolinas of the Nineteenth Century (Volume I). Madison, Wisconsin: Brant & Fuller, 1892 (Reprint 1972).

Davis, William C. *Rhett: The Turbulent Life and Times of a Fire-Eater.* Columbia: University of South Carolina Press, 2001.

Finkelman, Paul. *Slavery in the Courtroom: An Annotated Bibliography of American Cases.* Washington: Library of Congress, 1985.

Freeman, Douglas Southall. *Lee's Lieutenants: A Study in Command.* (Volume One: Manassas to Malvern Hill). New York: Charles Scribner's Sons, 1972.

Graydon, Nell S. *Tales of Columbia.* Columbia, South Carolina: The R.L. Bryan Company, 1967.

Gregg, Alexander. *History of the Old Cheraws.* New York: Richardson and Company, 1867 (Reproduction, n.d.).

Gregg, E. Stuart, Junior, compiler. *A Crane's Foot of Branches of the Gregg, Stuart, Robertson, Dobbs and Allied Families.* Columbia, South Carolina: The R.L. Bryan Company, 1975.

Hawker, Peter. *Instructions to Young Sportsmen, In All That Relates to Guns and Shooting.* Philadelphia: Lea and Blanchard, 1846.

Hennig, Helen Kohn. *William Harrison Scarborough, Portraitist and Miniaturist: "A Parade of the Living Past".* Columbia, South Carolina: The R.L. Bryan Company, 1927.

Holden, Charles F. *Holden's Book on Birds.* Boston: Charles Reiche and Brother, Publishers, 1873 (Reproduction by BiblioLife, LLC, no date).

Irving, John B. *A Day on Cooper River.* (Reprint edited by Louisa Cheves Stoney.) Columbia, South Carolina: The R.L. Bryan Company, 1969.

Jennings, Thelma. *The Nashville Convention: Southern Movement for Unity, 1848-1851.* Memphis, Tennessee: Memphis State University Press, 1980.

Johnson, Allen, editor. *Dictionary of American Biography* (Volume 1). New York: Charles Scribner's Sons, 1928.

Krick, Robert K. *Lee's Colonels: A Biographical Register of the Field Officers of the Army of Northern Virginia.* Dayton, Ohio: Morningside House, Inc., 1992.

Krick, Robert K. "Maxcy Gregg: Political Extremist and Confederate General." *The Smoothbore Volley That Doomed the Confederacy.* Baton Rouge: The Louisiana State University Press, 2002.

LaBorde, Maximilian. *History of the South Carolina College.* Columbia, South Carolina: Peter B. Glass, 1859 (Reprint by Applewood Books of Carlisle, Massachusetts, no date.).

Mathew, William M., editor. *Agriculture, Geology, and Society in Antebellum South Carolina: The Private Diary of Edmund Ruffin, 1843.* Athens: The University of Georgia Press, 1990.

Bibliography

McCarty, Louise Miller, compiler. *Footprints: The Story of the Greggs of South Carolina*. Winter Park, Florida: Orange Press, 1951.

Meyer, Jack Allen. *South Carolina in the Mexican War: A History of the Palmetto Regiment of Volunteers 1846-1917*. Columbia: The South Carolina Department of Archives and History, 1996.

Meyer, Jack Allen. *William Glaze and the Palmetto Armory*. Columbia: South Carolina State Museum, 1994.

Meynard, Virginia G. *History of Lower Richland County and Its Early Planters*. Columbia, South Carolina: The R.L. Bryan Company, 2010.

Mills, Robert. *Statistics of South Carolina*. Charleston, South Carolina: Hurlbut and Lloyd Publishers, 1826 (Reprint by The Reprint Company, Spartanburg, South Carolina, 1972).

Moore, John Hammond. *Columbia and Richland County: A South Carolina Community, 1740-1990*. Columbia, South Carolina: University of South Carolina Press, 1993.

Moragne, Mary Elizabeth. *The Neglected Thread: An Antebellum Journal from the Calhoun Community*. Delle Mullen Craven, editor; Reprint by Bobby F. Edmonds. McCormick, South Carolina: Cedar Hill Unlimited, 2006.

Neuffer, Claude, and Irene Neuffer. *Correct Mispronunciations of Some South Carolina Names*. Columbia: University of South Carolina Press, 1987.

O'Neall, John Belton. *Biographical Sketches of the Bench and Bar of South Carolina* (Volume II). Spartanburg, South Carolina: The Reprint Company, Publishers, 1975.

Oliphant, Mary C. Simms, and T.C. Duncan Eaves, editors. *The Letters of William Gilmore Simms* (Volume III). Columbia: University of South Carolina Press, 1954.

Palmer, Benjamin Morgan. *Address Delivered at the Funeral of General Maxcy Gregg*. Columbia, South Carolina: Southern Guardian Steam-power Press.

Parker, Eric, editor. *Colonel Hawker's Shooting Diaries.* No publication information.

Pryor, Elizabeth Brown. *Reading the Man: A Portrait of Robert E. Lee Through His Private Letters.* New York: Penguin Books, 2007.

Purvis, Edith Anthony. *The Gallant Gladden: The Life and Times of General A.H. Gladden.* Columbia, South Carolina: Palmetto Bookworks, 1996.

Reece, Bert Hendricks. *History of Pumpkintown-Oolenoy.* Greenville, South Carolina: A Press Printing Company, Incorporated, 1970.

Reynolds, Emily Bellinger, and Joan Reynolds Faunt, compilers. *The Senate of the State of South Carolina, 1776-1962.* Columbia: The Senate of the General Assembly of the State of South Carolina, 1962.

Scarborough, William Kauffman. *The Allstons of Chicora Wood.* Baton Rouge: Louisiana State University Press, 2011.

Scarborough, William Kauffman, editor. *The Diary of Edmund Ruffin (Volume 1: Toward Independence, October 1856 – April 1861).* Baton Rouge: Louisiana State University Press, 1972.

Schultz, Harold S. *Nationalism and Sectionalism in South Carolina, 1852-1860.* Durham, North Carolina: Duke University Press, 1950.

Bibliography

Scott, Edwin J. *Random Recollections of a Long Life, 1806-1876.* Columbia, South Carolina: Charles A. Calvo, Jr., Printers, 1884.

Selby, Julian A. *Memorabilia and Anecdotal Reminiscences of Columbia, S.C., and Incidents Connected Therewith.* Columbia, South Carolina: The R.L. Bryan Company, 1905.

Simons, Jane Kealhofer. *A Guide to Columbia, South Carolina's Capital City.* Columbia, South Carolina: The Columbia Sesquicentennial Commission, 1939.

Snowden, Harry Yates, editor. *History of South Carolina* (Volume II). Chicago: The Lewis Publishing Company, 1920 (Reproduction, no publication information).

South Carolina: The WPA Guide to the Palmetto State. Columbia, South Carolina: University of South Carolina Press, 1988.

Stoney, Louisa Cheves, editor. *John B. Irving's "A Day On Cooper River".* Columbia, South Carolina: The R.L. Bryan Company, 1969.

Taylor, David, editor. *South Carolina Naturalists: An Anthology, 1700-1860.* Columbia, South Carolina: University of South Carolina Press, 1998.

Taylor, Frances Wallace, Catherine Taylor Matthews and J. Tracy Power, editors. *The Leverett Letters: Correspondence of a South Carolina Family, 1851-1868.* Columbia, South Carolina: The University of South Carolina Press, 2000.

Taylor, Mrs. Thomas, editor. *South Carolina Women in the Confederacy.* Columbia, South Carolina: The State Company, 1903.

Thomas, Jno. P., editor. *Rivers' Account of the Raising of Troops in South Carolina for State and Confederate Service 1861-1865.* Columbia, South Carolina: The Bryan Printing Co., 1899.

Thorne, Samuel. *The Journal of a Boy's Trip on Horseback*. Cambridge, Massachusetts: The Riverside Press, 1936.

Wallace, David Duncan. *The History of South Carolina*. New York: The American Historical Society, Incorporated, 1934.

Waring, Joseph Ioor. *A History of Medicine in South Carolina 1825-1900*. Columbia, South Carolina: The R.L. Bryan Company, 1967.

West, Elizabeth Cassidy. *The Campus History Series: The University of South Carolina*. Charleston, South Carolina: Arcadia Publishing, 2006.

Williams, Jack K. *Dueling in the Old South: Vignettes of Social History*. College Station: Texas A&M University Press, 1980.

Wilson, Clyde N., and Shirley Bright Cook, editors. *The Papers of John C. Calhoun* (Volume XXIV). Columbia: University of South Carolina Press, 1998.

Wilson, John Lyde. *The Code of Honor or, Rules for the Government of Principals and Seconds in Duelling*. Charleston, South Carolina: Printed by James Phinney, 1858 (Reproduction, n.d.).

Woodruff, J. Report of the Trials of The Echo Cases, in Federal Court, Charleston, S.C., April, 1859; Together with Arguments of Counsel and Charge of the Court. Columbia, South Carolina: Steampower Press, 1858, 19. (http://www.loc.gov/resource/llst.038/?sp=15 Last viewed September 13, 2016.)

Woodward, C. Vann, and Elisabeth Muhlenfeld, editors. *The Private Mary Chesnut: The Unpublished Civil War Diaries*. New York: Oxford University Press, 1984.

The Writings of William Gilmore Simms, Centennial Edition (Volume III). Columbia, South Carolina: University of South Carolina Press, 1972.

PUBLISHED ARTICLES

Berry, Stephen. "Nathaniel Gordon." *The Civil War Monitor* (Volume 4, Number 4), 2014.

Biello, David. "3 Billion to Zero: What Happened to the Passenger Pigeon?" *Scientific American*, June 27, 2014.

McCrady, Edward Jr. "Gregg's Brigade of South Carolinians in the Second Battle of Manassas." *Southern Historical Society Papers*, Volume XIII (1885).

"Historical Notes." *South Carolina Historical and Genealogical Magazine*, Volume 7, Number 4 (October 1906).

Pursley, Larry E. "William Waters Boyce: Conscience of the Confederacy." *The Sandlapper Magazine*, December 1981.

Robertson, Mrs. A.G. "Gen. Maxcy Gregg." *Confederate Veteran Magazine*, Volume VIII (1900).

Rowbotham, Sally Smith. "Col. Charles Lunch and the Lynch Law." *Daughters of the American Revolution Magazine*, Volume 96, Number 1 (January 1962).

Stauffer, Michael. "Volunteer or Uniformed Companies in the Antebellum Militia: A Checklist of Identified Companies, 1790-1859." *South Carolina Historical Magazine*, Volume 88 (April 1987).

Takaki, Ronald. "The Movement to Reopen the African Slave Trade in South Carolina." *The South Carolina Historical Magazine*, Volume 66 (1965).

NEWSPAPERS

The Abbeville Press and Banner (Abbeville, South Carolina)

The Anderson Intelligencer (Anderson Court House, South Carolina)

The Anti-Slavery Bugle (New Lisbon, Ohio)

The Camden Journal (Camden, South Carolina)

Charleston Courier (Charleston, South Carolina)

Charleston Daily Courier (Charleston, South Carolina)

The Charleston Daily News (Charleston, South Carolina)

Columbia Daily Southern Guardian (Columbia, South Carolina)

The Daily Phoenix (Columbia, South Carolina)

The Edgefield Advertiser (Edgefield, South Carolina)

The Keowee Courier (Pickens Court House, South Carolina)

Memphis Daily Appeal (Memphis, Tennessee)

New York Daily Tribune (New York, New York)

The Newberry Herald and News (Newberry, South Carolina)

The News and Herald (Winnsboro, South Carolina)

Saturday Morning Visitor (City of Warsaw, Missouri)

The Somerset Herald and Farmers' and Mechanics' Register (Somerset, Pennsylvania)

The State (Columbia, South Carolina)

The Vermont Phoenix (Brattleboro, Vermont)

Yorkville Enquirer (Yorkville, South Carolina)

UNPUBLISHED MANUSCRIPTS

Bonham, M.L. (Junior). "A Boy's Memories of War Times and Other Times." Unpublished manuscript, no date; Fairfield County Historical Society Collection, Winnsboro, South Carolina.

Macaulay, Neill Webster. "Maxcy Gregg, Lawyer, Soldier and Savant." Unpublished manuscript, no date; South Carolina Confederate Relic Room and Military Museum, Columbia, South Carolina.

Marshall-Furman Papers (Mss. 2740, 4042), Louisiana State University Libraries, Baton Rouge, Louisiana.

South Caroliniana Library, University of South Carolina (SCL, USC)

  Alexander Cheves Haskell Papers

  Committee of Safety and Correspondence of Richland District

  Hampton Family Papers

  Henry Junius Nott Papers

  Hugh Kerr Aiken Papers

  James R. Gregg Papers

  Jonathan Maxcy Papers

  Maxcy Gregg Papers

  Milledge Luke Bonham Papers

  Robert W. Shand Papers

  Wardlaw Family Papers

  William Waters Boyce Papers

National Register of Historic Places Nomination Form, State Historic Preservation Office, South Carolina Department of Archives and History (NRHP, SCSHPO, SCDAH)

The Columbia Canal

Cooper River Historic District

Fort Motte Battle Site

Santee Canal

Santee Indian Mound and Fort Watson

South Carolina State Hospital Mills Building

MISCELLANEOUS

1840 Federal Census, Columbia, Richland District, South Carolina, National Archives and Records Administration (NARA), Washington, DC.

1850 Federal Census, Columbia, Richland District, South Carolina, NARA, Washington, DC.

1860 Federal Census, Columbia, Richland District, South Carolina, Roll M653-1227, NARA, Washington, DC.

The Constitution of the Aztec Club of 1847 and List of Members. New York: Aztec Club, 1900.

Governor Francis Wilkinson Pickens' Papers (1860-1862), S511001 (Stack Location 238L01), Box 2, File 124, SCDAH.

Last Will and Testament of Maxcy Gregg, 1862; Series S108093, Reel 0023, Frame 00707, SCDAH.

Letters Received by the Office of the Adjutant General, 1822-1860, Publication Number M567, Roll 0343, NARA, Washington, DC. (Fold3.com)

Letters of the Office of the Secretary of the Interior Relating to the Suppression of the African Slave Trade and Negro Colonization; M160, Record Group 48, NARA, Washington, DC.

"Records of Deaths in Columbia, South Carolina, and elsewhere, as recorded by John Glass, 1859-1877." http://genealogytrails.com/scar/richland/obituaries1861-1862.htm.

Unified Papers and Slips Belonging in Confederate Compiled Service Records, Maxcy Gregg, NARA, Washington, DC. (Fold3.com: http://www.fold3.com/image/251655761/).

Will of Cornelia M. Gregg; Series S108093, Reel 0023, Frame 00678, SCDAH.

INDEX

Index

Balsam Mountain, NC, 07/26/43, 07/27/43, 07/28/43, 07/28/43, 07/31/43

Balsam Pine tree, 06/17/48

Barber's Cut off, 02/04/45, 02/06/45

Barrett, J. Perkins, iii

Bartram, John, i

Baskin, William, 02/22/45, 08/04/45, 08/07/45, 08/21/45, 09/27/45, 11/15/45

Bateau, 12/22/42, 12/22/42n, 11/06/48, 05/18/58, 05/19/58

Bates, O.Z., 03/01/49

Battle Creek, Tennessee, 08/23/50

Bay, William, 02/18/43, 03/01/43

Bear, 07/28/43, 07/29/43, 07/31/43

Bear-hunt, 08/05/43

Beauregard, P.G.T., 05/09/48n

Bee, Barnard E., 05/09/48n

Bee Tree Landing, 10/28/43, 12/30/43, 02/04/45

Belser's plantation, 02/09/45

Bergara, 10/29/47, 06/29/48

Berryville, Virginia, xxi

Big Pigeon River, NC, 07/28/43, 07/31/43

Biggin Creek, 11/02/43

Birds: Alpine Lark, 05/09/48; Anhinga, 11/04/43, 04/22/53; Bald Eagle, 11/04/43, 04/25/45, 03/28/47; Balsam Bird, 07/30/43; Baltimore Oriole, 08/08/43; Barn Swallow, 08/15/42, S/A-08/30/44, 08/21/45, 05/10/48; Barred Owl, 12/22/42, 12/23/42, 02/07/45; Bartram Snipe, 05/05/42; Bee-Martin, 08/05/44, 08/17/44, 08/22/44, 08/21/45, 05/19/58; Black Duck, 01/09/44, 02/04/45; Black Tern, 11/02/43; Black Vulture, 04/27/51; Blackbird, 11/05/43, 12/23/46; Blackhead Duck, 10/31/43, 11/01/43; Black-throated Blue Warbler, 07/31/43; Blue-wing Teal Duck, 11/02/43, 11/03/43, 04/20/45, 09/05/46; Blue Grosbeak, 05/10/48; Blue Hawk, 12/22/42, 01/05/44; Blue Heron, 05/09/44, 07/30/44, 08/27/44, 04/22/44; Bluebird, 08/21/45, 05/09/48, 12/03/48; Booby, 10/24/47; Booby Gannet, 10/24/47; Brown Linnet, 12/23/46; Brown Titlark, 02/18/43; Buffel-head Duck, 01/20/44; Bullfinch, 12/23/46; Calandria, 05/10/48; Canada Geese, 10/29/47; Canary, 12/23/46; Canvasback Duck, 12/23/43; Caracara Eagle, 10/29/47; Carion Crow, 05/10/48; Carolina Turtle Dove, 10/29/47, 03/19/48; Catbird, 05/10/48; Chachalaca, 12/02/47, 05/09/48, 05/10/48, 06/05/48; Chaffinche, 12/23/46; Chewinker, 11/16/49; Chimney Swallow, 08/30/44, 05/10/48; Chuckwillswidow, 04/15/42, 06/24/42; Coopers Hawk, 01/26/52, 08/15/58;

Coot, 10/27/43, 10/31/43, 04/19/45; Cooter, 10/31/43; Cormorant, 11/04/43; Cowpen Blackbird, 11/15/46; Crane, 07/29/42, 11/04/43, 11/15/45; Crow, 07/29/42, 12/23/42, 04/21/43, 08/27/44, 08/29/44, 09/04/44, 09/27/45, 02/10/50, 02/20/52; Cuckoo, 09/05/44; Curlew, 11/05/43, 11/16/49; Didapper, 04/09/42, 07/29/42, 10/10/43, 10/31/43, 11/03/43; Dove, 04/15/42, 12/24/42, 12/31/42, 02/18/43, 04/11/43, 10/18/43, 01/02/44, 01/03/44, 08/27/44, 08/30/44, 09/05/44, 09/06/44, 09/07/44, 10/09/44, 12/25/44, 01/12/45, 03/18/45, 08/06/45, 08/22/45, 04/18/46, 12/03/48, 03/19/49, 03/23/49, 01/26/52, 02/04/52, 02/20/52; Downy Woodpecker, 07/31/43; Duck, 12/23/42, 10/14/43, 10/27/43, 01/08/44, 01/18/44, 11/03/44, 02/03/45, 02/09/45, 04/22/53; Eagle, 01/11/44; Egret, 10/25/47; English Duck, 12/22/42, 02/13/43, 10/30/43, 12/30/43, 12/31/43, 01/10/44, 01/11/44, 02/04/45, 02/05/45, 02/06/45, 02/07/45, 02/08/45, 03/04/45, 04/20/45; Field Sparrow, 03/04/44; Finch, 02/18/55; Fish Crow, 11/05/43; Fish Hawk, 09/04/44, 04/25/45, 10/29/47, 05/20/58; Florida Cormorant, 04/19/45; Flying Fish, 10/29/47; Frigate Bird, 10/24/47; Frigate Pelican, 10/29/47; Gannet, 10/29/47; Gobbler, 01/03/44; Golden Crowned Thrush, 08/15/42; Golden-Eye Duck, 11/02/43, 11/04/43; Golden Plover, 11/19/42, 11/16/49, 11/20/49, 10/21/50; Goldfinch, 12/-/46, 12/23/46, 02/18/49, 01/26/52; Gray Eagle, 07/31/43; Great Black-backed

Gull, 10/29/43; Great Blue Heron, 08/31/44; Great Crow, 11/05/43; Great Heron, 04/15/42, 08/26/44, 08/22/45, 02/07/45, 11/15/45, 10/28/47; Great Horned Owl, 11/03/43, 02/14/54; Great White Heron, 07/29/44; Great-footed Hawk, 11/05/43; Green-wing Teal Duck, 12/31/42, 01/25/43; Gull, 11/04/43, 02/03/45; Hawk, 11/19/42, 08/22/44, 04/27/51, 04/22/53; Hermit Thrush, 03/04/44, 02/24/54; Hooded Warbler, 04/23/45; Horned Owl, 12/23/42, 11/03/43; Humming-bird, 08/29/44; Hutchins Geese, 10/29/47; Ibis, 09/08/42, 07/20/44, 07/29/44, 07/29/44, 07/30/44; Indigo Finch, 07/31/43; Ivory-billed Woodpecker, 01/04/44, 01/12/44; Kildee, 05/09/42, 07/29/42, 10/21/50, 01/02/58; Kingfisher, 08/29/42, 04/11/43, 10/10/43, 08/29/44; Lark, 12/24/42, 01/08/44, 03/03/49, 02/20/52; Lesser Yellowleg, 05/09/42, 08/21/45; Longbilled Curlew, 03/28/47; Loon, 11/04/43; Marsh Hare, 01/20/44; Marsh Hawk, 12/31/42, 10/14/43, 11/03/43, 01/26/52, 01/20/58; Marsh Hen, 02/13/43; Martin, 05/30/42, 07/29/42, 08/15/42, 04/11/43, 08/02/44, 08/03/44, 08/05/44, 08/06/45, 08/07/45, 08/14/45, 07/06/52, 07/07/52, 07/08/52, 07/09/52, 07/28/52; Maryland Yellowthroat, 05/10/48; Merganser, 12/25/42; Mexican Ground Dove, 06/29/48; Mexican Partridge, 03/19/48, 03/26/48; Mexican Turtle Dove, 10/29/47, 03/17/48; Mississippi Kite, 04/25/45; Mockingbird, 07/29/42, 08/02/44, 08/26/44,

08/26/44n, 08/15/58; Mottled Owl, 11/21/49; Oriole, 05/10/48; Owl, 11/05/42, 11/19/42, 03/22/45, 02/19/54; Night Heron, 09/28/43, 09/05/44, 09/06/44, 09/26/45; Nightingale, 12/23/46n; Nighthawk, 05/30/42, 07/29/42, 08/15/42, 08/09/43, 09/07/43, 09/28/43, 08/02/44, 08/03/44, 08/05/44, 08/23/44, 08/26/44, 08/27/44, 08/29/44, 11/03/44, 08/06/45, 08/07/45, 08/11/46, 09/16/46, 04/02/48; Parakeet, 06/29/48; Parrot, 10/29/47, 06/29/48; Partridge, 12/24/42, 12/31/42, 02/13/43, 02/14/43, 07/19/43, 10/14/43, 03/04/44, 07/29/44, 08/17/44, 09/07/44, 12/25/44, 09/27/45, 09/16/46, 11/26/48, 02/14/54, 12/26/57, 01/14/58, 01/20/58, 01/02/58; Pectoral Sandpiper, 04/11/43, 04/13/43, 03/23/49; Pelican, 10/29/47; Peregrine Falcon, 11/02/43, 10/23/47, 01/26/52; Pheasant, 07/27/43, 07/29/43; Pigeon, 11/11/43; Pileated Woodpecker, 09/27/45; Plover, 11/02/43; Quebranthueso, 10/29/47, 12/03/47, 03/16/48, 04/23/48; Raven, 08/01/43, 12/03/47, 05/10/48; Razor-billed Blackbird, 05/10/48; Red bird, 05/10/48; Red-eyed Vireo, 05/09/44; Redheaded Woodpecker, 08/02/44, 08/03/44, 02/-
-/50; Red-shouldered Hawk, 11/05/42, 10/14/43, 08/22/44, 02/03/45, 06/29/48, 03/09/51, 08/15/58; Red-tail Hawk, 12/31/42, 10/14/43, 10/28/43, 03/28/47, 03/28/47, 01/20/58, 05/19/58; Red-tail, broad-winged Hawk, 04/24/45; Redwing Blackbird, 02/14/43; Ricebird, 05/09/44, 05/09/54; Ring-billed Gull, 11/04/43; Ring-neck Duck,

10/31/43, 11/01/43, 01/01/44, 01/04/44, 01/09/44, 01/20/44, 04/26/45; Robin, 12/31/42, 02/18/43, 03/01/43, 03/25/43, 07/31/43, 01/19/44, 08/02/44, 08/03/44, 08/26/44, 02/08/45, 02/18/49, 03/19/49, 02/10/50, 02/20/52, 02/24/54; Rose-breasted Grosbeak, 07/30/43; Ruby-crowned Wren, 01/17/58; Ruddy Duck, 10/28/43, 11/01/43; Rusty Blackbird, 01/01/44; Rusty Redbird, 02/14/43; Sandhill Crane, 11/08/42, 08/23/50; Sandpiper, 05/09/42; Screech Owl, 06/04/42, 11/21/49; Sea Gull, 10/29/43; Semi-palmated Snipe, 10/27/43; Sharp-shinned Hawk, 11/05/43; Sheldrake, 11/04/43; Shoveller, 04/22/53; Siskin, 12/23/46n; Snipe, 04/09/42, 02/14/43, 03/01/43, 03/25/43, 04/11/43, 04/13/43, 01/19/44, 01/20/44, 08/26/44, 03/19/49, 03/23/49; Snowbird, 07/31/43, 03/04/44; Solitary Sandpiper, 05/05/42, 05/09/42; Song Sparrow, 03/04/44, 02/18/55; Sparrow Hawk, 09/08/42, 10/09/43, 08/30/44, 09/05/44, 03/08/46, 05/10/48, 12/03/48; Spotted Sandpiper, 05/05/42, 08/21/45; Starling, 12/--/46, 12/23/46; Stone Curlew, 10/27/43; Sparrow Hawk, 10/29/47, 05/20/58; Summer Duck, 09/08/42, 12/31/42, 03/25/43, 09/28/43, 10/09/43, 10/10/43, 10/14/43, 10/27/43, 10/28/43, 10/29/43, 10/30/43, 01/03/44, 01/11/44, 01/12/44, 08/27/44, 08/29/44, 09/16/44, 10/09/44, 02/07/45, 04/19/45, 04/20/45, 11/15/45; Swallow, 07/29/42, 11/02/43; Swallow-tailed Hawk, 07/30/43, 07/31/43, 04/25/45, 05/20/58; Swamp

Index

Broad River Bridge, 03/18/45

Brooks, Preston S., 07/20/44n

Broom-grass, 05/09/44

Broom-straw,
12/22/42, 09/07/44

Brown University, 03/04/44n

Buena Vista, 12/03/47

Buffalo trail, 11/17/46

Buffalo-trail ford, 12/26/57

Bull Street, 02/23/45n

Bull's Bay, 12/30/43

Burgess, John, 08/03/43

Burgess, Sim, 08/03/43

Butchertown,
03/14/45, 03/14/45n,
05/09/54, 01/02/58

Butes bachmanii,
04/24/45, 10/30/47

Butler, Christopher
R.P., 03/28/47n

Butler, Pierce Mason,
11/15/45n, 03/28/47n

Buzzard-Rock
Mountain, 08/03/43

Cabin Branch, 12/24/42

Caesar's Head, 07/25/43,
07/25/43n, 08/01/43

Calico Branch, 08/14/45

Calomel, 04/24/44n

Camden, 07/29/44,
07/29/44n, 02/23/45

Camden Court, 04/01/49

Camden Debating
Club, 07/20/44n

Camp Barnes, VA, x

Campeche Banks, 10/28/47

Cane Branch, 12/25/42

Cane Creek, 12/26/57,
07/17/43, 08/04/45

Canebrakes, 01/11/44

Cannon's Creek, 08/12/43

Cantey's Cove, 01/14/44

Carey, J.F., 07/17/43,
07/17/43n

Carolina Titmouse, 07/31/43

Carp, 04/23/45

Carroll, James, 07/20/44n

Carson, William
A., 11/03/43n

Carson's Mill, 11/03/43

Cartridge of No. 7, 03/19/49

Cartridge of Blue
No. 7, 01/26/52

Cartridge of No. 8, 08/14/45

Cartridge of Blue
No. 8, 01/26/52

Carwile, (Major), 05/18/58

Catfish, 05/21/58

Cat-fish Meadow, 08/26/44

Cat, stray, 11/20/49, 02/10/50

Cat Squirrel, 12/23/42,
10/28/43, 10/29/43, 01/03/44,
01/18/44, 09/01/44, 11/03/44,
01/11/45, 01/12/45, 02/04/45,
04/06/45, 04/22/45, 11/15/45,
04/19/46, 11/22/46, 03/03/49

Catamount, 07/31/43

Catesby, Mark, i, 05/10/48

Catfish, 04/23/45, 04/24/45,
04/25/45, 03/01/49

Catfish Meadow, 08/02/44

Cayce House,
Lexington, 04/11/43,
04/11/43n, 03/23/49

Cayce's Pond,
04/9/42, 04/11/43

Cedar Creek, 07/17/43,
02/08/45

Cervus virginianus, 05/04/48

Chappell, Henry, 08/29/44,
09/05/44, 09/16/44

Chappell, Paul, 12/31/43,
01/09/44, 04/15/51

Chappell's plantation,
10/28/43

Charadrius marmoratus,
05/05/42, 11/16/49

Charadrius pluvialis,
05/05/42, 11/16/49

Index

Deer hunt, 08/03/43

Deer track, 10/27/43

Devil's Elbow, 10/29/43

Devil's Foot, 10/29/43

Devil's Pocket, 10/29/43

Devil's Pockethole, 10/28/43, 10/30/43

Dickinson, James P., 07/20/44, 07/20/44n, 11/15/45n

Distemper, canine, treatment, 03/04/44, 04/24/44

Dockon Creek, 11/03/43

Dogs: Blanco, 02/10/50, 02/--/50; Bob, 02/13/43; Brantley (Brant), 12/22/42n, 09/07/43, 11/33/43, 03/04/44, 04/24/44, 05/09/44, 05/12/44; Bruno, 07/29/42, 09/07/43, 09/28/43, 10/10/43, 10/14/43, 11/11/43, 12/23/43, 01/11/44, 01/14/44, 01/2/44, 03/04/44, 05/09/44, 07/29/44, 07/30/44, 08/05/44, 08/27/44, 08/30/44, 08/31/44, 09/06/44, 11/03/44, 11/03/44, 12/25/44, 01/12/45, 02/03/45, 03/04/45, 08/06/45, 08/14/45, 08/21/45, 09/26/45, 09/27/45, 09/16/46, 09/16/46, 11/07/48, 02/06/49, 03/19/49, 03/23/49, 02/10/50, 08/23/50; Cora, 10/27/43, 11/11/43, 02/23/45; Dash, 01/02/58; Drive, 08/06/43; Fan, 05/09/42, 12/22/42, 12/23/42, 12/31/42, 01/25/43, 02/13/43, 02/18/43, 03/01/43, 04/11/43, 07/17/43, 05/12/44, 02/10/50; Guard, 10/09/43, 10/27/43, 11/11/43, 02/03/45, 02/04/45, 02/08/45, 04/19/45, 04/26/45, 08/04/45,

11/14/45; Hock, 11/03/44, 01/10/45, 01/11/45, 01/12/45, 03/22/45, 11/17/46, 10/17/52; Jezebel, 04/15/51, 10/17/52, 04/22/52; Joe, 12/26/57; Lara, 04/15/42, 08/15/42, 10/09/43, 10/18/43, 03/04/44, 08/23/50; Lark, 02/06/49, 10/09/52, 10/--/54; Limery, 01/10/45, 03/22/45, 04/06/45, 11/17/46; Ramrod, 01/10/45, 01/11/45, 01/12/45, 03/22/45; Ranger, 08/04/45, 08/06/45, 08/07/45, 08/14/45, 08/21/45, 09/26/45, 09/27/45, 08/11/46, 02/10/50, 02/--/50; Rolla, 11/17/46; Snap, 10/28/43; Tige, 01/10/45, 01/11/45, 03/22/45; Trim, 07/29/43, 07/30/43

Double Dee Springs, 02/18/43

Douthitt, 08/01/43

Dr. Fisher's Pond, 08/14/45, 08/21/45

Drayton, John, ii, iv

Dublin, GA, 11/08/42

Dubose, Mr., 01/16/44

Duck hunt, 12/22/42

Duel, 07/20/44, 07/20/44n, 07/29/44, 07/29/44n

Dueling pistols, 10/29/47

Dulcimer, 07/31/43

Dummett, E.J., 03/28/47n

Dunn, Mr., 01/05/44

Earle, Edward, 08/05/43, 08/06/43

Earle, Sam, 08/05/43, 08/06/43

Ectopistes migratorius, 02/22/45n

Edgefield District, 03/28/47, 05/20/58, 05/21/58

Edisto River, 02/23/45, 05/21/58

Edwards, Edward, 01/12/45

Eel, 04/24/45, 04/25/45

Eley's cartridge, 08/22/44

Eleys Cartridges of Mould, 05/30/42

Elliott, Stephen, ii

Elmwood Avenue, 03/14/45, 11/20/49

Elmwood Cemetery, xxii

Encero, 12/03/47, 06/17/48

English, William, 07/06/52

Englishe, John, 05/30/42

Enoree River, 07/22/43, 08/11/43

Everett's Pond, 05/09/42, 06/04/42, 06/24/42, 07/29/42, 08/29/42, 10/10/43, 10/18/43, 05/09/44, 08/17/44, 08/27/44, 08/31/44, 09/16/44, 08/22/45, 11/25/48, 02/--/50, 03/09/51, 01/26/52

Ewell, Richard S., 05/09/48n

Fairfield District, South Carolina, iii

Index

Falco peregrinus, 10/23/47

Falco washingtonii, 07/31/43

Farm, The, 11/03/43n

*Fauna Americana,
Being a Description
of the Mammiferous
Animals Inhabiting North
America*, 03/01/43

Felder, Dr., 01/05/44

Fever: bilious, 01/20/44n;
catarrhal, 01/20/44n;
"Country," 01/20/44n;
Dengue, 01/20/44n;
intermittent, 01/20/44n;
malarial, 01/20/44n;
miasmatic, 01/20/44n;
remittent, 01/20/44n;
tertian, 01/20/44

First Presbyterian Church,
Columbia, xxii, 10/17/52n

First (Orr's) South Carolina
Rifles, 08/05/43n

Fishing expedition, 05/18/58

Fisher, Edward, 03/25/43n

Fisher's Pond, 03/25/43,
10/27/43, 11/06/48, 11/21/49

Fisher & Heintsch's
drug store, 02/23/52

Flagger's Ferry, 01/13/44

Flat Rock Creek, 08/03/43

Flemming, William, 09/08/42

Flora Caroliniana, ii

Fonti Flora plantation, iii

Fort Motte, 02/08/45

Fort Moultrie, Charleston
Harbor, 03/28/47n

Fort Sumter, xx

Fort Watson, 01/05/44,
01/05/44n

Fourteenth South Carolina
Infantry, xx, 05/18/58n

Fox, 08/05/43, 01/11/45

Fox Squirrel, 11/05/42,
01/01/44, 02/05/45, 03/08/46,
11/15/46, 05/21/58

Fredericksburg, battle of, xxii

Freeman, Douglas Southall, i

French Broad River,
Foreword, 07/26/43,
07/31/43, 08/01/43, 08/03/43

Fringilla melodia, 02/18/55

Frog, 02/13/43

Frost's Plantation, 12/26/57

Fulica americana, 10/27/43

Fuligula rubida, 10/28/43

Gadsden, 12/23/43, 02/08/45

Gaillard, Peter, 03/28/47

Gamble, F.J., 07/17/43,
07/17/43n

Gantt, Judge, 08/08/43

Gar, 04/22/45, 04/23/45

Gardiner, David, 03/04/44n

Garner's Ferry Road,
07/20/44n

Geiger's Lightwood
Landing, 02/03/45

General Hopkins'
Pond, 07/30/44

German bird dealer, 12/--
/46, 12/--/46n, 12/23/46

Giant's Stool, 08/05/43

Gibbes, Robert W., iii,
08/29/42, 08/29/42n,
07/31/43, 11/11/43,
12/23/43, 10/21/50

Gill's Creek, 10/14/43,
11/14/45

Gizzard Shad, 04/22/45

Gladden, Adley
H., 05/09/48n

Glaze, William, xvii,
10/27/43, 12/23/43, 05/18/58,
05/20/58, 05/21/58, 05/21/58

Glover, Ned, 10/30/47

Godman, John Davidson, iii,
xiii, 03/01/43, 03/01/43n

Goode, Pleasant, xviii,
03/01/43, 03/01/43n,
02/19/54, 01/14/58

Goodwyn, John, 08/22/44

Gopher, 11/08/42

Gough, Holly, 02/23/45

Granby, xiii, 04/9/42,
04/11/43n, 02/14/43,
04/13/43, 10/09/43, 10/27/43,
12/23/43, 12/30/43, 09/04/44,

Index

Index

Martin, John J., 03/28/47n

Martingale, 06/21/51

Maryland Legislature, 03/04/44n

Mattassee Lake, 01/14/44

Maxcy, Ashley, xviii, 12/31/48n, 10/17/52, 02/05/54, 02/07/54, 02/10/54, 02/12/54, 02/24/54, 02/28/54

Maxcy, Cornelia Manning, 08/04/45n

Maxcy, Desire Burroughs, 11/04/42n

Maxcy, Hart Samuel, xvii, 11/04/42, 11/08/42, 11/19/42n, 12/31/42, 02/14/43, 02/18/43, 03/01/43, 03/25/43, 04/21/43, 09/07/43, 09/01/44, 01/10/45, 01/11/45, 03/22/45, 04/06/45, 03/08/46, 11/17/46, 12/03/48, 12/31/48, 04/22/53, 12/06/53, 02/12/54, 02/14/54

Maxcy, Jonathan, i, xii, 11/19/42n, 02/23/45n, 12/31/48n

Maxcy, Jonathan, i, xviii, 02/05/54, 02/07/54, 02/12/54, 02/24/54, 02/28/54, 05/09/54

Maxcy, Martha, xviii, 12/31/48n, 02/05/54

Maxcy, Mary Bull, 08/04/45n

Maxcy, Mary Manning, 12/31/48

Maxcy, Susan, xiv, xvii, 12/31/48n, 02/05/54

Maxcy, Susannah Hopkins, 11/19/42, 11/19/42n, 09/07/43, 03/28/47, 03/28/47n

Maxcy, Virgil, 03/04/44n

Maxcy Gregg Park, 04/21/43n

Maybinton, 08/11/43, 08/11/43n

Mayo, Dr. William T., 12/23/42, 12/23/42n

Mayrant, Anne, 11/22/43n

Mayrant, Caroline, 11/22/43n

Mayrant, Frances A., 11/22/43n

Mayrant, Frances Ann Margaret Horry Guignard ('Fayette'), 11/22/43, 11/22/43n

Mayrant, James S. Guignard, 11/22/43n

Mayrant, John Gabriel, 11/22/43n

Mayrant, Laura Elizabeth, 11/22/43n

Mayrant, Robert P., xvii, 10/09/43, 10/09/43n, 10/27/43, 10/28/43, 10/29/43, 10/30/43, 10/31/43, 11/01/43, 11/02/43, 11/03/43, 11/04/43, 11/05/43, 11/11/43, 11/33/43, 11/33/43n, 12/23/43, 12/30/43, 01/04/44, 01/14/44, 01/20/44, 02/03/45, 02/04/45, 02/05/45, 02/06/45, 02/07/45, 02/08/45, 02/23/45, 03/04/45, 03/18/45, 04/19/45, 04/20/45, 04/21/45, 04/22/45, 04/23/45, 04/24/45, 08/04/45, 08/07/45, 11/14/45, 11/15/45, 03/28/47, 09/14/48, 11/06/48, 11/21/49

Mayrant, Robert Pringle, Jr., 11/33/43n

Mayrant, William Richardson, 11/33/43n

McClellan, George B., 05/09/48n

McGowan, Samuel, 05/09/48n, 05/18/58n

Meade, George G., xxii, 05/09/48n

Measles, x, 11/15/45

Menagerie animals, 12/23/46n

Meteor, 12/25/42

Mexico City, 12/03/47, 05/09/48, 05/10/48

Mexican War, 11/15/45, 11/15/45n, 03/28/47

Michaux, André and François André, i, ii, iii, xiii, 07/31/43, 07/31/43n, 08/06/43

Militia, brigade encampment, 09/26/45

Militia muster, 11/15/45

Mill Creek, 07/20/44

Mills, Robert, 02/23/45n

Minodioctes mitratus, 04/23/45

Moccasin, 04/25/45

208

Index

Pinckney, (Misses), 02/08/45

Pinckney, Shubrick, 07/17/43n

Pinckney's Lake, 02/08/45

Pink Beds, 07/31/43, 07/31/43n

Pine-Spur Ridge, NC, 07/27/43, 07/28/43

Pinus pungens, 08/06/43

Pisgah Ridge, 08/03/43

Pistol: Colt's six-shooting, 05/18/58; dueling, 02/18/49, 11/15/49, 02/18/55; rifled, 11/20/49, 02/--/50

Planter's Hotel, Charleston, 11/04/43, 11/04/43n

Playa del Rio, 12/02/47

Pleasant Creek, 01/20/44

Point Comfort Plantation, 11/03/43

Poke Swamp, xiv, 06/29/48

Polk, James K., 11/15/45n, 03/28/47n

Polybeous brasilinesis, 03/16/48

Porpoise, 11/04/43

Possum, recipe, 01/10/45n

Possum hunt, 11/04/42

Preston, Margaret Frances ("Sally"), 02/09/45, 02/09/45n

Preston, William C., 02/09/45n

Puebla, 05/10/48

Puente Nacional, 12/02/47, 12/02/47n

Pumpkin Town, 08/01/43, 08/01/43n, 08/02/43, 08/03/43, 08/06/43

Pumpkin Town Particular, 08/03/43, 08/05/43

Quitman, John, 05/09/48n

Rabbit, 07/29/42, 12/31/42, 02/13/43, 02/18/43, 04/13/43, 10/31/43, 02/06/45, 04/19/45, 04/19/46, 11/15/46, 03/01/49, 02/02/54, 02/05/54, 02/12/54, 02/24/54

Raccoon hunt, 01/10/45, 03/22/45, 04/05/45, 11/17/46

Raiford's Creek, 12/22/42, 10/28/43, 02/04/45

Railroad: Augusta, GA to Charleston, 05/21/58; Branchville to Columbia, 05/09/42n; Charleston to Columbia, 05/09/42n, 11/05/43, 06/24/42, 05/21/58; Charlotte to Columbia, 05/09/42n

Raleigh, NC, 08/23/50

Rallus elegans, 02/13/43

Randolph's Field, 03/01/43, 03/25/43

Rat trap, 02/02/54

Rattle Snake, 08/03/43

Ravenel, Henry F., iii

Red-bellied Perch, 05/19/58, 05/20/58

Redhorse fish, 04/23/45, 04/25/45

Reiche, Charles, 12/23/46n

Reiche, Henry, 12/23/46n

Republic of Texas, 11/15/45n

Rhett, Robert Barnwell, 08/23/50n

Rice cultivation, 01/18/44n

Rice plantation, 11/03/43

Richardson, Walter P., 03/28/47n

Richland District Court of Appeals, 04/11/43

Richland Volunteer Rifle Corps, 07/20/44n

Richland Volunteers, 12/22/42n

Rifle: brass-mounted, 11/22/46; double barrel, 11/05/42, 10/27/43, 11/33/43, 03/28/47, 12/03/48, 07/06/52; single-barrel, 10/27/43, 12/03/48, 12/31/48

Rio Frio, 06/05/48

Rio Zedeño, 06/15/48, 06/17/48

Ripley, Roswell S., 05/09/48n

River Bergara, 10/29/47

River cruise, 10/27/43, 12/30/43, 02/03/45, 04/19/45, 11/14/45

Roach, Dr., 09/05/46

Robinson, Murray, 05/18/58

Rockwood, xvii, 09/01/44, 11/03/44, 12/25/44, 01/12/45, 03/22/45, 04/05/45, 08/17/45, 03/08/46, 04/18/46, 09/05/46, 11/15/46, 11/17/46, 11/22/46, 03/28/47, 11/26/48, 12/03/48, 12/31/48, 01/14/49, 04/01/49, 10/17/52, 10/17/52n, 04/22/52, 12/06/53, 02/02/54

Rocky Branch, 06/04/42, 06/04/42n, 07/29/42, 09/05/44, 08/23/50

Roper, R.W., 11/03/43, 11/03/43n

Ruffin, Edmund, 03/25/43n

Rumph's Lake, 01/01/44

Rumph's Pond, 12/31/43, 02/06/45

Salamander, 11/08/42

Saluda Bridge, 11/11/43, 02/18/55

Saluda River, 08/15/42n, 12/31/42n

San Martín, 06/05/48

Sandhills Ball, 02/22/45

Santa Anna, 03/28/47n, 06/17/48, 06/28/48

Santee Canal, 10/31/43, 10/31/43n, 11/01/43, 11/02/43, 11/04/43, 01/09/44

Savanna Hunt, 04/19/45

Savanna Hunt Creek, 10/27/43

Savannah River, 11/08/42n

Scott, Jim, 11/03/44

Scott, Winfield, 10/23/47n, 05/09/48n

Scott's Bridge, 03/22/45, 11/17/46

Scott's Lake, 01/05/44

Sealops aquaticus, 10/17/52

Secession Convention, 05/18/58n

Secession Movement, 12/22/42n, 07/17/43n, 08/23/50, 04/27/51, 04/27/51n

Secession Party, 01/26/52

Seibels, Jake, 04/9/42

Seibels, John Jacob, 04/15/42, 04/15/42(n),

Seibels, Tom, 1842

Seymour, (Judge), 10/27/43, 10/29/43, 10/30/43

Shad, 03/01/49

Shark, 11/04/43

Sharpsburg, battle of, xxi

Shecut, John, ii

Shelton's Ferry, 07/19/43

Sheridan, Philip H., 05/09/48n

Sherman, William T., 05/09/48n

Shooting competition, 08/22/44

Sim's Deer Park, 07/19/43

Simms, William Gilmore, iv, x, xxiii, 05/18/58n

Sims, Nathan, iii, 07/19/43, 07/19/43n

Singleton, John, 02/10/50

Sketch of the Botany of South-Carolina and Georgia, ii

Slaves, Gregg family: Dennis, 08/04/45, 08/14/45, 08/23/50; Harriet, 08/04/45n; Hester, 08/04/45n; Leah, xviii, 11/20/49, 11/20/49n, 02/10/50; Peter, xviii, 07/17/43, 07/17/43n, 07/21/43, 07/22/43, 07/25/43, 08/08/43, 08/10/43, 08/11/43, 07/30/44, 01/12/45, 02/09/45, 11/15/45, 02/18/49, 11/20/49n, 07/28/52; Pleasant, xviii, 03/01/43, 03/01/43n, 02/19/54, 01/14/58

Smart, John, 07/20/44, 07/20/44n

The Smoothbore Volley That Doomed the Confederacy, xx

South Carolina Bar, 04/11/43

South Carolina College (University of South Carolina), i, iii, 07/29/42,

Index

Maxcy Gregg's Sporting Journal 1842 - 1858

Gum, 06/17/48; Sycamore, 02/08/45, 06/17/48; Wild Orange, 12/31/42

Trewet, 08/29/42

Trezevant, Daniel Heyward, 02/22/45, 02/22/45n

Trinity Episcopal Church, xix, 02/09/45

Troglodytes hyemalis, 02/18/55

Trout, 05/19/58, 05/21/58

Truesdell's Oyster plantation, 03/28/47

Tucker's Cut-off, 01/01/44

Turdus merula, 12/23/46n

Turkey Point, 08/23/50

Twelfth Infantry, US Army, 03/28/47n

Tyger River, 08/10/43, 08/11/43

Tyler, John, 03/04/44n

Union Court House, 08/10/43

Unionville, 08/10/43

University of Pennsylvania, ix

Upper Boundary Street, 03/14/45n, 11/20/49, 11/20/49n

Upshur, Abel P., 03/04/44n

US Princeton, 03/04/44n

Vance's Ferry, 10/30/43

Vera Cruz, Mexico, 03/28/47n, 10/23/47, 10/29/47, 06/15/48

Volcano of "La Herradiera," 04/01/48

von Hassell, B.J., 02/23/45, 03/12/45, 12/--/46, 12/--/46n, 11/07/48, 02/10/50, 08/23/50

von Hassell, Mrs., 02/10/50

Waldstein spy-glass, 04/19/46, 11/15/46, 01/26/52

Wallace, William, 12/26/57, 01/02/58

Walter, Thomas, ii

Walterboro, 03/28/47

Wappahoola Creek, 11/03/43

Waring, John, 07/17/43

Waring's Field, 03/01/43, 03/25/43

Washington Monument, Washington, DC, 02/23/45n

Washingtonian Temperance Society, 07/17/43n

Washingtonian Total Abstinence Society, 07/17/43n

Wateree Old River, 04/22/45

Wateree River, 10/30/43

Weather account for Columbia, 08/15/42, 11/19/42, 12/23/42, 12/24/42, 12/25/42, 12/31/42, 01/25/43, 02/13/43, 04/11/43, 02/14/43, 03/25/43, 09/07/43, 09/28/43,

10/09/43, 10/14/43, 10/18/43, 07/30/44, 08/17/44, 08/27/44, 08/31/44, 09/16/44, 11/03/44, 02/23/45, 03/14/45, 03/18/45, 08/04/45, 08/22/45, 09/16/46, 11/22/46, 12/--/46, 12/03/48, 01/14/49, 02/18/49, 03/03/49, 03/19/49, 03/23/49, 04/01/49, 02/10/50, 08/23/50, 01/26/52, 02/20/52

Wet-weather Pond, 06/24/42, 06/24/42n, 08/29/42, 08/30/44, 02/--/50

Whaley, William, 07/17/43n

Whip & Spur Gap, 08/05/43

Whitaker, Thomas, 07/29/44

White-top Mountain, NC, 07/29/43

Wigfall, Louis T., 07/20/44n

Wild Cat, 02/05/45

Wilson, Louis D., 03/17/48

Winnsboro, 07/17/43, 07/17/43n, 07/19/43

Winnsboro Court, 03/28/47, 04/01/49

Winnsboro Road, 08/04/45

Wolf, 08/05/43

Wolf's Pond, 10/27/43

Woodruff, (Dr.), 08/08/43

Wright's Bluff, 01/04/44, 01/05/44

Yellow fever, xv, 10/31/43n, 11/05/43, 06/29/48

213

ABOUT THE EDITOR

Suzanne Parfitt Johnson was born at Fort McPherson, Georgia, and spent most of her life living at United States Air Force and Army installations. While working for the Directorate of Engineering and Housing, United States Army South, she published several histories of the US military installations along the Panama Canal, including *An American Legacy in Panama*. She has worked as the Collections Manager of the Fairfield County Museum in Winnsboro, SC, since 2015.

www.ingramcontent.com/pod-product-compliance
Lightning Source LLC
Chambersburg PA
CBHW050237270326
41914CB00034BA/1961/J